MASTERS OF Jazz SAXOPHONE

MASTERS OF JAZZ SAXOPHONE   The story of the players and their music

A BALAFON BOOK   First British edition 2000
Published in the UK by Balafon Books,
an imprint of Outline Press Ltd,
115j Cleveland Street, London W1P 5PN, England.

ISBN   0-87930-622-X
Printed in Hong Kong
Art Director   Nigel Osborne
Commissioning Editor   Dave Gelly
Editor   Tony Bacon
Picture Research   Peter Symes
Production   Phil Richardson
Print and origination by Colorprint Offset
00 01 02 03 04 5 4 3 2 1

● *Countee Cullen Library Harlem 1976*

THE SAXOPHONE BREAKS THROUGH

JAZZ AND THE SAXOPHONE HAVE BEEN FIRMLY LINKED FOR THE BEST PART OF A CENTURY, BUT THEIR RELATIONSHIP GOT OFF TO A VERY UNCERTAIN START.

Masters of Chicago jazz: tenor saxophonist Bud Freeman's Summa Cum Laude band in 1938 (above), also featuring Eddie Condon (guitar), Pee Wee Russell (clarinet), Max Kaminsky (trumpet) and Brad Gowans (valve-trombone).

Consider the following jewels in the Belgian crown: Cesar Franck, Rene Magritte, Django Reinhardt, Georges Simenon, Tintin, moules frites, the Brussels sprout. For such a small country, Belgium has made many remarkable contributions to the arts and to civilised enjoyment, but perhaps the greatest, and certainly the most far-reaching, is the work of that peppery genius Adolphe Sax and the musical instrument which bears his name.

The saxophone is unique in one important respect. A violin sounds like a violin, a trumpet sounds like a trumpet, a barrel-organ sounds like a barrel-organ, but a saxophone can sound virtually any way the player wants it to. In the erudite words of the *Harvard Dictionary Of Music*, "Being intermediate between the timbres of wood and brass, it may pass from the softness of the flute to the broad, mellow tone of the cello to the metallic strength of the cornet." That is how the world of European orchestral music values the saxophone, for its versatility, but that is by no means the whole story.

It was jazz which discovered the truly magical quality concealed inside the saxophone: that it resembled the human voice. A voice expresses the style, mood, origins, age and all-round personality of its owner, and the same is true of the jazz saxophone. As we shall see in the course of this book, the variety of saxophone voices is infinite.

Since Adolphe Sax is responsible for the existence of this marvellous instrument, and hence for all the music that has ever been played on it, it would be churlish not to begin with a few words about the man himself. In the first place, his name was not really Adolphe at all; it was Antoine Joseph, but everybody called him Adolphe. He was born, the son of an instrument maker, at Dinant in 1814 and was brought up in Brussels. Sax appears to have been a singularly accident-prone child. He managed at various times during his youth to drink by accident a number of noxious substances, including arsenic. He swallowed a pin, was scalded by a frying pan, and blew himself up with gunpowder. Despite these tribulations, he became an excellent clarinettist and was already devising improvements to the instrument as a teenager. In his early 20s he designed the first reliable bass clarinet.

His saxophone began in about 1840 as an experiment in matching a clarinet mouthpiece to a cone-shaped tube. Sax's original idea was to make the whole thing in wood, but he soon adopted brass as his material. In 1842 he moved to Paris, to be near the centre of musical activity. Berlioz was so impressed with Sax's ingenuity that the composer lent him the money to start his own business. It was Berlioz who put on a concert in 1844, at his own expense, featuring Sax's inventions, including the first saxophone.

Like many original thinkers, Sax was impatient and contemptuous of other people working in the same field. He spoke his mind freely and made enemies as a result. There was even an attempt on his life, during which his assistant was stabbed to death by mistake.

In 1846 a complete family of eight saxophones, from tiny sopranino to elephantine contrabass, received a patent. The following year the instrument was officially accepted as part of the French military band. Within ten years saxophones were in general military use throughout Europe. A Professorship of Saxophone was established at the Paris Conservatoire in 1857. It seemed that Adolphe Sax was made for life, but in 1870 the Franco-Prussian war broke out, military bands were cut, and within three years Sax was bankrupt. His sons kept the business going on a reduced scale, and Sax himself survived until 1894, living on a small government pension, cursing his luck and the perfidy of his competitors.

Meanwhile, his invention was making its way in the world. By the time of Sax's death it had crossed the Atlantic to the United States and was thriving in the "wind bands" that were hugely popular at the time, the most celebrated being that led by the "March King", John Philip Sousa. A full-sized wind band employed several saxophones, mainly altos and tenors, and American manufacturers were not slow in responding to the demand. By the turn of the century the saxophone was among the main products of a thriving US band-instrument industry.

The saxophone also found a home on the American vaudeville stage. Its remarkable flexibility meant that it could be made to produce all manner of novelty or comic effects – laughter, sobbing, the neighing of a horse and other

The ever-dapper Bud Freeman, managing to look immaculate in braces.

farmyard noises, a peculiar popping sound known as "slap-tonguing", and so on. On a more elevated level there were the "saxophonic virtuosi" who astonished listeners with technical tricks and speed. The leading figure in this genre was Rudy Wiedoeft whose flashy but amazingly accomplished showpieces made him a big star in the years following World War I.

It was about this time that jazz and the saxophone first became acquainted. A lively form of popular music known loosely as ragtime had been in favour since around the turn of the century, and the word "jazz", meaning pep, vigour and enthusiasm, first appeared in print in 1913. The unbuttoned music of New Orleans arrived on the national scene soon afterwards, adding the unique rhythmic element which later came to be known as swing. The whole mixture was simply named "jazz". It grew into a craze during the hedonistic post-war years, allied to a widespread mania for social dancing.

The saxophone was not originally a New Orleans contribution, but was imported from vaudeville by the early dance bands of Art Hickman, Ben Pollack and others. The first records by New Orleans bands such as the Original Dixieland Jass Band (1917) and Ory's Sunshine Orchestra (1922) stick to the old cornet-trombone-clarinet format. King Oliver's Creole Jazz Band (1923), the first indisputably great jazz ensemble to record, followed a similar pattern, using two cornets, but it was already old-fashioned. If we glance forward three years we find Oliver leading a ten-piece band, the Dixie Syncopators, featuring three saxophones. Why did he make the change? Because by 1926 the idea of a hot dance orchestra without saxophones was unthinkable. The saxophone had become the icon of the Jazz Age.

"All night long the saxophones wailed the Beale Street Blues," wrote F Scott Fitzgerald in *The Great Gatsby*, published in 1926. Moaning or wailing saxophones feature largely in writing of the period. They stand as a kind of musical shorthand for the spirit of the age – for doomed youth, the Lost Generation, fashionable nihilism, and other high-minded excuses for getting drunk and having a good time. The fact that prohibition had been imposed in 1919 served only to add a mild but enticing flavour of criminality to the whole affair.

Young men bought saxophones in the 1920s in much the same way as their grandsons bought guitars in the 1960s. Possession of a saxophone identified the owner as a truly modern young person. Saxophones sold in tens of thousands, although they were by no means cheap. A new standard-model alto cost around $70 (about £45), but as used instruments in various states of dilapidation passed down through the nation's pawnshops and secondhand stores they gradually came within the reach of all classes.

A five-piece dance band of, let us say, cornet, violin, piano, banjo and drums could get by without much in the way of formal arrangement. Similarly, New Orleans jazz bands worked according to a tradition which allotted a specific role to each instrument. But once you have a couple of cornets, a trombone, two or three saxophones, piano, brass bass, banjo and drums, you are faced with a problem. That number of instruments playing together is bound to lead to chaos without someone to impose order. Enter a new figure, the arranger, who writes down what each instrument must play.

Among the leading early band arrangers were Ferde Grofé and Bill Challis of Paul Whiteman's orchestra and John Nesbit of McKinney's Cotton Pickers, as well as Don Redman and Fletcher Henderson. By the mid 1920s dance-band arrangers had settled on a standard format consisting of three elements:

Jimmy Dorsey leading his band in New York during 1938.

brass; saxophones; and rhythm. The brass and saxophone "choirs" (later known as sections) took the leading and backing roles by turns, interspersed with instrumental solos and whole-band passages – a method still widely used today. A practical tutor, *Arranging For The Modern Dance Orchestra* by Arthur Lange, was published in 1926 and reprinted nine times in its first year.

Yet for all its popularity and its identification with jazz in the public mind, the saxophone did not at first take easily or successfully to jazz. That, at least, is the impression one gains after listening to a selection of 1920s saxophonists struggling through attempts at jazz solos. The tone tends to be weak and diffuse, and even the best players seem unable to shake off the novelty connotations of the instrument. A good example is to be found in the work of Stump Evans (1904-28). His alto solo on Jelly Roll Morton's 'Wild Man Blues' (1927), for instance, reveals exceptional facility, but hampered by an apparent compulsion to cover the entire range of the instrument in a few brief phrases, liberally garnished with explosive slap-tonguing. Evans died young, so we have no way of knowing how he might have developed.

By contrast, Bud Freeman (1906-91) survived to become an imaginative compelling and splendidly idiosyncratic tenor soloist from the mid 1930s onward, but even as late as 1930 his solos had tended to proceed in a series of damp belches while his tone suggested a kazoo played into a rubber hot-water bottle. 'Barrel House Stomp' (1930) by The Cellar Boys is a prime instance.

Tenor saxophone pioneer Prince Robinson (above right) playing with Roy Eldridge's band in 1939. The other saxophonists are Franz Jackson (on tenor, left) and Joe Eldridge – Roy's brother – on alto.

In many respects the saxophone resembles the clarinet. It uses a similar single-reed mouthpiece, and the fingering system is akin to that of the clarinet. But the similarity is deceptive, as many clarinettists discovered when they took up the saxophone in the 1920s. The result of approaching the saxophone as though it were just a big clarinet is a strangled tone, appalling intonation and great physical discomfort for the player. Early saxophone sections – that of Oliver's Dixie Syncopators, for instance – often consisted of "doubling" clarinettists, and the effect could be quite woeful.

Nevertheless, there are exceptions to this gloomy picture. Prince Robinson (1902-1960) displays a clear, open tone and terse tenor style on 'Four Or Five Times' (1928) and other brief recorded appearances with McKinney's Cotton Pickers, while the alto of Joe Poston (1895-1942) proved to be an indispensable ingredient of Jimmie Noone's Apex Club Orchestra. On the face of it, Poston's was a rather thankless task. He punched out a straight lead while Noone's clarinet gambolled and capered around him like an excited puppy, but with such grace and restraint that he deserves to be remembered. 'I Know That You Know' and 'A Monday Date' (1928) are both little gems.

Poston's economical approach was highly untypical of saxophone style in the 1920s, particularly alto style. The ornate and inescapable influence of Rudy Wiedoeft made itself felt in many curious ways. For instance, Jimmy Dorsey (1904-1957), one of the finest alto players of the period, would sometimes interpolate passages of ready-prepared virtuoso material into his solos. Dorsey was also a technical innovator, pioneering the practice of multiphonics (playing two notes at once) and other tricks. So far we've talked about players of altos and tenors, the two members of the saxophone family which went on to become dominant in jazz. But the finest jazz saxophonists of the early period were exponents of less common varieties.

The bass saxophone is rarely heard nowadays. Its monstrous size renders it unwieldy to play and inconvenient to carry around, and there is no obvious role for it in contemporary jazz. In the early days, however, the bass saxophone had a number of uses. It was sometimes employed in the rhythm section, instead of a string or brass bass. At other times it took the place of a trombone or other melody instrument. Often, it just blundered around, getting in everyone's way. In the hands of Adrian Rollini, however, the bass

Frankie Trumbauer is pictured here with an alto saxophone at a concert in 1936. The other players are Jack Cardaro (clarinet), Jack Teagarden (trombone) and Larry Binyon (tenor).

saxophone found true eloquence. Rollini (1904-1956) developed a crisp, clean attack and a remarkably nimble technique, enabling him to build imaginative and coherent solos. At a time when most alto and tenor players sound as though they're wading through glue, Rollini gives the impression that he is dancing on tip-toe. He has rightly been hailed as one of the first truly original saxophonists in jazz, and made a large number of records to prove it. 'At The Jazz Band Ball' and 'Jazz Me Blues' (both 1927) by Bix Beiderbecke & His Gang catch him at his best. Rollini also had a disarming weakness for silly novelty instruments such as the "hot fountain pen" and the "goofus" which even he was unable to save from well-deserved oblivion.

Like the trumpet and the clarinet, the saxophone is a transposing instrument. That is to say that its "open" scale, equivalent to the white notes of a piano, is not C but B-flat (in the case of soprano, tenor and bass) or E-flat (alto, baritone). This is not the place to go into the technicalities of the matter, except to point out that transposition is confusing to beginners, and that players of transposing instruments cannot read off the same sheet of music as their accompanying pianists.

In an attempt to solve the problem, manufacturers came up with a saxophone between alto and tenor in size and pitched in C, named the c-melody. It proved quite popular with amateur players, and several professionals made use of it. In jazz the most prominent was Frankie Trumbauer (1901-56) whose charming, light tone is instantly recognisable on a number of classic records, notably the opening chorus of 'Singing The Blues' (1927) with Bix Beiderbecke. Trumbauer was also adept at the Wiedoeft-style showpiece solo, of which 'Trumbology' (1927) is a remarkable example.

Sidney Bechet jamming in New York in 1940, with Pops Foster (bass) and James P Johnson (piano and cigar). The record (below) is from Bechet's time in the 1940s with clarinettist Mezz Mezzrow.

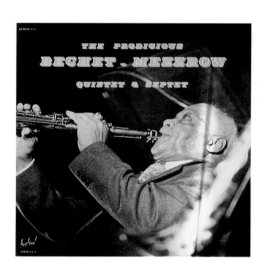

Trumbauer's other main claim to jazz fame is that he was an early idol of Lester Young. But the figure who towers above all others in the early history of the jazz saxophone is Sidney Bechet (1897-1959). Growing up in New Orleans during the first flowering of jazz, Bechet was recognised as exceptionally gifted while still in his early teens. Like many French-Creole children he was encouraged to learn an instrument, and began taking clarinet lessons from the New Orleans master-clarinettist Louis "Big Eye" Nelson. But Bechet preferred to teach himself. At the age of 20, having played with virtually every first-class band in New Orleans, he followed the general exodus of musicians to Chicago and soon became established there.

Throughout these early years Bechet changed bands with bewildering frequency, usually following a row of epic proportions. Indeed, he was driven by a personality so explosive and choleric that it made him virtually unemployable. He expected to be the centre of attention, the prodigy, the star – and would accept nothing less. Allied to this was a wanderlust which kept him constantly on the move. His travels took him across the United States and Europe – to Britain, France, Germany and even as far as Russia. He went as a featured virtuoso soloist, first with Will Marion Cook's Southern Syncopated Orchestra and later with the show *La Revue Negre*, starring Josephine Baker.

Bechet's music was the first jazz of any kind that most people in these places had heard, and such was the passion and vitality of his playing that they were often quite overwhelmed. The Swiss conductor Ernest Ansermet hailed him as a genius after hearing him play in London in 1919. It was during the same visit that Bechet bought a soprano saxophone and thus found his true musical voice. From it he produced a broad, commanding tone with a florid vibrato, ideally suited to the sweep and dash of his phrases. The soprano was also much louder than the clarinet, which enabled him to drown out any possible opposition.

In 1924, Bechet and Louis Armstrong found themselves together in a recording studio, as members of a pick-up band called the Red Onion Jazz

Alto saxophonists Benny Carter and Russell Procope (far right) at a reunion of former Fletcher Henderson band members at New York's Café Society in 1940.

Babies. The result, after a no-holds-barred contest and a series of stupendous solo breaks on 'Cake Walking Babies', was a dead heat.

Bechet's footloose life prevented him from building a career. At one point he was reduced to opening a tailor's shop in order to live. But he managed to record some superb music throughout the 1930s and '40s. The tracks by his New Orleans Feetwarmers are particularly fine, especially a hell-for-leather version of 'Maple Leaf Rag' (1932) which fully confirms the words of Bechet's pupil, Bob Wilber: "To grab the listener's attention, to carry him away on a continuously rising curve of excitement, that was Bechet's credo." Curiously enough, in view of Bechet's pugnacious character, some of his finest records are those on which he shares the billing as leader. The Spanier-Bechet Big Four (1940) with cornettist Muggsy Spanier and the Mezzrow-Bechet Quintet (1945) with clarinettist Mezz Mezzrow reveal his intense lyricism and a surprising gentleness beneath the bombast.

Bechet's fortunes were utterly transformed in the final decade of his life. In 1949 he appeared at the Paris Jazz Fair, the first-ever European jazz festival, and met with a reception so ecstatic that it amounted almost to an apotheosis. Not only was Bechet a bona fide jazz master, but as a New Orleans Creole he was also a species of Frenchman. He moved to France and graciously accepted his elevation to the position of National Treasure.

The sound of Bechet's soprano saxophone, throbbing with Gallic passion instantly conjures the atmosphere of 1950s Paris. When Bechet died, on his 62nd birthday, France mourned. A square near his home in Antibes was named in his honour and his statue still watches over it.

LOREN SCHOENBERG

COLEMAN HAWKINS

"WE ALL HAD OUR MENTORS," SAID BENNY CARTER IN 1983.
"FROM WHOM DID HAWKINS COPY? I DON'T THINK HE
FOLLOWED ANYBODY. HE WAS A CREATOR. HE LED."

Fletcher Henderson and his Orchestra (above) in Atlantic City, 1931. Back row, second from left, is Coleman Hawkins; on his left is Russell Procope; extreme right, back row, is guitarist Clarence Holiday, Billie Holiday's father. Pictured opposite is Coleman Hawkins jamming at the Greenhaven Inn, Mamaroneck, New York, in 1939. With him are Hot Lips Page on trumpet, clarinettist Joe Marsala, and Artie Shapiro on bass.

Coleman Hawkins single-handedly created the idiom for the tenor saxophone in jazz. He was not by any means the first person to play the saxophone. Before Hawkins came to maturity, Sidney Bechet and Adrian Rollini had already taken giant steps, establishing the idea that saxophones could be used to make great jazz. It was left to Hawkins to process the innovations of Louis Armstrong in an intensely personal way, and fashion out of them his own voice.

There are very few musicians in any genre who made as many transformations throughout their careers as did Coleman Hawkins. Not only was his chosen instrument considered a joke at best, there was as yet no model for coherent jazz improvisation. Miraculously, at the age of 35 he would have a hit recording that remains one of the most sophisticated and challenging items ever to come remotely near the bestseller list. And by the age of 59 Hawkins would more than hold his own in studio encounters with John Coltrane and Sonny Rollins – both of whose careers would have been unimaginable without Hawkins's precedent.

Coleman Randolph Hawkins was born in St. Joseph, Missouri, on November 21st 1904. There were many variations in African-American life during the early 20th century, though all too often the sort of poverty that Louis Armstrong experienced in New Orleans is thought typical of how other contemporary jazzmen were raised. Certainly, Hawkins's childhood was a comfortable and stable one, lived in relatively middle-class comfort. Young Coleman was given lessons on the cello and also played the piano before settling on the saxophone as a teenager. The attractive tone of the cello and the harmonic world made explicit by the piano would greatly benefit him over the next decade and a half as he moved toward musical maturity.

Hawkins continued to play the cello through his adolescent years as a student at the Industrial and Educational Institute in Topeka, Kansas, and he doubled on the c-melody saxophone with local dance bands and in theatre orchestras in nearby Kansas City.

Mamie Smith was still tremendously popular after the huge success of her 1920 recording 'Crazy Blues', and she came through Kansas City on a tour, supplementing her band with local musicians. The 16-year-old Hawkins immediately impressed her with his skills at reading music and improvisation. Although Smith's first attempts to take him on the road were rebuffed by Hawkins's grandmother, his mother eventually granted permission several months later – seemingly because she was only too happy to have her son part company with a certain local girl. The following year on the road with Smith's vaudeville troupe gave Hawkins a life's worth of professional and personal lessons. He was by now concentrating on the tenor saxophone, and though

Coleman Hawkins in concert in the 1950s.

still a teenager his incontestable mastery of the instrument made him a standout by the time he settled in New York in the summer of 1923. He soon came to the attention of bandleader Fletcher Henderson, who hired him for many recording sessions.

The early 1920s was a burgeoning time for jazz, and a virtuoso like Hawkins could make an excellent living freelancing in nightclubs, playing theatre dates and recording. Henderson was eventually able to offer Hawkins full-time employment, and the saxophonist remained a featured member of the band for a decade.

Musically, there is little to distinguish the Hawkins of 1922-24 from the other lively jazz tenor saxophonists of the time. He would spell out the basic chords, and articulate in a forceful manner known as slap-tonguing. It seems that his already growing reputation came more from his sheer volume and gusto, as well as his superlative skills as both a reader and a soloist. The arrival of Louis Armstrong in the Henderson band in late 1924 for a year-long stint was to have a profound impact on the music world in general and on the 20-year-old Coleman Hawkins in particular.

Armstrong created jazz phrases out of a vocabulary that drew heavily upon the blues and the "irrationalities" of African rhythms. This frightened some, and woke up many more. Within a decade there would be Armstrong-inspired singers and instrumentalists all around the world. Hawkins was one of the first to begin transforming Armstrong's example into personal terms, but it would be a lengthy process. He had given up the cello during his stint with Mamie Smith and picked up the cumbersome bass saxophone in the interim, even recording with it through 1926. He gradually concentrated on the tenor saxophone exclusively, only playing his "doubles" when called for in orchestrations.

There are Hawkins solos on literally hundreds of Fletcher Henderson recordings during the 1920s, in addition to sessions with Bessie Smith and others, and they reveal a very slow yet inexorable evolution. On Henderson's 'The Stampede' (1926) Hawkins played an inspired chorus that entranced the young trumpeter Roy Eldridge. Ultimately, this "saxophonistic" trumpet style would lead to Dizzy Gillespie.

But of all the recordings Hawkins made in the 1920s none reveals the scope of his conception at the time better than the Mound City Blue Blowers disc of 'Hello, Lola' and 'One Hour' (1929). On the first title, an up-tempo romp, he sounds animated, rhythmically agitated, and as emotionally subtle as a buzzsaw. The other side, however, contains the seeds of the tenor saxophone ballad, a style that he would cultivate for his greatest innovations. At once, the occasional jerkiness of his playing at more rapid tempos is eschewed for an over-arching lyricism and an almost operatic fervour. His harmonic imagination blossoms here in a fashion impossible at faster tempos – impossible, that is, for 15 years until Charlie Parker showed the way.

The early 1930s found Hawkins trying to adapt his ballad style to all tempos. This called for an extreme use of rubato: not in the original sense of the term of slowing down or cessation of tempo, but rather "robbing" from one part of a musical measure and "paying it back" in another (as has become commonplace in playing Chopin's piano music, for example). His ballad features were already widely known and loved by the time he recorded 'It's The Talk Of The Town' and 'I've Got To Sing A Torch Song' (1933). Jazz players around the world were taking these solos as models of every aspect of

improvisation. Tenor players such as Ben Webster, Chu Berry and Herschel Evans were all developing their own dialects within the expressive language that Hawkins was creating.

One facet of his musical personality was his competitiveness. As soon as a new man came anywhere near him, either on the road or at home in New York, there would be a jam session where, inevitably, Hawkins would predominate. This remained the case until one fateful night late in 1933 when Lester Young countered every punch that Hawkins aimed at him. In many ways, Young's style was an inversion of that of Hawkins. Hawkins's basic orientation was harmonic, whereas Young's was indisputably melodic. When it came to up-tempo playing, Young took his cue from Armstrong and would float as lightly as Hawkins trod heavily. And in terms of tone, where Hawkins was declamatory and fervent, Young seemed to be whispering and even, on occasion, just thinking his solos. What they shared was total originality and a seemingly limitless capacity for extended improvisation.

The Depression altered the entertainment business radically, and Henderson was having trouble finding steady work for his band as 1933 turned into 1934. In addition, since the departure of Armstrong in late 1925, Hawkins had been shouldering the great bulk of the band's solo load. The sheer responsibility of having to do so night after night and year after year must have been wearying.

A chance encounter with June Clark, a bassist just returned from an extended stay in Europe, led him to a contract with British bandleader Jack

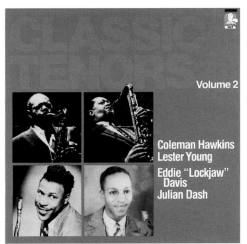

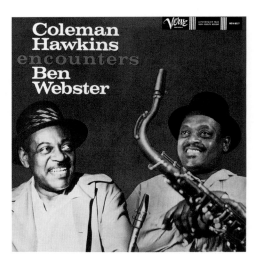

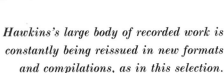

Hawkins's large body of recorded work is constantly being reissued in new formats and compilations, as in this selection.

Hylton. He spent the next five years in Britain and on the Continent, appearing as a featured soloist with a succession of dance bands and radio orchestras, while recording prolifically. There had been other visits by great American jazzmen – most notably Duke Ellington, Sidney Bechet and Louis Armstrong – but none of them lived and worked among European musicians to the extent that Hawkins did.

During this period he wrote many letters, and they provide much insight into his complex character. First brought to light in John Chilton's superb biography *The Song Of The Hawk*, they show him to be a highly literate and compassionate observer of the human condition. Hawkins kept up on musical happenings in America through recordings and radio broadcasts, and had good things to say about Benny Goodman, Roy Eldridge and Duke Ellington, among others.

In Europe he recorded in settings ranging from duets with a pianist to big-band sessions. He even sang on occasion, something he never did again. One session that has attained classic status took place in 1937, when Hawkins was reunited with his former Henderson bandmate Benny Carter (who spent three years in Europe) alongside the Belgian gypsy guitarist Django Reinhardt. 'Out Of Nowhere' and 'Crazy Rhythm' contain definitive Hawkins solos, full of drive and harmonic sophistication, where he plays like a man possessed.

During his European years, Hawkins not only enjoyed a lifestyle he could not experience back home, but he also had the opportunity to play concerts where he could begin and end his pieces with long, out-of-tempo solos – which would have been impossible in the almost exclusively dance-based music he'd been playing with Henderson. Nonetheless, a desire to play once again with his peers back home, as well as the imminence of war in Europe, brought him back to the States in the summer of 1939.

No one knew precisely what to expect from a Coleman Hawkins who had been away from jazz's native land for half a decade. Some thought his creative powers must have withered. It was partially to answer them that he recorded his masterpiece on October 11th 1939. 'Body And Soul' had long been a Hawkins feature, but the sheer perfection of the two choruses captured that day were extraordinary even by his own recorded standards. It is rare that any performer reaches their zenith within the confines of the recording studio, but 'Body And Soul' captured a truly perfect improvisation that has all the hallmarks of a great composition. Melodically and harmonically, it opened new musical vistas that remain timeless. Equally exceptional was the

London in the mid 1960s, and Jazz At The Philharmonic's touring group plays a concert. Pictured left to right: Coleman Hawkins, Dizzy Gillespie, Benny Carter, Clark Terry, James Moody, Zoot Sims.

fact that the record became something of a hit, indicating that a significant segment of the public were receptive to such a complex and sophisticated set of harmonic variations. This gave hope to a new generation of jazz musicians that their music might have wide appeal – although this was a hope that was ultimately unfulfilled.

Hawkins fronted a big-band for a couple of frustrating years, but he was just not cut out for that sort of job. A virtuoso with impeccably high standards, he found it distasteful to pander to what the various ballroom and theatre owners wanted. Despite the popularity of 'Body And Soul' and a significant following who respected his status as an artist, he was unable to sustain his career as a big-band leader.

Throughout the war years there evolved a pattern of single engagements with pick-up bands alternating with location jobs in New York. There were rumours that he would join Count Basie's band, making a two-tenor team with Lester Young. There were also many recording dates, and one of the most outstanding was a sextet of ex-Hendersonites with Roy Eldridge and Benny Carter which produced the classic ballad 'I Surrender, Dear' (1940).

Unlike most of his peers, Hawkins actively sought out young musicians with unorthodox ideas. Dizzy Gillespie, Max Roach and Thelonious Monk all received encouragement, nightclub work and recording dates from Hawkins at a time in their careers when they were far from celebrated. Bassist Oscar Pettiford was featured on Hawkins's inspired long-metre version of 'The Man I Love' (1943), on a pair of 1944 big-band (minus trombones) sessions that showcased Gillespie's music ('Woody 'n' You'), and on a series of 1945 small-group sides.

Much has been made of the bad reception for Gillespie and Parker when they played at Billy Berg's club in Los Angeles late in 1945. But it's often forgotten that Hawkins had a band out there a year earlier that played the new music coming from 52nd Street, to much acclaim.

After returning to New York, Hawkins continued to record with the best young players, showcasing Fats Navarro ('I Mean You' and 'Half Step Down, Please'), Hank Jones ('I Love You'), J J Johnson ('Indiana Winter') and Miles Davis (a short solo on 'Bean-A-Re-Bop') who was heard frequently with Hawk on 52nd Street. The jazz impresario Norman Granz came into Hawkins's life in the post-war years and was able to offer a healthy season of tours with the Jazz At The Philharmonic troupe – the first of which paired Hawkins with Lester Young – and the concomitant recordings, both live and in the studio.

Hawkins in his final years, bearded like a patriarch. Toward the end he virtually gave up eating, subsisting mainly on a diet of brandy and chicken soup, and appeared to lose all interest in life.

During the off times, Hawkins continued to appear as a single both in the States and abroad. In the 1950s he started an association with Roy Eldridge that was to last irregularly for the rest of his life. They made a great team, both on and off the bandstand. Hawkins was known to be super-sensitive about his age, which set the stage for all sorts of badinage with his bandmates. Stanley Dance captured a typical scene in his book *The World Of Swing*. "When the Eldridge-Hawkins Quintet was once playing the Heublein Lounge in Hartford," wrote Dance, "an eight-year-old girl insisted on getting the autograph of Coleman Hawkins, and his only. 'How is it, Roy,' he asked afterwards, 'that all your fans are old people? They come in here with canes and crutches. They must be anywhere from 58 to 108. But my fans are all young, from eight to 58 years old!' 'That little girl thought you were Santa Claus,' said drummer Eddie Locke. 'Is that so? Well, who's got more fans than Santa Claus?'"

One of the very best live recordings he made at the time is *Coleman Hawkins And Roy Eldridge At The Opera House* (1957). They are accompanied by pianist John Lewis, bassist Percy Heath and drummer Connie Kay. Two superlative studio sessions also appeared, made with Henry Red Allen (including trombonist J.C. Higgonbotham) and with Thelonious Monk (also featuring John Coltrane). And Hawkins played a major role in the best jazz TV show to date, *The Sound Of Jazz*, broadcast live on CBS in 1957. One of its joys was the reaction of the other musicians when Hawkins played – and his solo on 'Rosetta' was particularly fertile.

Hawkins weathered stoically the advent of rock'n'roll and the attendant diminution of work for musicians of his generation. Caught in between fetishes for traditional jazz and "the new thing", Hawkins only gradually got the kind of adulation and employment that was truly his due. He spent more and more time in his elegant apartment in New York City where he was surrounded by a world-class collection of classical music, with an emphasis on piano music and opera. Friends fondly recall the "musicales" Hawkins would host, always with superlative pianists (mostly from Detroit) present. He formed a quartet with just such a pianist, Tommy Flanagan, alongside bassist Major Holley and drummer Eddie Locke, and they recorded some outstanding albums for Impulse Records, as well as working sporadic live dates.

An appearance with his disciple Sonny Rollins at the Newport Jazz festival also spawned a record date, for RCA Victor. Rollins pulled no punches; after all, Hawkins was known for his love of the civil-but-very-serious cutting session. The younger man unleashed a barrage of eccentric, expressive devices, challenging Hawkins to re-assert the levels of creativity that had established him in the first place. What resulted was a vivid image of the late Hawkins's true identity as improviser, made starker by the startling context in which Rollins placed him.

As he approached his mid 60s Hawkins began to fall apart. For four decades he had been renowned for his sartorial splendour. Now he seemed indifferent to how he and his clothes looked. The music also suffered as he stopped supplementing his heavy drinking with the food necessary to act as ballast for the alcohol. A decade earlier he had struggled to get a sadly ailing Lester Young to eat. He did not heed his own advice. Hawkins eventually grew a beard that in its unkempt state made him look like a veritable Methuselah. Friends including Thelonious Monk and, notably, Eddie Locke did their best to steer him off this course of self-destruction, but to no avail.

His musical instincts never faltered. A vital key to his ability always to have fresh things to play was remembered by bassist George Duvivier in *Bassically Speaking*. "Despite his problems [in later years] Hawk never stopped listening," wrote Duvivier. "He took many of the new things and superimposed them on his own basic style. You never knew what would come out. It was almost unnerving how intently he could listen. You'd be playing and suddenly you'd be aware of someone standing off to your right. If you looked over you'd see him, arms folded and head down just a little, watching and listening to everything. He did that for as long as I knew him."

Probably we'll never know the reasons underlying those sad last few years, though the fact remains that Coleman Hawkins died on May 19th 1969, just days after a final concert with Roy Eldridge. But the vast majority of his life was spent spreading joy through his intense and intricate music that never went for the lowest common denominator. Hawkins explored the area where the best attributes of composition and improvisation intersected. He had truly learned Armstrong's lesson.

SWINGING OUT

AS BIG-BAND SAXOPHONE SECTIONS GREW IN SIZE AND VIRTUOSITY DURING THE SWING ERA, MANY GREAT SOLOISTS CAME TO PROMINENCE. EVERY LEADING PLAYER OF THE PERIOD SERVED AN APPRENTICESHIP IN THE RANKS OF A BIG-BAND.

Harry Carney (opposite) was Duke Ellington's longest-serving musician, a friend from his youth and his close confidant. The sound of Ellington's orchestra was built on Carney's massive tone and self-assured delivery.

The 1930s was a fertile decade for saxophonists, whether they were ambitious individual voices or dedicated section-men. While the brass players in the frontline already had much of their vocabulary mapped out by 1930 through such overbearing giants as Louis Armstrong and Jack Teagarden, the saxophone was still a relatively untutored horn.

Coleman Hawkins had established the primary sound for tenor players – and, indeed, many alto players too – but the saxophone was ready to accommodate an enormous stylistic range. Lester Young's emergence may have startled those who thought that the Hawkins gospel was not to be argued with, but that only made clear how broad and accommodating the instrument could be in admitting individual methods of delivery.

While Hawkins recreated himself as lone wolf after leaving Fletcher Henderson in 1934, many of the saxophone's most interesting exponents plied their trade in big-bands. The major swing orchestras could each boast sections of extraordinary capability: Lester Young, Herschel Evans and Marshall Royal with Count Basie; Babe Russin, Arthur Rollini and Vido Musso with Benny Goodman; Budd Johnson, Darnell Howard and Omer Simeon with Earl Hines; Eddie Miller, Matty Matlock and Gil Rodin with Bob Crosby.

Their work as section-players was what counted on a professional basis, a harmonious fraternising which essentially distinguished each band from another and set much of the tone in the sometimes misleadingly-named "swing era" (since many of the surviving records and airshots show how much the bandleaders relied on ballads and jazzless material). But it was the colour and shading of the reed sections which became a prime flavour in big-band music.

The most notable example was in Duke Ellington's orchestra, which entered one of its greatest periods from the mid 1930s onward. By then, Ellington was in charge of a saxophone section which had already been with him for many busy years: Johnny Hodges, perhaps the most eminent alto player in the music; Harry Carney, the imperturbable anchorman on baritone; the selfless veteran Otto Hardwick, who rarely took solos; and with the arrival of Ben Webster in 1940 – he had previously joined for a very brief spell a few years earlier – a major tenor soloist.

More than any other leader, Ellington saw the value of his saxophonists as both individual spirits and a richly integrated collective. The key man in this regard was Harry Carney (1910-74) whose sonorous baritone was effectively the signature sound in the Ellington orchestra for close to 50 years. Carney took relatively few solos then, but on almost every record by the orchestra of the 1930s and '40s it's the baritone which has the most multifaceted role, as bass counterpoint and harmonic ingredient: the tonal paterfamilias. Carney

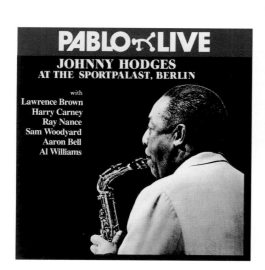

Johnny Hodges (right) looking typically inscrutable. His stone-faced demeanour contrasted strangely with the passionate romanticism of his music. Even away from Ellington's band, its members and ex-members tended to stick together, as for this recorded concert (sleeve, above).

remained to the end of his days an unobtrusive personality, even if his musical self was grandly powerful. The same could hardly be said for the dryly combative Johnny Hodges (1907-70). He began playing music in Boston, where Ellington first heard him, and took some lessons from Sidney Bechet. Although he only occasionally played soprano with Ellington – and gave it up altogether after 1940 – it was originally his first instrument, and in the alto's high register he never lost the singing attack which reminds one of the prodigious Bechet.

An early solo on the 1928 Victor version of 'Cotton Club Stomp' recorded during his first year with Ellington shows how masterful he already was at 21. Over Wellman Braud's fingerbusting beat he sails across the bar lines, unafraid to swoop on a note and, with a luxuriant dollop of vibrato, to hold it for a couple of beats. Barney Bigard, who comes next, seems so rattled that he lets off a dreadful reed squeak.

As the 1930s progressed, Hodges relaxed further into himself, honeying his tone and eventually fashioning such a shamelessly poetic sound on the alto that Ellington felt compelled to use him as his premier romantic – an amusing fate for a taciturn professional. Features such as 'Magenta Haze' (1946) were little more than recitations of a gorgeous melody; but Hodges had to keep himself interested, and he always had the blues close to hand in much of his improvising. The small-group dates from the late 1930s and early 1940s, under his nominal leadership, are superb examples of his mastery of blues phrasing within what was effectively an instrumental pop-song format, in the likes of 'Good Queen Bess', 'That's The Blues Old Man' (both 1940) and above all 'Squatty Roo' (1941), almost a concerto of stock phrases given riveting life by Hodges's sly variations as he bounces off Jimmy Blanton's bass parts.

Hodges was always going to be a master executant rather than a maverick. It was this comprehensive ability which made John Coltrane nominate him as the greatest saxophonist in jazz. Right up to his valedictory 'Blues For New Orleans', at Ellington's *New Orleans Suite* sessions (1970), he played for his context. Ben Webster, on the other hand, always sounded too

Two examples from Ben Webster's classic series of albums recorded in the 1950s.

big and hulking for whatever environment he was in. Ellington gave Webster his first really appropriate setting, but the saxophonist had already worked for several of the major black orchestras of the 1930s, and when he joined Duke he admitted that Hodges himself was a prime influence on his playing.

Webster (1909-73) took the Hawkins model and pared it back, turning his ballads into voluptuous hymns, his up-tempo vehicles into growling, cornered-animal statements of aggression. It was one of the ironies of his career that Ellington's main concerto for him, 'Cotton Tail' (1940), was actually set at a tempo which Webster disliked – far too fast. While Hawkins would always harvest chords for many-noted variations, Webster preferred a more stately progress. He had no shortage of harmonic curiosity, having trained as a pianist, but he liked to float his solos at a poised mid-tempo. 'All Too Soon' (1940) is a fine instance of Webster's early maturity with Ellington. In later years, the huge sound of his saxophone, with the vibrating husk of the air column seeming to surround every note, became almost too thick and congested. In this earlier period, although recording never quite catches its full measure, it is more mobile, more expertly languorous.

Every Ellingtonian who followed Hodges and Webster (Carney had no successors) was effectively obliged to follow in their blueprinted footsteps: Jimmy Hamilton, Russell Procope, Al Sears, Harold Ashby. Perhaps only Paul "Mex" Gonsalves, who arrived in 1950, forged a markedly different style, sidelong and resolutely avoiding cliché – although even his first inspirations were surely Hawkins and Webster. But that was the story of most big-band sections, who patterned their routines around in-built band lore as much as

through specific charts and arrangements. Where the orchestras had fewer individual stars in their section, they relied more on a swinging compatibility. Yet several saxmen of the period became familiar almost by default. There are few better examples than New Orleans-born Eddie Miller (1911-91), perhaps the central figure in the orchestral-Dixieland style which the Bob Crosby band perfected in the '30s. Miller took up a position somewhere between Hawkins's ebullience and the still brisk but more cajoling manner of Bud Freeman.

Miller was a very able clarinettist – his solo on Crosby's famous hit 'South Rampart Street Parade' (1937) is probably the most renowned thing he ever did – but tenor playing was his real forte. His ballad feature on The Bobcats's 'Can't We Be Friends' (1937) sums him up: measured, full-bodied, but fluid enough to keep the melody supple and make what was quite an exaggerated vibrato seem appropriate to the treatment. Miller could be a hard-driving tenorman, as in 'Stomp Off, Let's Go' (1939), but his liking for a long melodic line suggests a kinship with musicians such as Bobby Hackett, and it comes as no surprise to learn that in the 1950s he played on countless uncredited sessions, playing solos-to-order but keeping enough of himself in them to save the sound from complete anonymity.

Miller's name was, nevertheless, hardly known other than to die-hard Crosby fans, and he was one of many swing-era players whose achievements are now remembered mostly by scholars. Vido Musso (1913-82) made hundreds of records with – in turn – Benny Goodman, Gene Krupa, Harry James, Woody Herman, Tommy Dorsey and finally, as the swing era was closing, Stan Kenton. Yet he left scarcely any signature pieces behind him.

'Did You Mean It?' (1936), an early Goodman entry, has a brief but rather surprising solo which goes against the superficial politeness of the arrangement. That was Musso's rather cheeky method: he was a larger-than-life figure who chafed against the discipline of sight-reading and

Ben Webster built a new career in Europe during the 1960s, living first in Holland and later in Denmark. The shot of Webster opposite was taken at the Metropol Club in Oslo in 1965.

Ben Webster and pianist Billy Kyle recording with Jack Teagarden's Big Eight in New York, December 1940.

regimentation, and eventually faded away as a partial consequence. His contribution to Stan Kenton's 'Painted Rhythm' (1945) is a boisterous, rather bad-tempered development of the Webster manner, and hints at the rock'n'roll saxophone vocabulary which would grow up in the next decade. But Musso never really flourished under Kenton, or anywhere else afterwards.

Buddy Tate (b. 1915), two years younger than Musso, might have followed a similar path. But Tate's Texas-Tenor feet were more firmly grounded, and he liked to stay in places where he felt comfortable, such as the Basie band (nine years from 1939), or a long subsequent residency in a Harlem nightspot.

Where players such as Musso made styles out of disparate bits and pieces, Tate's implacable blues playing always anchored every solo. He didn't really become well-known until he struck out as a touring attraction in the 1960s and '70s. At that point he had honed his sound to a rich but muscular essence, with familiar licks coming to seem like effortless and inevitable parts of an unstoppable flow. Perhaps the legacy of the saxophonists who emerged intact from the big-band period was that sort of repertorial assurance. Untroubled by bebop's demands for a constant striving for newness and reinvention, they seemed rooted and nourished in the tradition, mountainous, and impervious to bad stylistic weather. Buddy Tate may be the consummate example.

Although there were only nine of them, The Savoy Sultans proved more than a match for many star big-bands appearing at Harlem's Savoy Ballroom.

Or perhaps that accolade should go to Joseph "Flip" Philips (b. 1915), who at 85 released in 2000 one of the best records of his career. In the 1930s he was working in Brooklyn clubs as an alto player, but when he switched to tenor in the 1940s he found his métier. For most of the last 50 years he has been somewhat miscast as an impetuous exponent of rabble-rousing marathon solos – of the type allegedly loved by the crowds who flocked to Jazz At The Philharmonic concerts, where he was a regular for many years.

It would be more fitting to turn to some of his lesser-known recordings to understand the real Flip. "You can be angry, you can be soulful, you can play soft, you can play loud…" he said. Philips loved the tenor's 57 varieties, and his booting side was softened by an ineffable touch on ballads, made the more effective by a certain obliqueness. If one expected him to be in thrall to Hawkins, it was Lester Young who was his real compadre: Flip's 'Salute To Pres' (1952) is one of the warmest homages from one tenorman to another.

The tenor never lacked for stylists in the swing period, even if many of them impressed more by their facility than their individuality. The brief solos which swing-era 78s allowed were just the medium for players such as Ray McKinstrey, Arthur Rollini and Dick Wilson to make their modest mark on jazz history. In the case of Gene "Honeybear" Sedric (1907-63), a tenorman enjoyed massive exposure on record without the audience ever much realising who he was. As the saxophonist with Fats Waller & His Rhythm, Sedric was featured on scores of sides, yet – like fellow frontliner, trumpeter Herman Autrey – he had to suffer the indignity of most of his solos being interrupted by Waller's yells of encouragement. As successful as he was in this band, it probably didn't bother Sedric too much.

Nor did comparative obscurity hamper the progress of the masterful Budd Johnson (1910-84), a Texas Tenor of supreme accomplishment who remained more of a musicians' musician for most of his life than a star property. Most were scarcely even aware of his powers as a soloist until he started making infrequent albums under his own name in the 1960s and '70s. Yet he was a considerable force as a section-leader and arranger in the Earl Hines band of the 1930s, and subsequently with Dizzy Gillespie and Billy Eckstine in the

A rare glimpse of Flip Phillips playing clarinet, the saxophonist's traditional "double", at Kelly's Stable on New York's 52nd Street in 1940. With him are Harry Prather (bass), Eddie Dougherty (drums), Frankie Newton (trumpet) and Pete Brown (alto saxophone).

1940s where he helped bridge the swing and bebop vocabularies. Johnson's own sound was lean, tonally opaque, yet curiously powerful – a Lester without the enigmatic depths. 'Blues By Budd', from his Prestige date *Let's Swing* (1960), shows how accomplished an improviser he was.

For the most part, swing-era saxophone was dominated by tenor players, with the great spectrum of shadings between the seemingly opposite poles of Young and Hawkins. But it's two alto players who bring this discussion almost full circle.

Among alto section-players, the supreme exponent in the period was surely Willie Smith (1910-67). Throughout the 1930s he was both the leader of the Jimmie Lunceford saxophone section and the outstanding soloist in Lunceford's outstanding orchestra. He was writing charts for Lunceford as early as 1934. In his hard, cutting tone one can hear the precision which set a benchmark for saxophone sections throughout the decade. At the same time, Smith was a soloist who could milk the emotions. His adroitness could be used to crowd-pleasing ends and, as with such different stylists as Musso and Philips, he proved to be a favourite with Jazz At The Philharmonic audiences.

He joined Harry James after leaving Lunceford, and was for a long time the major soloist in that band, after James himself. It is fascinating to hear him on the 1946 JATP performance of 'I Can't Get Started', where he immediately follows Charlie Parker. Bird sounds rather bleary and ill-at-ease in his solo, and Smith's rejoinder is in comparison very proper and symmetrical; yet it buttonholes the listener because of the fierceness of his delivery, every note articulated as if it's grabbed off the scale. Smith's professionalism is its own reward, but perhaps it says something about why,

Willie Smith was an alto saxophone virtuoso, a brilliant soloist and an immaculate section leader. He's pictured (right) with bandleader Jimmie Lunceford at New York's Kit Kat Club in 1938.

for all his undoubted talent, he seems a far less interesting player than Parker.

Some of that paradox attends the reputation of Benny Carter (b. 1907), the other leading swing alto. Carter is a survivor from the original jazz age, arranging for Henderson and even Ellington by the late 1920s, doubling on trumpet and piano, and leading an occasional band which worked almost as a graduate school for the better players in New York. Carter's methods, scrupulous in their finesse, seemed indivisible from the man and his style of playing. Everything about him proposed jazz as a civilised, higher activity: there was no more reliable pro in the game, yet most of his work was done for commercial situations – he never proposed jazz as art music.

In the early 1930s he worked for various bands and led a handful of record dates, but he found wider exposure on record when he went to Europe in 1935, eventually ending up in London and working as staff arranger for the BBC Dance Orchestra. His own originals, such as 'Blues In My Heart' and 'When Lights Are Low', are memorable works which cross the bridge between jazz and tin-pan-alley standards. He returned home in 1938 to New York and his orchestra: the only other alto player who also led a big band of any

moment was Jimmy Dorsey, something of a stylistic kindred spirit. But where Dorsey's group had great success, Carter's was, hindsight has suggested, too good to succeed. Records such as 'Midnight' and 'My Favorite Blues' (both 1941) are impeccable extensions of Carter's style, a cultivated balance between what was by then a rather old-fashioned hot feel and a sophisticated balancing of the orchestral colours. In the end, it made little difference to Carter's career that the band didn't succeed: from 1945 he stayed permanently in Hollywood where his skills found reward in film and TV work, as well as occasional foraying into more hardcore jazz work.

His manner on the alto – with its genteel vibrato, unfailingly courteous relationship to the beat and smooth, consistent tone – is unmistakable. Even into his great old age (he eventually gave up the trumpet) his chops remained intact, and only occasionally does he really indulge himself in an exaggeration – a slurped note or a heavy-handed phrase. His 1950s sessions with Oscar Peterson, *Cosmopolite* and *Plays Pretty*, are some of the best examples of his work as a featured soloist. To pick one example, 'I've Got The World On A String' (1952) is a melody he has fun with, guying its jauntiness with a series of variations that are as clever as they are faultlessly delivered.

But that very urbanity has arguably hindered Carter's standing. He has never been much of an influence on players or arrangers. Some critics have seen his sound as "Republican", a conservatism which for some might be antithetical to what jazz ought to be about. Carter's fine taste has forever isolated him from the eminence which more colourful jazz characters have enjoyed, and it is even hard to think of defining moments in his discography.

Perhaps that mix of elegance, professionalism and exuberance is, though, the quintessence of swing-era saxophone. Its exponents were among the last jazz musicians who would be obliged to play strictly by the rules, and their consummate craft, in the years before the arrival of bebop, is a unique part of the language of the music.

Benny Carter was a musical phenomenon who played reed and brass instruments, as well as being a first-class arranger. He is seen (left) leading his own band in 1941. Despite his brilliance, he never had much success as a bandleader.

PETER VACHER **STILL SWINGING**

ENDLESS TRAVELLING AND INTENSE COMPETITION FOSTERED
THE DEVELOPMENT OF INDIVIDUAL, HIGHLY RECOGNISABLE
STYLES. BUT MANY FINE MUSICIANS FAILED TO ACHIEVE DUE
RECOGNITION BECAUSE THEY WERE IN THE WRONG PLACE AT
THE WRONG TIME, WITH NO OPPORTUNITY TO RECORD.

When publicists first came up with "swing" as a descriptive term for the music they were seeking to promote, they were concentrating on the output of the great big-bands of the 1930s. Their brief was clear: keep the bands and their leaders in the public eye, and high record sales and well-attended engagements would surely follow. Happily, the dancing public knew a good thing when they heard it, and swing took off. It generated new levels of prosperity for some prominent bandleaders, and allowed their better sidemen a fair crack at fame as well.

Since those heady days, "swing" has proved to be a useful portmanteau term to describe much of the jazz played and recorded from 1930 through to 1945. These were the pre-bebop years, of course, when rhythm sections stayed closer to an unvarying four-four beat and soloists began to improvise with increasing certainty on the harmonic structures of standards and originals.

While most of the musicians earned their living in the touring orchestras which proliferated in this period, it was in small groups that their solo capabilities were best able to flourish. If Louis Armstrong cast an ample shadow over jazz as a whole, it was as we've already seen the ground-breaking efforts of Coleman Hawkins which inspired the tenor saxophonists. In 1929, Hawkins had set out a new solo approach for the instrument on 'Hello Lola' and 'One Hour', building a series of choruses which appeared fully-formed and seamless – and incidentally providing a new definition of excellence for aspiring jazz saxophonists.

It became commonplace for these younger instrumentalists to try out their skills at jam sessions, often going head-to-head with an established player like Hawkins. There's a well-documented tale of an encounter in Kansas City in December 1933 when Hawkins (then playing with Fletcher Henderson) came up against Lester Young, Ben Webster and Herschel Evans at the Cherry Blossom Club, an after-hours spot. These three were then up-and-coming tenor saxophonists with strictly local reputations, but they gave the visitor such a hard time that he made himself late for Henderson's engagement in St Louis the following night. Drummer Jo Jones, who was present, claimed: "That was the first night that Hawkins was really challenged."

If Hawkins was a prime target for such a musical ambush, other incidents of lesser impact were taking place in Kansas City all the time, fuelled no doubt by KC's legendary "wide-open" reputation. In fact any town or city with a substantial black population – from Seattle in the North-West to San Antonio in Texas – had its share of late-night spots where soloists from visiting bands could engage with local men. Most areas of the US supported a number of "territory" dance bands, white and black, some minor-league and

The Pete Brown Sextet/
The Jonah Jones Sextet
HARLEM JUMP AND SWING

*Pete Brown was a pioneer of "jump jazz",
and is shown (left) at Jimmy Ryan's club
in New York during 1942. Brown's
forceful style marked the early stirrings of
what was to become R&B.*

likely to remain so, others with ambition and an eye on national success. Each
might contain a selection of committed jazz players who were anxious to pit
themselves in friendly musical combat against the best opposition of the day.
These informal get-togethers often allowed lesser-known musicians to surprise
established jazz stars. The tenor man Teddy Edwards, then playing alto with
the Ernie Fields Orchestra from Tulsa, Oklahoma, came up against the little-
known Harry Pettiford, brother of Ellington's great bassist, Oscar Pettiford.

"[Pettiford] was just one of the greatest saxophonists that ever lived," said
Edwards. "We'd go through Tulsa a lot and that's when we'd run into Harry.
There'd be guys from about four bands there and we'd jam the whole night.
At the end, it would be just Harry that was playing. He was fantastic."
Edwards was illustrating one of the truisms of jazz, that personal
circumstances and the failure to be in the right place at the right time
sometimes combined to keep outstanding musicians away from the limelight
and out of the recording studio.

One combative individual who knew his way around a jam session was
Leon "Chu" Berry (1910-41), whose career was cut short at the early age of
31. It has been argued that Berry was the only tenor saxophonist to mount a
serious challenge to the omniscience of Hawkins in the swing era. He had the
same rich and voluptuous tone, and loved to test himself against all-comers.
Born in Wheeling, West Virginia, Berry had the build to make it as a
footballer but decided on music while at college.

His nickname was a reference to the 1930s movie character Chu-Chin-
Chow, called to mind by the goatee beard and moustache that Berry wore as a
young man. Summoned to Chicago to join Sammy Stewart's band, he first
arrived in New York in 1930 when Stewart played the Savoy Ballroom. Berry

West Coast tenor saxophonist Teddy Edwards, pictured playing in London in 1993, began his career in the travelling swing bands of the South-West.

stayed on and began to attract the attention of leaders like Benny Carter and Charlie Johnson. After a period with Teddy Hill, in 1935 he joined the famed Fletcher Henderson orchestra (where Hawkins had made his reputation).

The British writer and arranger Spike Hughes was among the first to recognise Berry's talents and used him to good effect (in tandem with Hawkins) on a 1933 session. Berry was also featured on a John Hammond date for English Parlophone, again in 1933, under the name of The Chocolate Dandies. Records such as 'Blue Lou' with Henderson reveal a confident soloist, warm-toned and surging. Berry went on to cut many more fine sides before hitting the headlines when he joined Cab Calloway in 1937.

Something of a Calloway favourite, Berry was given many chances to shine by the vocal prankster, most notably on 'A Ghost Of A Chance' (1940), a rhapsodic ballad feature. He was also the star turn in the orchestra's band-within-the-band, The Cab Jivers. Inevitably, given his tendency to unfettered solo playing, Berry was at his best in small groups, such as the magnificent 'Shufflin' At The Hollywood' (1939) with Lionel Hampton, often cited as his definitive achievement. He was killed in a car crash in October 1941. Hawkins provided an appropriate, if laconic, epitaph: "Chu was about the best."

Another shortlived talent, Herschel Evans, left fewer recordings than Berry yet is remembered with almost equal enthusiasm, as much for his version of 'Blue And Sentimental' made with Count Basie in 1938 as for his influence on a later generation of Texan saxophonists. Evans (1909-39) was born in Denton, Texas, and came to musical maturity early in his teens, performing with territory bands from 1926 onwards. He made his first recordings with Troy Floyd's 10,000 Dollars Gold Orchestra in 1929, although the tenor solos scarcely hint at his later qualities.

In 1933 Evans travelled to Kansas City where he played alongside Lester Young in the Bennie Moten band. After Moten died on the operating table, many of his musicians dispersed, Evans to Chicago and then to Los Angeles in 1935. Once there he took part in the burgeoning Central Avenue scene, working with Lionel Hampton and trumpeter Buck Clayton in their big-bands. Sadly, neither of these was recorded.

Three top saxophonists of the swing era: Bud Freeman, Johnny Hodges and Chu Berry. Berry's early death in a road accident robbed jazz of a major talent.

Clayton was invited to join the Willie Bryant band in New York; on his way East he stopped off in Kansas City, accepted an offer from Count Basie, and persuaded Basie to send for Evans, who was thus reunited with Young. The contrast in their styles was an essential ingredient in the band's rising success. Evans soloed in the grand manner, influenced by his idol Hawkins, but with his own windswept, slightly wheezy approach, while Young favoured a lighter sound with unusual rhythmic placements.

Aside from some well-received small-group sessions, one with Hampton, another with trumpeter Harry James, the Evans legacy is best represented by his contributions to Basie's Decca sides. 'Texas Shuffle' (1938; composed and arranged by Evans himself) and 'Doggin' Around' (1938; co-composed by Evans and trumpeter Edgar Battle) are among his finest recordings.

His eventual successor with Basie was George "Buddy" Tate (b. 1914), another Texan, born in Sherman. Tate, who today lives in quiet retirement in upstate New York, has always paid tribute to Evans as both a formative influence and a distinguished role model. "He was immaculate, looked as though he had stepped out of a bandbox. When Herschel died, Basie wanted someone who would fit with the band. Herschel and I always did sound

Buddy Tate, doyen of "Texas Tenors", at a London concert (above) in 1969. With him are Charlie Shavers and Bill Coleman (trumpets). Tate is also pictured (right) outside Harlem's Celebrity Club, where he led the band for many years, successfully defying passing fashions by sticking to solid, danceable swing music.

alike," he said. There were other similarities, too: Buddy Tate played for Troy Floyd, with whom Evans had made his debut on wax, and moved from band to band in the South-West in much the same way as Evans had done. Tate was working with the Omaha-based Nat Towles orchestra when Count Basie's call came along in the spring of 1939. On Tate's first night with his new employer, the crowd kept calling for him to play 'Blue And Sentimental' as a tribute to Evans. Basie balked at this but Tate coped, his muscular sound and blues-feeling firmly in the Texan tradition.

Tate stayed with Basie for ten years and then went on to build a successful career as a club bandleader and touring soloist. He recorded often with Basie but came into his own once the mainstream movement of the 1960s took off, making many albums in Europe. *When I'm Blue* (1967) with organist Milt Buckner won the French Prix du Jazz. Tate's final round-up included a lively collaboration with ex-Basie trombonist Al Grey which proved popular throughout Europe. Tate was also part of a loosely organised 1980s festival act known as The Texas Tenors, with Arnett Cobb, Budd Johnson and Illinois Jacquet. Each of these outstanding instrumentalists employed the rousing, blues-based tenor style first made explicit by Evans. Jacquet stated unequivocally, "[Evans] was *the* Texas Tenor. [He] had such a big tone, you couldn't get near him."

Budd Johnson (1910-84), equally proficient as an arranger and instrumentalist, favoured a lighter touch than his confreres, but there was still no doubting his Texan origins. Born in Denton, he debuted with local groups and by 1932 was good enough to join Louis Armstrong's band in Chicago. He then became a fixture with the superb Earl Hines orchestra at the Grand Terrace, contributing arrangements and running things musically for Earl.

By the mid 1940s, Johnson was aligned with the younger modernists in Billy Eckstine's big-band, and was writing for everyone. His fluency and swing-to-bebop tenor aptitude commended him to many leaders. He also produced a number of excellent "name" albums, and his successful European tours helped to correct earlier critical neglect.

Illinois Jacquet (b. 1922) was born in Louisiana but was brought up in Houston, Texas. A kid dancer with his father's Legion Steppers, Illinois graduated to the alto and played as a teenager in The California Playboys with his brothers. He eventually made it to California proper after kicking off his career in Houston with the splendid Milt Larkin orchestra, billed as the

"Greatest Band Of All Time". His father's railroad job allowed the youngster a travel pass and he opted for Los Angeles, arriving there in 1939.

Befriended by bassist Charlie Mingus, Jacquet made some waves locally, but it was his selection for the new Lionel Hampton band which brought him the fame which has attended him ever since. Hampton converted Jacquet to tenor in 1942 and allotted him a feature on 'Flying Home', a recording which took off nationwide, powered by Jacquet's extraordinary solo (complete with its Evans quotation). Its success brought Jacquet all sorts of opportunities: high-profile engagements with Count Basie and Cab Calloway; participation in films; a key role in the initial Jazz At The Philharmonic concerts in Los Angeles; and the chance to run his own combos.

Jacquet combined exceptional mobility with a bluesy, full-toned Texan sound, but it was his predilection for upper-register harmonics which seemed to register with the fans. It was their enthusiasm which made Jacquet a club and concert smash in the later 1940s. His pianist John Lewis recalled, "Jacquet was making suitcases of money. I never saw so much." Since those days Jacquet has continued to lead his own groups. Recording regularly, he has a substantial array of albums to his credit. Hugely popular in Europe, he is effectively the last of the great swing tenor stars, as impressive in his maturity as he was in his 1940s heyday. With the formation of his big-band in 1984, re-energised and triumphant, Jacquet found new success with festival dates and international tours. And yes, he does still play 'Flying Home'.

With so many swing bands to choose from, each with its roster of soloists, the student of jazz history might well conclude that the swing years were truly "the tenor sax era", as Duke Ellington put it. There was Julian Dash and Paul Bascomb with Erskine Hawkins, Henry Bridges with Harlan

Sleeves of three top tenors who kept the flame of swing alive for more than half a century: Buddy Tate, Illinois Jacquet and Georgie Auld.

Leonard, Baker Millian with Boots & His Buddies, Joe Thomas with Jimmie Lunceford, the Berry disciple Herbie Haymer, and Californians Hubert "Bumps" Myers and Ulysses "Buddy" Banks. Each left evidence of laudable creativity on wax and deserves closer attention.

Benny Goodman's principal tenor soloist Georgie Auld (1919-90) was another robust, hard-swinging instrumentalist who fell under the spell of Coleman Hawkins. His tracks with the Goodman Sextet alongside trumpeter Cootie Williams and guitarist Charlie Christian amply demonstrate what critic Gunther Schuller called his "native vitality". Auld's later big-band bristled with young beboppers and emphasised his openness to new ideas. His on-screen role in the film *New York, New York*, for which he coached Robert De Niro and handled the soundtrack, made him enough money to ensure a comfortable retirement. Another fine tenorist, Jerry Jerome, also enjoyed the solo spotlight with Goodman, although his mentor was Lester Young rather than Hawkins. Jerome has continued to perform and record well into his 80s.

One-time postman Andy Kirk founded an excellent big-band in the mid 1930s and based it in Kansas City, taking it to national prominence. Its principal distinction arose from the sparkling arrangements by band pianist Mary Lou Williams and the solos of Dick Wilson (1911-41), another tenor saxophonist whose career was cut short by chronic illness. In the beginning he was a pupil of reedman Joe Darensbourg in Seattle, but Wilson left town with Gene Coy's Happy Black Aces and moved through the ranks of several bands before settling with Kirk. Kirk's 'In The Groove' (1937) and some neat combo sessions with Williams highlight a talent comparable to Lester Young. Fluent, silky-smooth yet vigorous, the quality of Wilson's solo performances made his early demise in 1941 at the age of 30 a tragedy comparable to those which beset Berry and Evans.

Georgie Auld playing tenor saxophone in trumpeter Bunny Berigan's orchestra in 1938. Auld would later work with Artie Shaw, Benny Goodman and other leading figures of the swing era.

Up in Harlem other less-publicised tenor heroes earned a crust on record and in small-group work. Players like Lem Johnson, Bob Carroll, Big Nick Nicholas, Benny Waters with Hot Lips Page, Kenny Hollon (on record with Billie Holiday and Slim Gaillard) and Hal Singer went on to benefit from the expansive 52nd Street club scene, often mixing with if not aping the younger modernists before settling for Dixieland or R&B. Gene "Honeybear" Sedric (1907-63) had his heyday with Fats Waller's small band in the late 1930s on many record sessions, alternately tender or tough. After Waller's death, Sedric dabbled with Dixieland and toured Europe with Mezz Mezzrow.

Although the tenor saxophone became the principal voice of choice for reed soloists in the swing era, it would be wrong to assume that alto and baritone soloists were necessarily in short supply. However, the protean achievements of Johnny Hodges and Benny Carter on alto and Ellington's stalwart Harry Carney on baritone have tended to mask the accomplishments of other lesser figures. Even so, among the altoists James "Pete" Brown (1906-63) cut quite a dash in Harlem, developing an abrupt, syncopated approach and kick-starting the jump style that was later taken to new heights by Louis Jordan. Principally associated with bassist John Kirby and trumpeter Frankie Newton, Brown wrestled abortively with the complexities of bebop, and died just as the mainstream revival was gathering momentum.

Brown's successor with Kirby was Russell Procope (1908-81), a New Yorker whose tailored exuberance was just right for Kirby's skilful combo. Procope, who recorded with Jelly Roll Morton in 1928, spent almost three decades in the Duke Ellington orchestra, sitting next to Hodges. Another altoist who made a mark on 52nd Street was St Louis native Don Stovall (1913-70), who started out in riverboat bands but whose main claim to fame arose from his seven-years with trumpeter Red Allen's hot New York band.

Down in the South-West there was Buster Smith (1904-90), known as "Prof". He was an altoist of great distinction, but chose to retreat into obscurity, leading blues bands in Dallas rather than challenging for supremacy in Harlem. Now best remembered for his tutelage of the teenage Charlie Parker, who joined Smith's combo in 1937, he was a visionary arranger and bandmaster. He helped Basie in Kansas City, soldiered with Jay McShann, and worked with various leaders in New York. His few recorded solos from the 1940s demonstrate his warm sound and attractive fluency – echoed, inevitably, in Parker's early work.

The tightly-knit John Kirby Sextet, with Russell Procope on alto saxophone, broadcasting from New York's Onyx Club in 1938. Vocalist is Maxine Sullivan.

Over in Kansas City, Tommy Douglas also influenced Parker, and his original ideas and full tone are represented on a handful of records. Cab Calloway's Eddie Barefield (1909-91) was another who cut his teeth in Kansas City (Barefield composed 'Toby', recorded by Bennie Moten in 1932) before moving to New York to work with the best bands around. Proficient on all the reeds, Barefield was hot on alto and equally effective on the tenor to which he switched later in his career.

Swing-era bandleaders largely used the baritone saxophone to add colour in section voicings. Only rarely were baritone players offered extended solo space, although Basie gave Jack Washington some moments to savour on 'Topsy' (1937) and 'Doggin' Around' (1938), while Jimmie Lunceford afforded Jock Carruthers occasional opportunities, notably on 'Harlem Shout' (1936).

Haywood Henry (b. 1913) bucked the trend to some degree in his 20-year association with the Erskine Hawkins orchestra, later moving into lucrative rock'n'roll studio work and touring as a mainstream soloist. Of course, any neglect of the baritone was corrected once Gerry Mulligan made his breakthrough in the 1950s. But that, as they say, is another story.

LESTER YOUNG – "PRES" – BROUGHT A NEW APPROACH TO THE TENOR SAXOPHONE AND, IMPORTANTLY, A NEW SENSIBILITY TO JAZZ, VASTLY EXPANDING ITS EXPRESSIVE RANGE.

In 1937 recorded jazz was 20 years old. In those two decades it had changed almost beyond recognition, to the extent that the word jazz itself was now hopelessly old-fashioned and used only patronisingly, as though referring to some aged relative of coarse and embarrassing habits.

The modern term was swing, and swing was rapidly developing into a diverse and flexible musical language. It was the popular music of the day, the music of social dancing, but it also attracted a growing audience of knowledgeable listeners, and an attendant corps of expert commentators and critics. In these circles, it was accepted that the sound of the tenor saxophone was broad and rugged, with a beefy vibrato and a bustling, assertive approach to phrasing. Since every tenor saxophonist laboured under the giant shadow of Coleman Hawkins, and these were the hallmarks of his style, this assumption is quite understandable. Equally understandable is the baffled silence which, early in 1937, greeted the first appearance on record of Lester Young.

The record in question bore the title 'Shoe Shine Boy', a cheery old ditty from the 1930 show *Hot Chocolates*. It had been recorded in Chicago on October 9th 1936 by a five-piece band calling itself Jones-Smith Incorporated. This was, in fact, a small group drawn from Count Basie's orchestra, but Basie himself was still virtually unknown at the time. So 'Shoe Shine Boy' arrived, unannounced, as an enigma from nowhere. More than 60 years have passed since then, but it takes only a small effort of imagination to experience some of the frisson those early listeners must have felt on first hearing it. Basie plays a good but unremarkable introduction and opening chorus, supported by superlatively buoyant bass and drums. Then, 45 seconds into the piece, Lester Young bursts upon the world.

The first impression is one of blazing energy and complete self-assurance as his solo drives unhesitatingly forward. It has all the patrician confidence of the young Louis Armstrong, and the passing years have not dimmed this in the slightest. But the solo was also deeply disconcerting at the time. To appreciate why, it is necessary to listen to the universal hero, Hawkins, and then hear 'Shoe Shine Boy' again, because Lester Young is the antithesis of Hawkins in all respects. Young's tone is light and airy, his vibrato delicately shaded, his phrases glancing and mercurial. Where Hawkins digs deeply into the harmonies of a tune, extracting every drop of harmonic juice, Young seems intent on avoiding harmonic embroilment altogether. At several points in 'Shoe Shine Boy' he toys with just two notes for several bars on end – and very basic notes, too.

To many people in 1937 it just didn't make sense. And yet those two choruses of 'Shoe Shine Boy' form a completely convincing, unified musical statement, involving tone, articulation, notes, rhythms, and all the other inseparable elements of a jazz musician's style. In introducing Lester Young to the world, 'Shoe Shine Boy' also made an important aesthetic point: that to be original you don't have to be complicated. At the time of this recording Lester Young was 27 years old, quite an advanced age for a debut. Behind him lay an eventful childhood and youth, passed in the now-vanished world of the itinerant entertainer. His father, Willis (Billy) Young, was the leader of a travelling carnival band. A talented and self-educated man, Billy Young recruited his entire family to form the nucleus of the band.

Lester, born on August 27th 1909, was the eldest of six and began his showbusiness career at the age of five, handing out flyers when the carnival

Lester Young with pianist Joe Sullivan, pictured together at New York's Vanguard Club in December 1940.

arrived in town. A few years later he graduated to playing the drums, switching to saxophone in his early teens because, so he later claimed, the drums were hampering his social life. By the time he had packed them away after the show, all the prettiest girls had gone.

His children all inherited Billy Young's acute musical ear, but Lester's was quite phenomenal. He had only to hear a piece once and he could reproduce it note-for-note. As a result he did not bother to learn to read music. He simply got his sister, Irma, to play his part through, and he memorised it. Eventually, Billy Young suspected what was going on and confronted Lester with a fresh sheet of music, which might as well have been Greek verse for all the sense he could make of it. Humiliated, he was banished from the band until his reading was up to standard.

This seemingly trivial incident touched on a key aspect of his personality, one which was to determine the course of his life and the nature of his art. Young was exceptionally sensitive to other people and their attitude toward him. He craved approval and acceptance, suffered anguish at the slightest hint of rejection, and strenuously avoided confrontation of any kind. He never got

*Lester Young's extraordinary sidelong
stance with the tenor saxophone looked
awkward but obviously suited him. Later
he held the instrument lower, but retained
the twist in the mouthpiece, so that he was
playing with his head tilted to one side.*

over that first humiliating rejection, and would bring it up in conversation for
the rest of his life. But in congenial company, safe among friends, Young was
a different person – exuberant, quirkish, comical, the life and soul of the
party. He often exasperated his friends by his improvidence, his vagueness
and his semi-detached attitude to everyday life. But there is no record of his
ever having made a single enemy.

At 18, unable to face a proposed tour through the Deep South with its
insults and privations, he left the family band and started a wandering career
around the Mid-West and South-West. In Salina, Kansas, he joined Art
Bronson's Bostonians, and switched from alto to tenor saxophone. "As soon as
I got my mouth round it I knew it was for me," he recalled.

As he drifted from band to band, his name was increasingly passed around
as being a young man to listen out for. He worked with the legendary Blue
Devils orchestra, and briefly with the great New Orleans pioneer King Oliver
who was then in his declining years. Young's love of playing was insatiable.
He turned up at jam sessions in bars and hotel lobbies, even in a shoe-shine
parlour on one celebrated occasion. Those who heard him were regularly
struck dumb by the force and eloquence of his playing. It was during this

wandering period that the style which was to be unveiled in the recording studio in 1936 came together. We have no way of telling exactly when that happened, or through what stages it passed, but we do know which players Young admired at the time. His two favourite saxophonists were Jimmy Dorsey and Frankie Trumbauer. "They were the only ones telling a story I liked to hear," said Young. "Trumbauer always told a little story. And I liked the way he slurred the notes. Did you ever hear him play 'Singing The Blues'? That tricked me right then, and that's where I went." Trumbauer played charming, slightly whimsical solos on c-melody saxophone, quite the reverse of the earthy, blues-inflected style of the South-West. It was probably his unassertive grace as much as his flawless technique that caught Young's ear.

Early 1933 found Young established in Kansas City, a town prospering

Lester Young, Roy Eldridge and Harry Edison

mightily under the corrupt regime of gangster-politician Tom Pendergast, booming amid the surrounding Depression. Entertainment blazed for 24 hours a day and it was said that there was no such creature as an unemployed musician in the whole of KC. Reputations were won and lost at the marathon jam sessions which took place almost every morning as musicians drifted in after work. Young was in his element.

Pianist Mary Lou Williams recalled the epic night when Coleman Hawkins, on tour with Fletcher Henderson's orchestra, challenged all-comers. "The word went round that Hawkins was in The Cherry Blossom, and within half an hour there were Lester Young, Ben Webster, Herschel Evans, Herman Walder and one or two unknown tenors piling into the club to blow." According to her account, Hawkins's royal progress had an unexpected setback, particularly at the hands of Lester Young. "It took him maybe five choruses to warm up, but then he'd really blow. Then you couldn't handle him on a cutting session... Yes, Hawkins was king until he met those crazy Kansas City tenor men."

Exploits such as this spread Young's fame among touring musicians right across America. Many would not actually have heard him play, but they knew of him by reputation. Early in 1934 he joined the small band led by pianist Bill Basie (not yet elevated to the aristocracy as a Count). He had scarcely settled in when a telegram arrived from Fletcher Henderson. Hawkins had left to try his luck in Europe and Henderson was offering Young the vacant job. This promised to be his big break, and Basie urged him to accept. On March 31st he joined Henderson in Detroit. Very soon it became clear that something was seriously wrong. Henderson's saxophone section consisted of

Three studies of Lester Young in later life. Left to right: on a European tour in 1952; wearing his trademark pork-pie hat; and laughing with Roy Eldridge during a 1958 recording session.

two altos and a tenor, plus clarinet. It had worked very well anchored by Hawkins's weighty sound, but once that ballast was removed the ensemble fell apart. The band members complained bitterly about the newcomer's "thin tone". Henderson's wife, Leora, took it upon herself to administer a crash course in Hawkins Studies. She played Young various Hawkins records and chased him around music stores in search of magic mouthpieces and reeds, but all to no avail. Young could not turn himself into Coleman Hawkins, even if he had wanted to. Criticised, singled out for blame, excluded – it was all too painfully reminiscent of the traumatic episode with the family band. Before leaving, he asked Henderson for a letter certifying he had not been sacked.

He worked his way back to Kansas City and eventually back into Basie's band, now resident at the Reno Club. A live broadcast from the club was picked up by producer and talent scout John Hammond, and in 1936 Basie signed agency and recording contracts. He expanded his band from nine to 14 members and left Kansas City for New York and the big time. En route, the small Jones-Smith contingent recorded four numbers, including 'Shoe Shine Boy' and its equally fine companion piece 'Lady Be Good'.

Without doubt, the years with Basie, between 1936 and 1941, were the happiest of Lester Young's life. They also produced some of his finest recorded work, both with the band itself and with various ad hoc small groups such as The Kansas City Six. The quality of his playing is so astonishingly consistent that it is impossible to pick out any obvious "best" moments. Young claimed that his favourite solo with Basie was the opening chorus of 'Taxi War Dance' (1939). It certainly is a marvellous creation. One is struck once again by his poise and absolute sure-footedness as he flips deftly through the harmonies, drawing an elegant, unbroken line of melody. Even at the fastest tempo, as in 'Clap Hands, Here Comes Charlie' (1939), he never sounds hurried.

Rudolf Nureyev once remarked that a dancer of genius is not one who makes a difficult step look easy, but one who makes an easy step look interesting. In these brief solos with the Basie band, Lester Young contrives to do both. The apparent simplicity is deceptive, with tricky intervals and teasing rhythm patterns negotiated with ease. As for making easy steps interesting, look no further than the first two bars of the 'Clap Hands' solo: a single note, repeated exactly on the beat eight times, but played with such dynamism and tonal variety that they send the whole solo flying forward.

Young's originality of mind revealed itself in a kind of lateral thinking, both musical and otherwise. For instance, noticing that some notes on the saxophone could be produced using more than one fingering, and that different fingerings produced different densities of tone, he developed the practice of alternating "thick" and "thin" versions of the same note – "ooh, ah" – not as an applied effect but as an integral part of his style.

Then there was his highly personal use of language. He was the first to use the term "bread" to mean money. "Eyes" meant enthusiasm, "bells" meant enjoyment, white musicians were "grey boys". As he grew older this linguistic inventiveness evolved into virtually a private language, impenetrable to outsiders. "I feel a draft," he would say, meaning that he sensed hostility. Later this was replaced by "Von Hangman is here."

He was also adept at bestowing nicknames, the most celebrated being "Lady Day" for Billie Holiday, with whom he had an extraordinary closeness, at once platonic and passionate. She, in return, named him "Pres", short for "The President", and these names have stuck to both of them beyond the

A gentle and essentially shy man, Young appeared withdrawn with strangers but expanded among friends. This shot from a 1957 session (opposite) catches his character perfectly.

grave. The records they made together in the late 1930s act out their relationship in music and are among the most beautiful jazz performances ever recorded. Holiday's small, knowing, unsentimental voice and Young's smoothly laconic saxophone conduct little conversations, so exquisite in their subtlety that they never lose their capacity to surprise and delight. On pieces such as 'Me, Myself And I' and 'A Sailboat In The Moonlight' (both recorded on June 15th 1937) the two voices move together in such perfect unity that they seem to be thinking each other's thoughts.

The Billie Holiday sessions and other small-band recordings of the time reveal a truly revolutionary aspect of Young's art. He opened up a whole new range of emotional territory to jazz. Until he came along, jazz dealt largely in simple, strong modes of expression – the sweeping majesty of Armstrong or Hawkins, the lithe grace of Bix Beiderbecke, the headlong delight of Fats Waller. With Young, we encounter ambiguity for the first time – passion combined with wit, energy combined with reticence and, increasingly in his later years, weariness, resignation and self-doubt. He was a uniquely sensitive individual; his playing faithfully reflected his complicated emotional make-up.

Young left Basie's band in December 1940, for undisclosed reasons. It was reported at the time that he had been sacked for refusing to record on Friday 13th. This ridiculous story caused him great anguish, and his wife, Mary, wrote a furious denial to the editor of *Down Beat* magazine. He now formed a small band of his own and secured a job at a New York club, Kelly's Stables. But it would be difficult to imagine a more unsuitable person as a bandleader, and the venture fell apart after a few months. In May, Young left New York for Los Angeles to join the band led by his brother, the drummer Lee Young.

Lee Young's band made no records, but in July 1942 Lester recorded four numbers in LA with Nat King Cole on piano and Red Callender on bass. They are startlingly different from anything he had done before: softer and more reflective, with far less spring in the step. His tone is thicker, too. Whatever caused this change – and several theories have been put forward – it proved to be permanent. A recording strike by the union kept him out of the studios until December 1943. Then came a run of superb small-band sessions, mostly with former Basie colleagues. Young always insisted that a jazz solo should "tell a story", and on these recordings he seems to be speaking directly from experience. The youthful exuberance may have evaporated, but the simplicity and candour of his improvisations make them irresistible. Compared with 'Shoe Shine Boy', 'Just You, Just Me' (1943) is sparse and severe, a gravely elegant exploration of a simple melody. This was also the period when he began to work with slow ballads. 'Ghost Of A Chance' (1944), the first of many, is a wonderfully dark, brooding performance which, even a few years earlier, would have been quite unthinkable as a Lester Young creation.

Shortly before recording 'Ghost Of A Chance' Young had rejoined Basie, the only band in which he'd ever felt truly at home. In September 1944, while they were playing at a club in Watts, LA, Young was caught by the wartime draft and sent to an army induction camp in Alabama. Various dubious substances were discovered among his possessions, there was a court martial, and he was sentenced to a year's detention. With remission, he served eight dreadful months in the detention barracks at Fort Gordon, Georgia.

His post-army career has been the subject of endless debate over the years. It used to be said that his experience at Fort Gordon was so traumatic that he never recovered, ending up "a broken man", drunken and incoherent.

Toward the end of his life, declining health and uncontrolled drinking badly affected Young's playing, although he could still play beautifully on occasion.

His sustained, seamless, three-minute improvisation on 'These Foolish Things' (1945), recorded soon after his release, gives the lie to that. But he certainly became increasingly wary and withdrawn, and drank more and more.

His playing reflected his changing moods and fluctuating state of health, but at least until 1956 he was capable of beautifully subtle and touching performances – for example 'Polka Dots And Moonbeams' (1949), 'Undercover Girl Blues' (1951) and 'Pres Returns' (1956). Two nervous breakdowns, drink, increasing shortness of breath; these and other afflictions all took their toll, yet he could rise magnificently to the occasion when the circumstances were right. A week-long engagement at a Washington DC club in 1955 was privately recorded and the results, released many years later, could almost have come from the pre-army days. Significantly, Young enjoyed the company of his young Washington accompanists and spent hours regaling them with tales of his early career.

His final years were marked by both physical decline and a sense of failure which no one else could quite understand. Throughout the 1950s he was in roughly the same position as Hawkins in the 1930s: hugely influential and widely revered. But this brought no pleasure; he did not find imitation flattering. "They're picking the bones while the body's still warm," he said.

He was taken ill during a solo engagement in Paris, flew home and died the following day, March 15th 1959. He was 49. He had predicted that he would not live to see his 50th birthday.

CHARLIE PARKER

***THE LANGUAGE OF JAZZ CHANGED IN THE FORTIES. TO SOME IT
WAS GRADUAL, BUT TO MANY IT WAS UNPREDICTABLE, SUDDEN
AND VIOLENT – AND THE MOST DECISIVE FACTOR IN THE
BEBOP REVOLUTION WAS THE PLAYING OF CHARLIE PARKER.***

*Every surviving note played by Charlie
Parker has been rescued and at one time or
another issued on record.*

The acceptance of the new bebop style by the average jazz listener was destined to be gradual. In the early 1940s the most popular saxophonists were Coleman Hawkins, Lester Young and Don Byas (who initially replaced Young in the Basie band), along with their followers such as Illinois Jacquet and Flip Phillips. There was also Ellington's first featured tenor star Ben Webster, and his section-mate Johnny Hodges, then rising to his greatest personal popularity, along with fellow altoists Willie Smith of the Jimmie Lunceford band and Benny Carter.

It seemed unlikely that another altoist, with a radically different approach, could rival these men either in their general appeal or their influence on other players. Yet listeners who experienced the sound of Parker, either in the flesh or on record, all had an extreme reaction. Some welcomed him as a new messiah; others dismissed him as crazy. There were, as we shall see, aspects of his life that might support the latter theory. But the net effect of his music was positive. Far from being destructive, his work consolidated the earlier achievements of others while adding something new and personal.

The musician who did all this was not the most likely candidate. Born in 1920, Charlie Parker was the son of a travelling man. Charlie's father apparently had some talent as a singer and pianist, but perhaps was most creative working as a cook on the Pullman trains. Charlie's mother had to earn her living as a night cleaner after being abandoned by her husband. One of Charlie's few advantages in life was his realisation, at least by his very early teens, that he could exploit his mother's unquestioning support. She would let him spend all his time on the streets without criticism, she would buy him a secondhand instrument, and when he married at 16 she would house and support the happy couple plus his mother-in-law.

Another undoubted advantage came from being brought up in Kansas City ("KC"), with its wall-to-wall jam sessions and lively nightlife (as depicted, along with the municipal corruption that created them, in Robert Altman's film *Kansas City*). So it was that Parker – unimpressed by the high-school band in which he played the euphonium-family "baritone horn" – found that there was absorbing music all around him. A school-friend encouraged him, and Parker soon made up for lost time, acquiring his first alto at 13, gigging with friends by the following year, and soon attending major-league jam sessions. Here he heard leading local saxophonists Tommy Douglas and Buster Smith (who became his mentors) as well as the notably avant-garde Lester Young, before any of them were widely known beyond the city or appeared on records. Soon, he got the nerve to sit in himself and, while his rather basic musical competence initially met with hostility, he persevered

Parker plays in Sweden during his second, and last, European visit, in 1950.

and redoubled his practice routine. During the summer that he turned 17, Parker was employed for the season by top Kansas City bandleader George E Lee in a lake resort some 100 miles away. Parker had quickly discovered the seamier side of music-making in KC, and was already into hard drugs. An abnormally strong constitution enabled him to tolerate regular intakes of heroin and alcohol, often simultaneously. It was only later in his short life that they would catch up with him.

When Charlie moved in 1938, first to Chicago and then to New York, a small circle of hip musicians was astounded by his newly acquired technical ability. But he didn't find many paying gigs. Indeed, he took the only non-musical job of his life, washing dishes at a Harlem night-spot in order to hear its resident pianist, Art Tatum. Tatum's great harmonic knowledge and versatility even influenced the doyen of jazz saxophonists, Coleman Hawkins, and was probably a factor in Parker's major musical discovery of this period. Ten years later, Parker described how in a jam session he found that "by using the higher intervals of a chord as a melody line and backing them with appropriately related changes, I could play the thing I'd been hearing". Dexter Gordon, who played with Parker in 1945, noted more specifically that where Lester Young had already used accented 6ths and 9ths, Parker "extended that to 11ths and 13ths, like [Dizzy Gillespie], and to altered notes

Backstage at the 1949 Paris Jazz Fair,
Parker plays for a group of visiting
British fans and musicians.

like the flatted 5th and the flatted 9th". Gillespie, with Cab Calloway's band, was already working on some of the new harmonic and rhythmic ideas that went toward the formation of bebop. Gillespie was full of admiration and amazement when, on tour with Calloway in 1940, he heard the self-taught Parker incorporating similar ideas, while still retaining a natural feel for saxophone phrasing.

In 1980, with hindsight, Gillespie declared: "Charlie Parker, as we all know, was the catalyst. He was the establisher of the style... After we started playing together, I began to play rhythmically more like him. In that sense he influenced me, and all of us. Because what makes the style is not what you play but how you play it."

Parker had returned to Kansas City and joined a former colleague, pianist Jay McShann, who in 1940 formed a Basie-style big-band to which Parker contributed both ensemble ideas and his rapidly coalescing solo style. The band gave him the nickname Yardbird, soon shortened to Bird. It also provided him with a chance to make records and, when they played the famous Savoy Ballroom in 1942, a second chance to visit New York.

Pioneer bebop drummer Kenny Clarke, resident at the famous Minton's Club, said: "They began to talk about Bird because he was playing like [Lester Young] on alto... until we found out that he had something of his own to offer." What he had to offer was both harmonic and rhythmic. In addition

Dizzy Gillespie toward the end of his life, almost half a century after his revolutionary partnership with Parker.

to adopting Young's relaxed approach to the beat, Parker brought the ability to play phrases of widely varying lengths, starting at any part of the bar, and to impart a great variety of timing within individual phrases.

It was natural that he and Gillespie should form an informal partnership, which for a few years spearheaded the development of the bebop style. Partly this took place within a big-band format during their joint membership of the orchestras of Earl Hines (for some eight months in 1943) and Billy Eckstine (an even shorter period in 1944). As well as constantly practising together and seeking out jam sessions while on the road, they regularly inspired each other in their contributions to the band shows. Dizzy included his written arrangements such as the classic 'Night In Tunisia' while Bird played dynamic solos in the limited space allotted to him.

However, bebop was to be fundamentally a small-group music for quintet or quartet. Its huge potential was obscured while the big-bands retained their popularity during World War II, although it was ready to surge forward in the succeeding Cold War period. The equally new consolidation of what became R&B took over many of the more basic and immediately entertaining aspects of big-band swing, such as the novelty vocals and the obvious emphatic rhythm-section work. But bebop was conceived as a more artistic endeavour, essentially concerned with breaking up the regularity of much earlier jazz, not only in the melody lines themselves but in the interplay of the hornmen with the rhythm players. As a result, the role of pianists and drummers in particular became that of accenting (often in a different way from each other) the lines of the melody instruments. It was not a surprise, then, that the textural variety of the best big-band music gave way to a streamlined unison sound, or that Gillespie and Parker were both interested in the explicit cross-rhythms of Afro-Latin bands.

Gillespie's penchant for bandleading, both in terms of musical organisation and showmanship, meant that he usually obtained the gigs. At first these were on New York's 52nd Street, in the winter of 1943-44 and again in winter 1944-45, and then in California during the winter of 1945-46. Parker's talents were not directed toward fronting a group or finding work. Indeed, he missed that first quintet season, being on his last extended stay in Kansas City. But in these small-group settings he created superb improvisations with their own spontaneous organisation. And, with Gillespie's help, he created some of the first composed material in the bebop style: 'Dizzy Atmosphere', 'Shaw Nuff',

Max Roach (right), drummer with Parker's great quintet of the late 1940s, pictured in concert during 1989.

Charlie Parker in concert in the late 1940s.

'Thriving On A Riff' ('Anthropology') and the harmonically and rhythmically ambiguous 'Koko'. All these were recorded during 1945, along with Dizzy's 'Groovin' High' and 'Salt Peanuts' and Tadd Dameron's 'Hot House'. For those who hadn't previously picked up on Parker's brief solos with Jay McShann, these records became the new bible.

Trumpeter Art Farmer, who first met Parker at this period, observed: "He could play [Lester Young]'s solos, note for note, and probably Coleman Hawkins's, too. But he did that to find out what was in them, not to copy them." Parker's combination of Young with the harmonic expertise of Hawkins and Don Byas was executed with a masterly precision, enhanced by his unique tone that was at first derided by some for its apparent harsh edge. But it reflected his great love of the blues. Indeed the first record session under his name included two 12-bar numbers, each destined to be famous in its own right: 'Billie's Bounce' and the more riff-based 'Now's The Time'.

Musicians already converted by seeing Bird live cherished these sacred texts, while those confused by what they'd heard were now able to study the discs at length. Among those who did so were James Moody, Sonny Criss and Art Pepper. (There has always been a question-mark over Sonny Stitt, since both he and Bird agreed he was working along similar lines before they met, but his achievements were only those of a less inventive imitator.)

Even musicians of earlier styles were not hostile and, as well as being heard on several records with swing players, Parker eventually exerted an influence on elders such as Hawkins and Benny Carter. While in California in early 1946, he made his first guest appearances with the swing-oriented Jazz

At The Philharmonic concert-group organised by producer Norman Granz. At the same time, in a seemingly unplanned move, he made the break from Gillespie. Dizzy went on to achieve considerable popularity as the public face of bebop. Bird, however, was about to reach a low point. He became the frontman of a shortlived quintet with the young Miles Davis and then of another group put together by trumpeter Howard McGhee. But he ended up living rough, and short of the regular supply of heroin which he now needed.

He made two recording sessions in 1946, one with each group. With Miles Davis there was his stunning solo on 'Night In Tunisia' as well as further original material: the new 'Moose The Mooche', the several-years-old 'Yardbird Suite', first created for Jay McShann, and 'Ornithology', a theme created by Benny Harris from Bird's solo on the McShann record 'Jumpin' Blues'. The date with McGhee, however, saw Parker in many ways close to the edge. His playing was mostly incoherent, while the painfully assembled solo on the famous ballad 'Lover Man' was executed with an untypically flabby tone and barely controlled fingering. After failing to complete the session, he created a scene at the hotel where he had been installed and as a result was forcibly subdued and arrested.

Parker ended up in the Camarillo mental hospital for six months. Although he apparently submitted with equanimity to the restorative aspects of the regime there and emerged fit and well, he could by no means be said to have learned a lesson. He continued to indulge in many and varied forms of dissipation, and was often difficult to work with.

Returning to New York in spring 1947, he formed a new quintet that, for a while, earned its enduring reputation as the best group he was ever associated with. Miles Davis was the trumpeter, Max Roach the drummer, with bassist Tommy Potter and pianist Duke Jordan.

As well as regular, well-received live dates, the group produced a quantity of excellent recordings (1947-48) for the Dial and Savoy labels. For the records there were slight fluctuations of personnel. The first session had Bud Powell, the last two John Lewis on piano; trombonist J J Johnson was added on one occasion; and on another, set up to feature the playing and composing of Miles, Bird was on tenor rather than alto. The overall quality of the performances, and their suitability as a setting for Parker himself, created one of the most revered bodies of work in the whole history of jazz. Bird's own improvisation is flawless and ceaselessly inventive, as the later release of alternate takes of the tunes amply demonstrated. The contrast between him and the moody Davis, who is technically less than magnificent, adds a piquant balance not found in Parker's work with Gillespie. A similar contrast existed in the rhythm section between the hot playing of Roach and the relatively cool piano work. The new material included items soon to become bebop standards, including 'Scrapple From The Apple'. More striking still was the first appearance on records of Bird the slow-tempo stylist, on tunes like 'My Old Flame', 'Out Of Nowhere', 'How Deep Is The Ocean', 'Embraceable You' and, especially, the slow blues 'Parker's Mood'.

Yet it was not a happy band. Jordan noted that the drug-pushers followed Bird everywhere, distracting him from music, while Miles and Max Roach suffered from his indifference both to their performance and to paying them regularly. Davis, the youngest member, commented that he was the only one to rehearse the group. He composed the tune 'Donna Lee' for their first record date and probably created the introduction to 'Don't Blame Me'. When Davis

This live recording of Parker with Bud Powell and Dizzy Gillespie was recorded at Birdland in 1949.

tried to get Duke Jordan replaced in the working group by John Lewis, he was slapped down by Parker, who told him "that he [Bird] chose the guys and Miles could form his own outfit if anything displeased him". Davis proceeded to do just that, with Roach on drums, and while they both would return to Parker, the musical link was broken. By late 1949 Miles had been replaced by Kenny Dorham, then Red Rodney, and Roach gave way to Roy Haynes.

During that same year Parker also started to appear on record away from his own group. He made notable if brief contributions to a Metronome All Stars session, hooked up again with Jazz At The Philharmonic, and signed a recording contract with Norman Granz who paired him with Machito's Afro-Cuban band and, more controversially, with a string ensemble. The fact that the first album with strings included a relatively popular single, the standard

  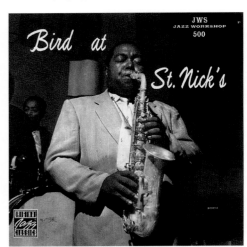

Typical compilation albums of Parker's work (above) first issued during the 1960s.

'Just Friends', was perhaps less significant for Bird than his week with the quintet in Paris, as one of the stars of the second Paris Jazz Fair. The adulation of European fans led to a further trip on his own to Sweden the following year – but it also helped to underline the fact that, as the middle of the century approached, neither bebop nor its black innovators (not even Gillespie) were receiving that kind of acclaim in the United States.

His management's temporary solution was to feature Parker with a big-band at Harlem's Apollo Theatre and then to tour him with a string quintet. But both ended up increasing his musical frustrations, particularly the latter which necessarily included several non-jazz players. The fact that he could no longer call on a regular group of sidemen capable of providing interest and contrast, as with Miles and Max Roach, led to a downward spiral in his well-being. Increasingly dependent on stimulants, he was also more and more unreliable in public appearances, and when he was in a position still to choose the guys, he often turned up with a hastily-thrown-together band of wholly unworthy fourth-rank players.

What many regard as the last time Bird did himself justice musically was an all-star "Quintet Of The Year", assembled in 1953 at Massey Hall, Toronto. Parker, Gillespie, Bud Powell, Max Roach and Charles Mingus romped through some old bebop favourites, and the uplifting results were recorded and issued on the small label jointly started by Mingus and Roach.

Less than two years later, however, in March 1955, a similar quintet (with Gillespie and Roach replaced by Kenny Dorham and Art Blakey) played two nights at New York's Birdland – the club named in honour of Parker yet which had often banned him from appearing. By all accounts, the second night was an embarrassing fiasco during which Parker argued with Powell on the stand and refused to play. Mingus said to the audience, "This is not jazz. These are sick people." Sadly, he was right. A week later Bird was dead from a heart-attack at the age of 34.

But his music lives on. The classic records have been constantly reissued, and a treasure-trove of live sessions has been discovered and released publicly. The Parker sound and the style are a constant touchstone for musicians and listeners around the world, bebop is widely recognised as a classic form of jazz, and Parker is revered as the player who brought it to the peak of its achievement. In addition, except for the occasions when he was manifestly not in control, his command of the saxophone was second to none. Whether

playing on a brand new instrument or one borrowed from a hapless bystander. he sounded immediately like himself and no one else.

At the start of jazz's second century, Parker is only the second jazzman (after Duke Ellington) to have a plaque on the wall of his New York home – at 151 Avenue B on the Lower East Side. In fact, there are two plaques and although one draws attention to the architecture of the building, both duly mention Parker's importance as a player and as co-founder of bebop Meanwhile, the plastic saxophone he used at Massey Hall is in the museum of his hometown, Kansas City. Yet more significant is the fact that people are still listening to him and trying to play like him.

Parker jamming with the young Chet Baker in Los Angeles in 1952.

BEBOP SAXOPHONES

THE INFLUENCE OF CHARLIE PARKER PROVED IRRESISTIBLE, ESPECIALLY TO ALTOISTS, ALTHOUGH SOME MANAGED TO DEVELOP A PERSONAL APPROACH. THERE WAS A GREATER VARIETY OF STYLES AMONG TENOR PLAYERS, INCLUDING SUCH GREATS AS DON BYAS, WARDELL GRAY AND DEXTER GORDON.

Essentially a swing player, saxophonist Charlie Ventura popularised bebop through his Bop For The People band.

Not the least measure of bebop's impact was its almost instant attraction to up-and-coming musicians. Over half the musicians discussed here were born during the early 1920s and were therefore in their late teens when the new music burgeoned so rapidly. No doubt other youngsters were drawn to more traditional forms of jazz, but few made any sort of a name for themselves.

Even those musicians who may be said to have begun their careers as swing-oriented players rapidly assimilated both the harmonic and rhythmic innovations of bop. Two prime examples discussed elsewhere are Paul Gonsalves and Stan Getz. But we begin with a tenor saxophonist who had effected a mature style before the advent of bop.

Don Byas (1912-72) had started out with Bennie Moten and Walter Page, and by the time he replaced Lester Young in the Basie band in 1941 he had worked with Lionel Hampton, Buck Clayton, Lucky Millender and Benny Carter. A wide-ranging and highly intelligent musician, Byas was attracted to bop from the outset, becoming centrally involved in its advance. It is no accident that Dizzy Gillespie chose him for his seminal sextet recordings of 1946. Indeed, during this time Byas was regarded as "Boss Tenor", his output judged as superior to both Hawkins and Young.

Byas's tone was an artful variant of the Hawkins swagger, but his harmonic grasp was deceptively subtle, recalling Lester Young; conversely, while he swung prodigiously, he did not share the boppers' interest in serpentine patterns and oblique accents, but favoured an on-the-beat attack.

In short, Byas was a real original, and it is not easy to explain why his reputation is not larger. One reason may be his emigration to Europe in the late 1940s. Although he prospered there, he cut himself off from the recording opportunities that were beginning to proliferate in America, especially once the LP had come of age. Consequently the Byas catalogue is more modest than it should be, and his story is a poignant one, set in a minor key.

He had something of a revival shortly before his death, winning great acclaim at the Newport Festival of 1970 and touring Japan with Art Blakey in 1971. As an exemplar of both his gifts and his importance, try 'All The Things You Are' on *Jazz At The Philharmonic In Europe Vol 1* (1960). Byas takes the second solo, following Hawkins and preceding Getz. All three are majestic; together they encapsulate a rich slice of the history of jazz tenor.

Charlie Ventura (1916-92) was essentially a swing musician whose style approximated a somewhat vulgarised version of Chu Berry's approach. He is chiefly known for his work with Gene Krupa, whose band he joined in 1942 and with whom he was reunited on several subsequent occasions. Nevertheless he championed bop, and while his own playing displays a limited assimilation

One of the first bop tenor saxophonists, Don Byas moved to France in the 1950s and had great success with a series of albums featuring slow, sensuous ballads.

of the new language, he often played with bop musicians (Kai Winding, Bennie Green and Illinois Jacquet) and in the late 1940s led a band billed as Bop For The People. The arrangements were clever, especially those in which bop themes were performed by voices and instruments in unison, and the outfit was quite successful for a while.

Although only a minor figure, Ventura is interesting in that his career epitomises the meteoric rise of bop and its hardly less rapid demise as a commercial proposition. He was a forward-looking musician who was clearly charmed by bop's harmonic innovation and melodic adventurousness; rhythmically, though, he was a good deal more traditional, and by the early 1950s his playing had reverted to its conservative roots.

Byas was already a leading light when bop happened and Ventura was also an experienced sideman who absorbed some of the bop idiom. Younger musicians had different stories to tell. The separate but decisive influences of Young and Parker proved simultaneously liberating and tyrannical. Their radicalism opened up vast new territories for aspiring musicians; the problem, however, lay in discovering a truly distinctive way of exploring them. To master one's craft and gradually to become established is always difficult enough. To attempt the task under the giant shadows cast by Young and Parker was something else again. One stratagem was to go back a little as well as forward, as Byas had instinctively done. More deliberate was the way several bop novices gravitated to Ben Webster's work in Ellington's early-1940s orchestra. That was the governing inspiration for Lucky Thompson, Gene Ammons and Eddie "Lockjaw" Davis, who attempted to combine the new and more traditional styles of playing.

Lucky Thompson (b. 1924) was christened Eli; the sobriquet Lucky has a grim irony to it. Originally a Byas disciple, by the mid 1940s he had developed a much lighter tone and a style which caressed rather than hammered. He also had a sense of time that owed something to Young but which he made all his own: his swing was as deceptive as it was hard. He worked with Lionel Hampton, Count Basie, Dizzy Gillespie and Charlie Parker during the 1940s, Milt Jackson, Oscar Pettiford and Quincy Jones in the 1950s, and later recorded with Art Blakey. Consistently creative and much admired by musicians of all persuasions, his exposure was nevertheless patchy, and from the mid 1970s he was inactive as a musician.

All this adds up to a considerable shame. Thompson could be as rhapsodic as Webster on ballads, albeit with a silkier touch, and on up-tempo numbers his stealthy power and beautifully-judged phrasing never fail to satisfy. He brought the same originality and flair to his occasional work on soprano sax: 'Spot Session' with Art Blakey on *Soul Finger* (1965) is a definitive example.

Gene "Jug" Ammons (1925-74), son of the renowned boogie-woogie pianist Albert, drew on Young as well as Webster, and for all his harmonic sophistication his work has a simple directness associated with the pre-bop era. In the 1940s he worked with his father, with Billy Eckstine and Woody Herman, and went on to lead a two-tenor band with Sonny Stitt in 1952; nearly a decade later they were reunited on the thoroughly satisfying *Boss Tenors* (1961). He also made a number of fine records for Prestige and became a notable influence on Johnny Griffin and Clifford Jordan. Exhilarating swinger though he was, Ammons was arguably at his best on ballads and medium-tempo tunes where the plangency of his tone and his delightful nuances of phrasing are heard to maximum advantage. His soulful approach guaranteed him continued popularity up to his premature death from cancer.

The self-taught Eddie "Lockjaw" Davis (1921-85) owed his sobriquet to an early recording session whose titles – 'Surgery', 'Fracture', 'Maternity' and so forth – had a medical theme. 'Lockjaw' was one such piece and, needing something to distinguish him from another Eddie Davis, the tenorist borrowed the term and it stuck. He first caught the jazz world's attention with his 1946 Savoy date with Fats Navarro, and was soon working regularly with his own groups. With roots in R&B, from the outset he evinced a highly sophisticated harmonic grasp and an idiosyncratic variant of Webster's approach.

Davis is probably best known for his various tenures with Count Basie. He had something of a hit with 'Paradise Squat' in 1952 during his first period with the band, was the undoubted star of *The Complete Atomic* (1957), Basie's greatest post-war album, and was no less outstanding during his final stint in the late 1960s: 'Corner Pocket' on *Standing Ovation* (1969) contains perhaps his single best solo anywhere. In between his spells with Basie, Davis recorded extensively with organist Shirley Scott and formed an exhilarating quintet with fellow tenorist Johnny Griffin. He also made albums with Coleman Hawkins and in harness with arranger Oliver Nelson. In the latter years of his life he was widely featured on Norman Granz's Pablo label. Davis remains an undersung tenorist of considerable originality. No one else sounds remotely like him, and that tonal uniqueness is strengthened by what Humphrey

Sonny Stitt (pictured in 1964) was a virtuoso of both alto and tenor saxophones. His alto was reminiscent of Parker – although he claimed to have developed his style independently – and many found his tenor playing the more distinctive.

Lyttelton memorably termed the "dirty slurred insolence" of his phrasing. Davis could be as tender as his formative master Webster, as ferocious as the Basie band he graced so many times. Sheer excitement may not be a definitive criterion in jazz, but it is important, and for eviscerating power few have matched Lockjaw at his best.

The name of Lester Young has already appeared several times, but his influence was fundamental to the next four saxophonists under scrutiny: Wardell Gray, Dexter Gordon, Sonny Stitt and James Moody. Gray (1921-55) was arguably the most talented; he was certainly the least fortunate, his life ending in mysterious circumstances (probably murder) at the age of 34. In the 1940s he worked with Earl Hines, Benny Carter and Billy Eckstine; in 1949 he joined Benny Goodman, who may have been ambivalent about bop but was not in the least so about the tenorist. "If Wardell Gray plays bop, it's great,"

Tall, imposing and stylish, Dexter Gordon had natural star quality. Toward the end of his life he received an Oscar nomination for his acting-and-playing role in the movie Round Midnight.

Goodman said, "because he's wonderful." Gray had always been an assiduous student, and he was more than proficient on alto and clarinet; that may partly account for the purity and innate lyricism of his tenor work. His tone was light yet full, the phrasing languorous but supple, the overall approach relaxed, almost insouciant. However, there is nothing flabby about his rhythmic grasp. Gray could really stomp, and he swings infallibly at all times, most famously evident on 'The Chase', 'The Hunt' and 'The Steeplechase', all made (1947) with Dexter Gordon. In some ways it is a pity that these are Gray's best-known performances, for exhilarating though such "tenor battles" are, they offer limited insight into both players. That said, the contrast is fascinating. There is no mistaking Gray's subtler approach for the harder, more aggressive Gordon lines. Evidence of Gray's more varied cogency can be found in abundance on the two *Memorial* albums (1949-53) and also on the

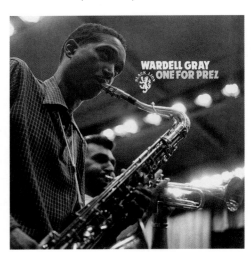

Like many of his contemporaries, Dexter Gordon found great success in Europe during the 1960s. He came to play a two-week engagement and stayed for 14 years. Wardell Gray (opposite), often hailed as the finest of all the bop tenors, died at 34 before fulfilling his great potential.

long-unavailable jam session he cut for Norman Granz in 1953 alongside among others Buddy de Franco, Benny Carter, Harry Edison and Stan Getz, with a rhythm section led by Count Basie. Gray's masterly range of idiom suggests that, had he been less ill-fated, the chances are he would have gone on to become one of the leading tenors of his generation.

Dexter Gordon (1923-90) had a somewhat chequered career, though he enjoyed a spiriting renascence in his later years. His first jobs – with Lionel Hampton, Fletcher Henderson, Louis Armstrong and Billy Eckstine – suggest a musician whose roots were in swing, and that indeed characterised his time-sense throughout. But he quickly displayed an aptitude for bop harmonics and lines, and the resultant tension led to a style that Brian Priestley has called "excruciatingly enjoyable".

Young's rhythmic influence was enormous; tonally, though, Gordon was much hotter, especially on ballads, where his sound can seem almost intimidatingly authoritative. It was that power which made him an important mid-1940s influence, notably on Sonny Stitt and the young Stan Getz and John Coltrane, yet it would not be long before the latter two, and Sonny Rollins, eclipsed him. While Philip Larkin's description of Gordon as "a good punching player of no great originality without whom jazz would be immeasurably poorer" might appear harsh, it is nearer the truth than accounts which lionise him unduly.

After his numerous though informal partnerships with Gray, Gordon was absent for much of the 1950s due to two separate prison sentences for drug

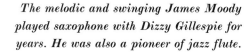

The melodic and swinging James Moody played saxophone with Dizzy Gillespie for years. He was also a pioneer of jazz flute.

offences, but he returned with a vengeance in the early 1960s, recording a string of albums for Blue Note. He moved to Copenhagen in 1962, where he stayed for 14 years, and despite regular work his overall reputation faded. However, he had a hugely successful return to America in 1976, enshrined by the aptly titled album *The Homecoming*. He worked regularly with trumpeter Woody Shaw and in 1986 achieved unexpected fame when he starred in Bertrand Tavernier's film *Round Midnight*, a superior performance given added depth by the character's resemblance to Lester Young.

Evaluating Sonny Stitt (1924-82) is invariably problematic as he seems to be two quite different players, according to whether he's on tenor or alto. His tenor playing is steeped in Young's influence, especially in his conception of time; on alto, however, the influence of Parker appears to be total and exclusive. In fact, there's a much closer relationship between the "two Stitts" than casual listening reveals.

Several reliable sources suggest that Stitt had carved out his style before he ever heard Parker, and for all their undoubted similarity in tone, the two altoists differ considerably in their phrasing and rhythmic attack. It would be wrong to call Stitt's rhythmic conception "old-fashioned", but the album *Only The Blues* (1957) offers definitive evidence of the saxophonist's swing roots. It is significant anyway that his frontline confrère is Roy Eldridge. More specifically 'Blues For Bags' – a Stitt composition that is a thinly disguised paraphrase of Sonny Rollins's 'Tenor Madness' made with John Coltrane the previous year – reveals Stitt's approach as altogether more mainstream than Rollins's or anything one could imagine Parker doing with the tune. That is not to belittle what is a marvellous performance, but to place it – and Stitt – in proper context. Similar commendation and stylistic observations apply to his work with Dizzy and Rollins, where it is the latter who adjusts, not Stitt.

Stitt's reputation has declined since his death. The number of people who remember his blistering performances in clubs and concerts gets fewer every year, and his recorded work does not consistently reflect what a magnificent improviser he could be. Sessions with frontline partners are invariably splendid, but for his quartet dates he was too often landed with (or chose) inferior rhythm sections and an uninspired repertoire. It was Stitt's fate to be thought of as the man who was Parker yet wasn't; a lot of people who ought to have known (and listened) better dismissed him as a pale imitation of the "real thing", even a copy-cat. Who better to counter that canard than Oscar Peterson, with whom in 1959 Stitt made arguably his finest album, and who cited the saxophonist as one of his two favourite players to accompany. (The other was Gillespie.) The story is Maynard Ferguson's: "I remember Oscar Peterson listening to Sonny Stitt, and someone was being kind of critical. He heard a lot of Bird clichés just then, he said. And Oscar said, 'Listen to that – he's taken a lot of Bird clichés, and a lot of Lester Young clichés, and a couple of things of Diz's, and I thought I heard something of mine in there, I'm not sure, and he's just smashed them all together, and god, isn't it gorgeous?' And I really drank to that one."

James Moody (b. 1925) is probably the least significant of the four saxophonists under review, though an engaging and satisfying performer, reminiscent of a softer-toned Dexter Gordon. Although he had a surprise hit on alto with 'I'm In The Mood For Love' (1949) he is renowned for his work in Gillespie's 1940s and '60s bands. Moody is another who comfortably assimilated bop while remaining faithful to pre-bop origins. Recent albums are essentially mainstream yet imaginative, but determinedly accessible.

Several high-quality bop saxophonists were closely associated with the Basie orchestra. Lockjaw Davis was perhaps the most distinctive saxophonist of the band's post-war years, but there is much to enjoy and admire in the work of Frank Wess (b. 1922), Frank Foster (b. 1928), Billy Mitchell (b. 1926) and Eric Dixon (1930-89). Frank Wess is an attractive soloist on tenor and alto; curiously, his flute work – for which he is probably best known – is less bop-influenced than his style on the other horns. Frank Foster, who now leads the Basie orchestra, is a fine writer as well as a vigorous and literate tenorist. The 1960 LP *Easin' It* impressively showcases both talents.

Billy Mitchell played in Dizzy Gillespie's State Department band, but it was his five-year tenure with Basie until 1961 that established him. His style is straightforward bop, lithe and linear, and his tone incisive. He went on to become Stevie Wonder's musical director and a jazz educator of some distinction. Finally, Eric Dixon's work has proved highly durable, albeit a little constricted. He responds especially well to the writing of Quincy Jones: his solo on 'Nasty Magnus' from *L'il Ol' Groovemaker* (1963) is probably his best, though he plays nearly as well on Jones's own 'Quintessence'.

Charlie Rouse (1924-88) had a CV both broad and long, but he is ineluctably associated with the music of Thelonious Monk with whom he worked for 12 years. Fans of Rouse tend therefore to be fans of Monk; those less enamoured of the pianist's approach often find the tenorist similarly unlovable, not least because of his nasal, thinnish tone. Nevertheless, he had considerable imagination and proved a durable, highly effective foil. He was not the hardest or most natural of swingers, but then neither was Monk, and Rouse's angular, witty paraphrases of Monk's lines can be absorbing. Away from Monk he assisted on those Basie *Easin' It* and *Groovemaker* albums, two memorable sessions that illuminate Rouse's quirkily independent style.

The sense of muted achievement that attends many of the musicians discussed thus far particularly characterises the work of altoist Sonny Criss (1927-77). Rather like pianist Phineas Newborn, he had everything but luck. Based on the West Coast, he was labelled a Parker clone, a judgement as

Alto saxophonist Sonny Criss, photographed in Paris during 1962.

damaging as erroneous; despite some superficial resemblances his style is entirely discrete, and his tone is much further from Parker's than is Stitt's – warmer, richer and with a more prominent vibrato.

Those properties, together with Criss's plangent emotionalism, are well captured on his *Portrait* (1967), while *I'll Catch The Sun*, made two years later with Hampton Hawes, is an impressive testament to his ability to transcend vacuous material. The sad fact remains that Criss was largely unappreciated (he often found it difficult to get work), and it is all too telling that he took his own life just as his career showed signs of burgeoning anew.

While most bop saxophonists favoured tenor or alto, three significant musicians majored on baritone. Cecil Payne (b. 1922) came to prominence with the Gillespie big-band; later he was a stalwart member of one of Woody Herman's most exhilarating outfits, recording *Concerto For Herd* (1967). Payne was technically fluent, always melodious. His work offered pioneering evidence

West Coast altoist Sonny Criss (right) was a Charlie Parker disciple. The Flamingo (anniversary sleeve, far right) was one of London's leading bop venues in the 1950s.

that the instrument could be adapted to the new demands of bop, opening the way for better-known figures such as Serge Chaloff and Gerry Mulligan.

Like Lockjaw Davis and John Coltrane, Leo Parker (1925-62) was originally versed in R&B but quickly made the transition to bop. It seems likely that he switched to baritone from alto (on which he was a more than passable performer) to avoid inevitable comparison with his namesake. On the larger horn he produced a lithely robust sound and swung effortlessly. In the 1950s he faded somewhat, partly because of drug problems. Blue Note signed him in 1961 with auspicious results, especially *Let Me Tell You 'Bout It* (1961), and it was a sad loss when he died suddenly from a heart attack.

Sahib Shihab (1925-89) enjoyed a wide-ranging career that mirrors his multi-instrumental virtuosity. He changed his name from Edmund Gregory on converting to the Muslim faith in 1947. A musician of considerable stamina and imagination, he is best known in Europe for his long tenure with the Clarke-Boland band, though his 1950s work with Monk and as a leader is also noteworthy. Shihab was at his most distinctive on baritone, though his work on flute, as mellifluous as it is lissom, is hardly less edifying.

Finally, Ronnie Scott (1927-97). He will long be remembered as a club proprietor extraordinaire, distinguished for his entrepreneurial courage and artistic vision, and as a stand-up comedian who could rival anyone on his best nights (and those were many). But over, above and beneath all that he was a world-class tenorist: indeed, it was that which made all the other things possible. His tone and natural affinity for the blues recall another superb white player, Zoot Sims, but his phrasing and attack are closer to Sonny Rollins, with whom he played on many occasions. Scott was at home in any context and any company. The recently reissued *All Stars At Montreux* (1977) showcases his imagination and range as both leader and improviser.

In a compressed survey of this kind it is not only difficult to do full justice to those cited, it is impossible to include every musician who merits attention. Though they appear in the list of recommended records at the rear of the book, no room could be found here to discuss those fine tenorists Teddy Edwards (b. 1922), Jimmy Heath (b. 1926) or Don Lanphere (b. 1928) and the altoist Ernie Henry (1926-57), and no doubt there are several more who will come to others' minds. But in the end that is cheering. Whether writing or listening, it is better to have to choose from an embarrassment of riches than to wonder where the next sentence or pleasing note is coming from.

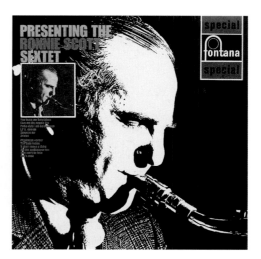

Ronnie Scott (left) playing at his original London club in 1962. One of the finest jazz saxophonists of his generation, he became better known as a clubowner and wit.

ALUN MORGAN **THE COOL SOUND**

IN CONTRAST TO THE VEHEMENCE AND PASSION OF PARKER,
PLAYERS OF THE "COOL SCHOOL" EMPHASISED DELICACY,
RESTRAINT AND A SOMEWHAT DETACHED APPROACH.
INITIALLY A NEW YORK DEVELOPMENT, IT LATER FLOURISHED
AMONG THE STUDIO MUSICIANS OF THE WEST COAST.

In jazz, "cool" is one of the most misunderstood and misused terms. Generally, it has once again become a common form of approbation, signifying the essential rightness of something. But in jazz it has a specific meaning for those whose knowledge of the music goes back to the 1940s, perhaps earlier.

In his seminal work *Inside Bebop*, published in 1949, Leonard Feather wrote that "Lester [Young] was a radical in that he symbolised the gradual evolution from hot jazz to 'cool' jazz... . Lester was rejecting the harshness and blatancy of the earlier jazz in favour of a new relaxation and restraint."

Although Young did not play as significant a part in the evolution of bebop as did Charlie Parker and Thelonious Monk and Dizzy Gillespie, his sound nevertheless became the focus for many younger musicians. Lee Konitz described the sound of Lester Young on the old Basie records as "real beautiful tenor saxophone sound, pure sound". That smooth tone and lack of vibrato appealed strongly to an entire generation of jazz soloists. Konitz wondered just how many people Young had influenced, and claimed: "He is definitely the basis of everything that's happened since. And his rhythmic approach [is] complex in its simplicity. How can you analyse it? Shall we tag some words on it? Call it polyrhythmic?"

It is a truism that the musical influence of Lester Young was more marked among white musicians than black players, and in particular affected the school which grew up around the blind pianist Lennie Tristano. Konitz (b. 1927) was probably the best-known of all Tristano's students, and he set himself the task of finding an individual voice on alto at a time when the blanket influence of Charlie Parker was very strong. He achieved this by applying the tenets of Young's teachings to the smaller horn, producing a consistent tone throughout its range and building his extemporisations largely on melody, eschewing the use of harsh rhythmic phrases.

The same disciplines formed the basis of the style of Warne Marsh, the tenor saxophonist who studied with Tristano alongside Konitz. Marsh (1927-87) developed to the point where he was one of the greatest pure improvisers jazz has ever known. Nothing seemed beyond his capabilities, and he made extensive use of high harmonics, extending the range of the tenor seemingly with ease. Like Konitz he accepted Tristano's firm teaching methods. "A student who has any listening experience first gets an education in Louis, Pres and Bird," said Marsh, "before any theory. From there [Tristano] applies the basic ingredients: harmony, ear training, rhythm – the understanding of what goes into improvising without actually telling the student what to play."

Tristano's strict methods did not appeal to all his students, some of whom abruptly terminated their lessons. But he had particular success with the saxophonists. Apart from Konitz and Marsh, the tenor saxophonist Ted Brown (b. 1927) studied with Tristano from 1948 to 1955 and produced a style of playing almost indistinguishable from that of his two colleagues. The handful of recordings he made are important, particularly his 1999 collaboration with Konitz on *Sound Of Surprise*. Regrettably, Brown found it necessary to work outside music (in computers) in order to earn a living.

Tristano's students – including those three saxophonists, the trumpeter Don Ferrara, guitarist Billy Bauer, bass player Peter Ind and pianist Sal Mosa – tended to work together as a compact, inward-looking school during the 1950s. It was Konitz who first achieved acclaim. In September 1948 Miles Davis formed a nine-piece band for a two-week engagement at New York's Royal Roost. He initially chose Sonny Stitt to play alto. But it was Gerry

Mulligan, a key figure in the formation of the Davis group, who suggested Konitz, "because he had a light sound rather than a hard, bebop sound," as Miles recalled later.

The importance of the dozen recordings made in the studio in 1949 and 1950 by the Davis nonet is well established. Gerry Mulligan (1927-96) was central to the music as composer, arranger and baritone-saxophone soloist. Despite his comparative youth he had already worked as writer and player with the bands of Elliott Lawrence, Claude Thornhill and Gene Krupa. Initially Mulligan's baritone playing was simply adequate, but his interest in arranging gave his solos an identity of their own, and when he moved to the

Lee Konitz, one of the few alto saxophonists of the bop era to develop a style independent of Parker.

Warne Marsh was a frequent partner of
Lee Konitz on the avant-garde sessions
led by Lennie Tristano.

West Coast in 1952 he was fortunate to find an intuitive, talented soloist in trumpeter Chet Baker. With Baker, Mulligan was able to bring to fruition his ideas to form a compact small band in which the piano played no part. "The piano's accepted function of constantly stating the chords of the progression makes the solo horn a slave to the whims of the piano player," was Mulligan's justification for the pianoless quartet.

Throughout his working life Mulligan's parallel careers as arranger and soloist were successfully combined; he had the ability always to think in terms of the group sound and ensured that each individual voice played its part. His own baritone playing improved to the point where he was pre-eminent on his instrument and could challenge any soloist when it came to facility of expression, irrespective of tempo. In later years he added the soprano and produced a warm tone on this notoriously difficult instrument.

It was probably more by design than accident that bandleader Stan Kenton employed a number of cool saxophonists over the years. Maybe he wanted to display the contrast between his powerful brass team and the smoothness of the reed players? An example occurs on the Shorty Rogers work 'Viva Prado' (1950) where the excitement of the brass "wall of sound" gives way to the comparatively restrained solo playing of Art Pepper and Bob Cooper. Previous Kenton bands had contained Vido Musso, a big-toned bustling tenor player capable of taking on the might of the Kenton trombones. But from the late 1940s onward the band featured such saxophonists as Pepper and Cooper, Bud Shank, Bill Holman, Charlie Mariano, Bill Perkins and Lennie Niehaus.

These men went on to carve out individual careers, but most acknowledge the help and experience they had gained while working with Kenton. Lee Konitz was a member of the Kenton band in 1952 and 1953, sitting in the saxophone section immediately in front of a brass team that included Maynard Ferguson, Conte Candoli, Frank Rosolino and Bill Russo. Understandably, Konitz learned to project his sound more forcefully and left the band as an increasingly impressive soloist.

Art Pepper (1925-82) was arguably the most important saxophonist ever to play with Kenton, and his career as a soloist from 1952 until his death 30 years later featured many outstanding recordings. He had the ability to perform at the peak level with groups of all sizes and types, including Miles Davis's rhythm section, handcrafted units devised by arranger Marty Paich, and big-bands assembled for the studio. Toward the end of his life he broadened the scope of his playing, reflecting his interest in the work of John Coltrane, but his ability to produce warm-toned ballads of great emotional intensity remained undiminished.

In Pepper's shadow for a time was Bud Shank (b. 1926), but he came to make a name for himself as one of the finest jazz flautists – as well as being a capable tenor player and a surprisingly virile baritone soloist. Eventually Shank elected to concentrate on the alto saxophone and has produced many fine albums, including two outstanding releases for the Spanish Fresh Sound label devoted to the music of Bill Evans and Gerry Mulligan.

Bob Cooper sometimes played oboe in duets with Shank on flute, but was a truly underrated tenor player, in the same league as Zoot Sims. Cooper (1925-93) had a warm, full tone throughout the range of his instrument and the ability to swing with the ease of such masters as Sims and Richie Kamuca. Bill Holman (b. 1927) was occasionally featured as a soloist on tenor

CHAPTER EIGHT

Gerry Mulligan brought a lightness and fluidity to the baritone saxophone, and introduced a new group sound with his piano-less quartet.

by Kenton, but his main contribution to the band was as a composer and arranger. However his small-group work on record with such men as Conte Candoli and Lee Katzman mark him as a soloist of importance.

Bill Perkins (b. 1924) came to prominence with the Woody Herman band in the early 1950s, having taken his first featured solo on record with a Shorty Rogers big-band (on 'Blues For Brando' in 1953). With Herman he was heard on the Ralph Burns ballad 'Misty Morning' and the swinging 'Autobahn Blues' (both 1954). After leaving Herman at the end of 1954 he joined Stan Kenton and remained with the band for four years, commencing his featured recording stint on Bill Holman's fine arrangement of 'Yesterdays' (1955).

During his stay with Kenton, Perkins also made a number of outstanding records with small groups for the Pacific Jazz label, the best of which is certainly *Grand Encounter* (1956) where he was joined by John Lewis, Jim Hall, Percy Heath and Chico Hamilton. Perkins's pellucid tone and fractionally-behind-the-beat phrasing are features of the album's 'Easy Living' and 'Two Degrees East, Three Degrees West', a blues by Lewis.

With the passage of time Perkins's sound has changed, the light, floating Lester Young-like quality replaced by a deeper tone not unlike that of tenorist Benny Golson. However, Perkins was coaxed into recreating his earlier and distinctive style by producer Dick Bank for an outstanding album made in 1995 and dedicated to Lester Young, *Perk Plays Prez*.

Charlie Mariano (b. 1923) was an important figure on the Boston jazz scene in the late 1940s before he left to work with Chubby Jackson and Bill Harris in New York. His alto playing has always been marked by a rare degree of passion and his stay with Stan Kenton resulted in several outstanding recorded solos including an intense version of 'Stella By Starlight' (1955). He also worked very successfully with drummer Shelly Manne's quintet and various Charlie Mingus units. During the 1960s he had a series of residencies in various countries including Japan and Belgium. He also studied Indian music and worked with jazz-rock bands, but whenever he has appeared with Stan Kenton tribute bands he has shown that his ability to create authentic jazz solos remains safely intact.

Like Mariano, Lennie Niehaus (b. 1929) gained his early big-band experience with Stan Kenton. He joined in 1952 and remained until he was called for military service. He rejoined Kenton in 1954 and remained with the

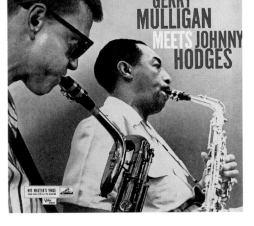

West Coast jazz (three example sleeves here) had a clear, open sound that blended well with older styles and had a broad general appeal.

band for five years, concurrently leading his own quintet with Bill Perkins. His major contribution to Kenton was a considerable library of arrangements, but his recorded solo playing, particularly on such pieces as 'Cherokee' (1955) and 'The End Of A Love Affair' (1959), is excellent.

In 1954 Niehaus started to record a series of albums for the Hollywood-based Contemporary label, and the initial quintet release had a considerable impact on the jazz scene. The fluency and creativity of Niehaus's work comes across on such numbers as 'I Remember You' and 'Whose Blues' (both 1954). In more recent years he has produced film scores for his old army colleague Clint Eastwood, notably for *Bird* (1988), based on the life of Charlie Parker.

For 16 years Paul Desmond's name was inextricably linked to that of Dave Brubeck, with Desmond's composition 'Take Five' (1961) becoming a considerable success for Brubeck's quartet. Many felt that Desmond (1924-77) would achieve more personal recognition if he left Brubeck to appear as a soloist or group leader in his own right, especially after the long line of albums he made for the RCA and A&M labels in the 1960s under his own name. Even after he and Brubeck parted company in December 1967, Desmond kept returning to work with Brubeck on special projects or tours.

Desmond's attraction was his very melodic approach to improvisation and his smooth, clear tone. He also made wide use of the extended upper range of the alto, maintaining perfect control over the high harmonics. A very amusing and witty man, he claimed that he tried to make his solos "sound like a dry martini", while another jazz humorist, guitarist Eddie Condon, said Desmond's playing "sounded like a girl saying yes".

With Brubeck's quartet, Desmond always took the first solo – he said he didn't want to play after Brubeck. The best albums by the group were those recorded live, notably *Jazz At Oberlin* and *Jazz At The College Of The Pacific* (both 1953). The former has spectacular and spontaneous interplay between alto and piano on 'Perdido' while the latter has memorable versions of 'All The Things You Are' and 'Laura'.

Away from Brubeck, Desmond's preferred group setting seemed to be that of the pianoless rhythm section, with a guitar to provide the necessary harmonies. His RCA albums use this format for the most part, with Jim Hall supplying that interplay. His final recordings, made for A&M, have the Canadian guitarist Ed Bickert, who proves to be an ideal partner. Meanwhile, during the 1950s California was the focus for a jazz phenomenon that became

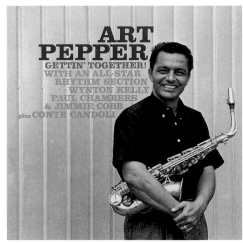

Art Pepper's sparkling tone and limpid phrasing survived a turbulent life, including several prison sentences.

known as West Coast Jazz. With many large orchestras disbanding or reforming there and with plenty of work to be found in the Hollywood studios, the area soon became a haven for many noted jazz soloists. Herb Geller (b. 1928) was actually born in Los Angeles, which gave him more of a proprietorial right to be there than most. Best known for his alto work, Geller has always possessed a full, warm tone on the instrument and his elegant phrasing often brings Benny Carter to mind. During his California days he recorded with Clifford Brown and such leaders as Maynard Ferguson, Shorty Rogers and Billy May. In 1962 he left for Europe where he spent many years working with German radio orchestras. Since retiring from studio work he has made a number of albums with small groups, all of which indicate that he has lost none of his expertise as a superior soloist. One of his best was *Plays The Al Cohn Song Book* (1996), a tribute to the arranger. Geller is a connoisseur of songs, many of which might otherwise have been forgotten. His albums usually contain rare tunes lovingly restored by his musical brilliance.

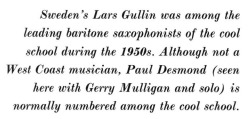

Sweden's Lars Gullin was among the leading baritone saxophonists of the cool school during the 1950s. Although not a West Coast musician, Paul Desmond (seen here with Gerry Mulligan and solo) is normally numbered among the cool school.

One of America's leading dance orchestras made intelligent use of cool tenor players during the 1940s and 1950s. Les Brown has always led a most musicianly band with good jazz soloists and arrangers. In 1944 Ted Nash (b. 1922) joined the band as the featured tenor player and was soon demonstrating his command of high harmonics on the instrument. (Nash wrote a primer for students on the subject.) He also cultivated a smooth tone, and both aspects of his work were to be heard during his solo on Brown's hit recording of 'I've Got My Love To Keep Me Warm' (1946).

Nash left the band in 1946, and two years later Dave Pell (b. 1925) became Brown's tenor soloist. Like Nash he made use of a smooth, cool sound not unlike that of a 1950-vintage Stan Getz. Pell was heavily featured with the band from 1948 to 1955, when he left to form his own octet, making neat, tuneful music primarily designed for dancing. In the late 1970s Pell formed Prez Conference, dedicated to transcribing from record and playing classic Lester Young solos, in the way that Supersax did with Charlie Parker's solos.

Among musicians the importance of Lester Young has never been forgotten, and one tenor saxophonist in particular played in a style so close to Young's that he was dubbed the Vice-Prez. Paul Quinichette (1916-83) got to know Young in Denver during the 1930s when he was starting out; the two would often practice together, and that initial contact remained with Quinichette throughout his career. Inevitably, record producers made use of

him in neo-Basie settings when he would be teamed with such men as Buck Clayton and Jo Jones. But Quinichette was more original than that, as he proved with the many discs he made for Decca and Mercury during the 1950s.

Inevitably, it seems, the cool approach found favour among European jazz musicians, notably in Sweden and Britain. Baritone saxophonist Lars Gullin (1928-76) was a most important soloist, irrespective of geographical boundaries. He developed a distinctive sound on his instrument and was a composer of considerable merit. Like a number of Scandinavians he showed an early interest in the music of Lee Konitz and Lennie Tristano. In November 1950 Konitz went to Sweden to play a number of concerts featuring his own music, accompanied by compatible players including pianist Bengt Hallberg and tenor saxophonist Hacke Björksten as well as Gullin.

In Britain one of the earliest cool players was the Getz-influenced tenor saxophonist Keith Bird, while Tristano's music was the inspiration for both Gray Allard and Chas Burchell. In Germany Hans Koller indicated an admiration for Warne Marsh in his own tenor playing, and in 1956 he recorded an album in Cologne with Lee Konitz and Lars Gullin.

In terms of its popularity among musicians and audiences alike, cool reached its zenith in the 1950s. It lost ground under the assault of the more aggressive hard bop style, but its most dedicated surviving disciples continue to produce fascinating music.

Dave Brubeck and Paul Desmond, one of the most commercially successful partnerships in jazz. Desmond's composition 'Take Five' is the best-selling jazz instrumental record ever.

STAN GETZ AND THE BROTHERS

JIM TOMLINSON

"THE BROTHERS" WERE THE SPIRITUAL CHILDREN OF LESTER YOUNG, ADOPTING HIS LIGHT TONE AND MERCURIAL PHRASING AS THE BASIS OF THEIR OWN PLAYING, AND EVOLVING A NEW APPROACH TO JAZZ TENOR. STAN GETZ WAS THE MOST PROMINENT MEMBER OF THIS GROUP, CLOSELY FOLLOWED BY ZOOT SIMS AND AL COHN.

Stan Getz pictured performing at the Metropol Club in Oslo during 1960.

The big bands of the 1930s and '40s provided the training grounds for many of the greatest instrumentalists and composer-arrangers in jazz. Some were particularly rich in talent. One has only to think, for example, of the personnel of the Count Basie band of the late 1930s for names such as Harry Edison, Buck Clayton, Jo Jones and Lester Young to spring to mind.

Woody Herman's Second Herd, formed in 1947 and brimming with youthful exuberance, was another such organisation. Its principal soloists and arrangers were inspired largely by the emerging music of the East Coast, bebop. But the defining sound of the band came from its unique saxophone section. Instead of the usual two altos, two tenors and baritone, Herman employed a section of one alto, three tenors and baritone. For the standard ensemble passages, the alto would take the lead. But on occasion the section would drop the lead alto, with the first tenor taking the lead and the remaining two tenors and baritone playing close-position harmony.

The effect was to produce a light, perfectly-blended and mobile sound, capable of executing melodically intricate passages in harmony. This was ideally suited to the bop-oriented style of the band and came to be one of the most recognisable sounds in jazz. The signature tune that brought this new sound to the listening public was 'Four Brothers' (1947).

'Four Brothers' came not only to define a particular style of saxophone-section writing, but also to identify a group of saxophonists. The original Brothers were Herbie Steward, Zoot Sims, Stan Getz and baritone saxophonist Serge Chaloff. Other names can be added to this list, either because they came through Herman's sax section at the time or were associated stylistically: Al Cohn, who replaced Steward in the original section; Jimmy Giuffre, composer of 'Four Brothers'; Brew Moore; Richie Kamuca; and Bill Perkins.

What did the Brothers have in common? They all played, at least at the outset of their careers, in a style that was very much downwind of Lester

A selection of Stan Getz album sleeves from records issued in the 1950s and 1960s.

Young. Young's playing was at variance with the prevailing tenor saxophone influence of Coleman Hawkins. Young eschewed the chesty, wide vibrato that dominated the tenor saxophone of the late 1930s in favour of a lighter, more lucid sound, not entirely unlike the c-melody saxophone sound of Frankie Trumbauer. It is not only the sound, however, that identifies Lester Young's disciples. Young also played with a more "horizontal" melodic approach. Where Hawkins would tend to craft his improvisations by ranging vertically through the notes of the chord sequence of the tune, Young would take a more linear route.

Listening to that classic recording of 'Four Brothers', recorded on December 27th 1947, it is hard to distinguish between the tenor players as their solos follow on seamlessly from one another. Sims is the first out of the blocks, followed by Chaloff. Steward, whose motific solo is perhaps the most convincing of the statements, is followed by the fluid Getz.

It was in his ballad playing, however, that Getz distinguished himself in the Herman band. Ralph Burns, pianist and composer, created the 'Summer Sequence' suite for the Herman band, the fourth part of which came to be known as 'Early Autumn' (1948). It is a slow ballad that features the three tenors and baritone, with Getz on lead and performing the solo duties. Getz's solo is exotically dreamy and is of such crafted perfection and maturity that it is hard to believe it came from a man of 21 years.

However, these sessions with the Second Herd were anything but a recording debut for Getz (1927-91). He had been a precocious musical talent at school, playing bassoon in the school's symphony orchestra as well as the

The easy-swinging Zoot Sims in his prime.
His effortless delivery and seemingly
endless flow of ideas made him a hero to
several generations of jazz lovers.

other reeds. This enabled him to take casual gigs to supplement his family's modest income. The gap between a working wage and the earning potential of a successful musician was such that when the 15-year-old Getz was offered a regular job with Dick Rodgers' band at $35 per week (about £23) his parents allowed him to drop out of school. This was soon followed by a $70 offer from Jack Teagarden, and it was with Teagarden that Getz first recorded, on August 18th 1943. Stints with Stan Kenton, Jimmy Dorsey and Benny Goodman followed, so when Getz joined Herman in the autumn of 1947 he was no freshman. As well as picking up musical skills along the way, he also acquired an addiction to heroin and alcohol that was to dog him for years.

The saxophone section of the Second Herd originally came together in a rehearsal band organised in New York by arranger Gene Roland. It consisted of four tenor saxophones. This was re-formed out on the West Coast as part of Tommy di Carlo's band – and it was this band, containing Getz, Steward, Sims and Giuffre, that Woody Herman heard and liked. Herman hired the section, with Giuffre replaced by Serge Chaloff on baritone. The Second Herd, and the Four Brothers sound, had been born.

Getz did not stay with the Herman band for long. With the responsibilities of a wife and young child, he left the band and the rigours of the road to settle near his family in New York early in 1949. 'Early Autumn' had not yet been released and Getz found himself taking odd gigs to make ends meet. When it did appear later that year the record was such a hit that it instantly launched him on a solo career that would last over four decades.

It is his sound that first strikes one about Getz's playing. Certainly it evolved throughout his career, but it remained at all times a thing of agonising beauty. In his earliest quartet recordings he has a thicker, more metallic sound, rather like that of Dexter Gordon's at the time. In 'And The Angels Swing' (1946) we hear an already dazzling technique with perfectly executed double-time runs, but it is not until the 1949 'Indian Summer' session that we hear the lightness of touch and lyricism that distinguished Getz's playing of this period.

The success of 'Early Autumn' enabled Getz to form a working quartet, with Al Haig, Horace Silver and Duke Jordan consecutively in the piano chair. With these groups he made a series of recordings for the Roost label which define his playing in the early 1950s. By this time there is a consistency of tone: light, with a warm glow. This was achieved by the use of a mouthpiece that did not allow the reed to vibrate widely, so that the sound we hear is dominated by the resonating sound of the brass rather than the sound of the reed. It was a hard reed, to give evenness of tone, especially in the middle and upper registers. And the embouchure – the shape that the mouth forms around the mouthpiece and reed – dampened the higher partials of the notes. Together, these factors combined to give the unmistakable Getz tone: airy, warm and pure, with a brassy glow that is sometimes almost trombone-like. This formula remained more or less consistent throughout his career, although Getz's tone did evolve a richness and range of expression that was absent for much of the 1950s.

Among Getz's first recordings on leaving the Herman band was a series of Brothers sessions in April 1949 with Sims, Cohn, Allen Eager and Brew Moore on tenors. 'Four And One Moore' from this session is a Gerry Mulligan composition based on the chord sequence of 'Indiana'. It reveals the opening soloist Brew Moore to have absorbed the Parker style, and he even refers to

the Parker tune 'Donna Lee' (itself based on 'Indiana'). Moore (1924-73) also draws on a number of Lester-type devices, for example in the 13th and 14th bars of his solo where he plays a phrase highly reminiscent of Young's solo on 'Jive At Five'. Later Moore plays an elongated phrase in which three-beat groups of notes are repeated over the four-to-the-bar structure of the tune to create an exciting rhythmic tension: barring the bop inflections, this could be said to be pure Pres.

Zoot Sims, who plays next, has more of Young's relaxed rhythmic feel but fewer of his mannerisms. It was this relaxed style of playing, as well as a warm, gravy-like tone, that distinguished Sims throughout his long career. Sims (1925-85) began his professional career at the age of 15. In the ensuing 45 years he worked off and on with many of the big-band leaders, especially Herman and Goodman. He was also a successful solo artist whose forthright and appealing style seemed to fit all occasions without need for adjustment. Whatever the musical context, whether playing harmonically-adventurous Bill Evans compositions or simply blowing a blues, Sims always made it sound effortless, with phrases that were both logical and unhurried. He never sounds rattled or trapped into playing unnecessarily by a demanding musical situation – rather like a good batsman doggedly refusing to venture outside the off stump. His greatest musical collaboration was with fellow Brother, Al Cohn. The quintet they co-led was formed in 1957 and lasted until the 1980s.

Al Cohn is next at the microphone on 'Four And One Moore'. He sounds more obviously Young-inspired than Sims. His lines are fluid and flow across the beat rather then locking into it. Cohn (1925-88) was a tenor player more revered by other musicians than the public, and it was perhaps this lack of recognition that encouraged him to devote himself for a large part of the 1950s to the studios and to writing. But he did bring his arranging and writing skills to his work with Zoot Sims. This and an enviable flair for imaginative improvisation made for a sublime pairing. Although his tone

Three brothers: Zoot Sims, Al Cohn and Jimmy Giuffre at a Woody Herman reunion gig in New York, 1976.

hardened a little in later years and his rhythmic feel became more taut, the melodic flow of the Young tradition remained intact.

Stan Getz is next. He plays consistently in the upper register and sounds a little thin in comparison to the others, though he is by far the most distinctive. Last up is Allen Eager (b. 1927) whose solo has more bop than Pres. This is hardly surprising: he spent most of 1948 playing with Tadd Dameron, the pianist, arranger and bop guru. After freelancing throughout the 1950s, Eager gave up music in the 1960s and '70s to pursue other interests (including sports-car racing, at which he was very accomplished). He resumed playing in the 1980s, occasionally partnering Chet Baker.

Getz's most important musical partnerships of this period were not with other tenor players but with guitarists Johnny Smith and Jimmy Raney. Like

Al Cohn was the simplest and most funky of the Brothers-style tenors, but at the same time probably the most sophisticated all-round musician. He was also a highly successful arranger and musical director.

'Early Autumn', Getz's next significant hit was a ballad. Recorded with Smith, 'Moonlight In Vermont' (1952) is a romantic and impressionistic melody with an odd structure, due to its lyric being in the form of a haiku poem. The tune is played and harmonised in Smith's distinctive, almost Hawaiian-sounding guitar style, with Getz playing an improvised counter-melody. Getz's solo contribution is a meagre six bars, but his is the dominant voice that turns what would otherwise have been a sugary novelty into something with emotional depth. The record was such a hit that on the basis of its success Getz was earning upwards of $1,000 per week (about £650), a staggering sum in the early 1950s.

The best Getz band of this period was the one formed with guitarist Jimmy Raney, an associate from the Herman band. They played with an empathy that bordered on the telepathic. The way in which they executed unison and counterpoint is best demonstrated on their Roost sessions recorded live at Storyville. In the early 1950s, on the back of Miles Davis's *Birth Of The Cool* and the pianoless Mulligan/Baker Quartet, the term "cool jazz" became current and Getz, with his lyrical style and light sound, seemed to fit the bill. However, on 'Parker 51' (1951), an up-tempo, contrapuntal composition of Raney's based on the chord sequence of 'Cherokee', Getz reels off chorus after chorus of perfectly executed improvisation while sounding anything but cool.

Recordings a few years later with Dizzy Gillespie and Sonny Stitt gave Getz the opportunity to demonstrate a technical facility and imagination comparable with the very best of the bebop masters. And yet whatever the tempo and harmonic demands, there is always a lyricism at the heart of his playing – and, of course, that sound.

For Getz the 1950s are characterised by remarkable professional and artistic achievement, but against a backdrop of drug abuse that periodically disrupted his career, most notably earning him a spell in jail in 1954. However, the six months he spent inside appeared to revitalise Getz. In the October following his release he took part in his first tour for jazz impresario Norman Granz. The quintet's frontline included valve trombonist Bob Brookmeyer, with whom Getz would make a number of fine recordings. (They

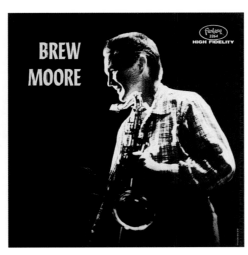
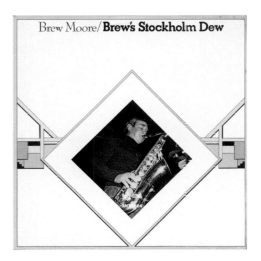

would pair up again for two of Getz's best recordings, their joint 1961 album *Fall 61*, and Brookmeyer's 1964 LP *And Friends*.)

On the album *Stan Getz At The Shrine* (1954) the audience receive Getz warmly, perhaps put at ease by Duke Ellington's faintly ironic and ice-breaking introduction. Listening to Getz's own introductions, it is easy but perhaps fanciful to imagine a contrite tone. But there is nothing contrite in his playing: if anything, Getz's sound becomes darker and heavier from here on. By the time we hear *Stan Getz With The Oscar Peterson Trio*, recorded on October 10th 1957, and the Herb Ellis session *Nothing But The Blues*, recorded the following day, the long, lucid lines are now interspersed with bluesy interjections and possess an emotional range lacking earlier in the decade.

At the end of 1958, with the birth of daughter Pamela to his new wife Monica Silfverskiold, and on the basis of rapturous receptions from European audiences, Getz decided to move to Copenhagen. This marks a period of personal stability that is reflected in his playing. Recordings made in 1960 with pianist Jan Johansson's trio and issued as two volumes of *Stan Getz At Large* show Getz's playing to be relaxed and fluent. Meanwhile, a ballad album *Cool Velvet* made the same year with Russ Garcia's string arrangements marks the arrival of the mature Getz sound of the 1960s: warm and sensuous in the lower and middle register, with a capacity for an edgy intensity in the upper. But when considered in the light of Miles Davis's *Kind Of Blue* and John Coltrane's *Giant Steps*, recorded a year earlier, these albums start to sound little more than accomplished. Whether prompted by a feeling of artistic isolation, as suggested by Donald Maggin in his excellent biography of Getz,

Serge Chaloff was the baritone-playing Brother. Brew Moore, a dedicated Lester Young disciple, lived a wandering life which kept him out of the limelight.

Dexter Gordon (left) and Stan Getz meet up at the Nice Festival in 1981.

or simply by homesickness, Getz moved back to New York in January of 1961. Thus began a period that would produce Getz's greatest work. If one had to pick a single Getz album that demonstrates his musical prowess more completely and emphatically than any other, it would be *Focus* (1961), the LP he made with writer and arranger Eddie Sauter. Getz had not found his return to America as easy as he might have hoped. His drawing power in the clubs was diminished, perhaps on account of his two-year absence, but also because of the fashions for hard bop and avant-garde modal music, neither of which Getz represented. Jazz tastes had moved on while he had not.

But in the fall of 1961 Getz went into the studio to record the album that would restart his career in the States and remains to this day one of the most remarkable achievements of improvisation. Getz commissioned Sauter to write original string music over which he would improvise his part. The result is one of stunning originality and perfection, and is the truest realisation of the fusion of the classical and jazz traditions.

Focus is an improvised concerto consisting of seven movements ranging from the angular 'I'm Late, I'm Late', based on Bartok's *Music For Strings, Percussion And Celeste*, to the lush and romantic 'A Summer Afternoon'. Throughout, Getz's playing meshes so perfectly with the string parts that it is hard to believe that his own part is not written. The album was given a full five stars in *Down Beat* (as was his reunion album with Brookmeyer, *Fall 61*), restoring Getz to his rightful place among the great creative geniuses of jazz.

The 1960s mark a period of continued musical excellence for Getz. His regular quartet often included Roy Haynes on drums, an associate from the Roost recordings with whom he can be heard sparring with an intensity reminiscent of that generated by John Coltrane and Elvin Jones. Listening to the exchanges on 'Green Dolphin Street' from the recorded concert *Stan Getz Quartet In Paris* (1966) we hear a rhythmic playfulness more like that of Sonny Rollins. And the edginess that first appeared in the upper register is now freely employed throughout the entire range of the instrument. This was not a result of a change of technique or equipment so much as a new willingness to explore the full tonal possibilities of the instrument. It is perhaps Getz's best small-group playing. He is the consummate improviser, capable of playing with a musical, tonal and emotional range to which only a handful of other musicians have come close.

And yet this most powerful of Getz's playing is overshadowed by the work for which he remains best known, the bossa nova albums. Persuaded by guitarist Charlie Byrd, in 1962 Getz made an album of Brazilian tunes titled *Jazz Samba*. To everyone's surprise it scored an enormous success, especially the single 'Desafinado'. This was followed by a pairing with Brazilian musicians Joao Gilberto and Antonio Carlos Jobim. On the resulting album *Getz/Gilberto* (1963) Getz's serenely melodic improvising has a beauty that transcends genre. The LP, which contained the hit song 'The Girl From Ipanema', remained on the pop charts for an amazing 96 weeks, rising to number two – the kind of achievement rivalled only by The Beatles. The commercial success of the albums was entirely deserved but set an unrealistic standard for Getz's record sales. While his working band remained a vibrant jazz unit with such young talents as Gary Burton and Chick Corea, much of his recorded output became more commercial, with orchestral albums covering current pop material. But Getz was not happy to rest on his musical laurels.

Richie Kamuca played with Stan Kenton and Woody Herman before becoming one of the leading West Coast tenor soloists.

The next musical shock wave to hit the jazz world came from the jazz-rock explosion. From the 1920s to the 1950s jazz had remained in close touch with the popular music of the time, drawing on it for repertoire and forms. The 1960s were something of a departure. While popular music was dominated by rock'n'roll, jazz moved into areas of modal, free and protest music that had less to do with what was happening on the pop scene than before.

But the jazz fusion of the 1970s represented a fresh convergence of jazz and popular music and provided a challenge that Getz did not ignore. He was able to play the rock grooves with conviction and never sounded as though he had simply sold out, although his bands of this period have an electric sound that is strangely at odds with Getz's dark tone. On his 1977 album *Another World* we hear him sounding not entirely at ease as he experiments with digital delay and Echoplex; however, recorded in the more acoustic context of Woody Herman's 40th Anniversary concert around the same time (1976) he sounds more comfortable and convincing, swinging out on 'Blue Getz Blues'.

Throughout his career, the distinguishing feature of Getz's playing was his sound, which had become more and more distinctive through the years. So his experimentation with electronics seems like an act of sacrilegious interruption to that process of refinement. Perhaps it was a response to this when in 1982 his playing took an abrupt turn with the acoustic-quartet format of the pointedly titled album *Pure Getz*. He would keep to this format until the end of his life. Getz died of cancer on July 6th 1991. He was battling the illness throughout this period, and his playing never reached the audacious heights that it had in the 1960s. But there is a mature gathering of resources that gives his playing a depth and an impact that make many of the recordings from this time among his best. The Grammy-winning album *Serenity*, recorded in 1987 in Copenhagen, deserves to be in any serious jazz collection.

Described by his hero Lester Young as "the best of the grey boys," Stan Getz contributed not only to the history of the jazz saxophone but also to jazz history itself. He set standards of technical mastery and artistic beauty that some might aspire to match but none could hope to surpass.

TONY RUSSELL

HONKERS AND SCREAMERS

SUBTLE THEY WEREN'T, BUT THE PLAYERS WHO WORKED ON THE BORDER BETWEEN JAZZ AND R&B PROVED UNBEATABLE WHEN IT CAME TO EXCITEMENT. THEIR VERY NAMES – BIG JAY McNEELY, HAL "CORNBREAD" SINGER, WILLIS "GATOR TAIL" JACKSON – EVOKE THE FIFTIES AND THEIR HEYDAY.

Arnett Cobb (above) still enlivening Lionel Hampton's band with his forceful, rocking tenor at the age of 61, in London, 1979. From R&B to Count Base's band, Jimmy Forrest (opposite) had a blues-filled style that suited both to perfection.

"If one should ever have cause to erect a memorial to the whole school of rhythm and blues," the English critic Albert McCarthy mused in an essay in *Jazzbook 1955*, "I can think of no more fitting one than crossed tenor saxophones with the simple epitaph 'we honked'."

Since then the term "rhythm and blues" and its abbreviation "R&B" have been appropriated by the music industry for music only distantly related to McCarthy's examples of Tiny Bradshaw, Wynonie Harris or The Ravens. Even 45 years ago, as that trio of names suggests, there were varied interpretations of it. But McCarthy's instinct was surely right: when it comes to R&B, the tenor saxophone is the jam in the doughnut; the spirit, if you like, in the machine.

In common with most jazz pundits of his era, McCarthy had little good to say about R&B purely as music. He quoted, but regrettably did not name, a "well-known jazz tenor player who commented that if one could teach the apes in the zoo the way to play tenor, they would sound like rhythm and blues men. Rhythm and blues," he went on, "is the music of gimmicks and cheap excitement.... It expresses perfectly the basic emptiness of modern America," and more in that vein.

On the other hand, he wrote, it had impeccable sociological credentials. "It is inevitable that [the Negro's] music will become more cosmopolitan. Rhythm and blues are the welding of the Negro blues with the material of Tin Pan Alley and represents, in the truest sense of the word, the commercialisation of the blues.... Behind the honking tenors, the fabulous altos and the electric guitars whining interminably, there is a core of the blues that serves to remind one of greater things."

McCarthy recognised that saxophone-fronted R&B grew naturally from performance practices in certain black orchestras of the early 1940s, particularly the Lucky Millinder band with Eddie "Lockjaw" Davis and the Lionel Hampton band with Illinois Jacquet and later Arnett Cobb. Jacquet (b.1922) played a solo on Hampton's 1942 recording of 'Flying Home' that is often regarded as an R&B landmark, and with its slightly unshaven tone and the repeated notes in the second chorus it does indeed contain some of the material that would make up a blueprint for R&B tenor. But it was in concert that details were accentuated or added, as may be heard in airshots, so that the tune grew by accretion into a sort of compendium of R&B devices: squeals, rasps, teetering stacks of riffs.

Within a few years Jacquet was deploying those devices with the economical repetitiveness of the born honker'n'screamer: witness the note repeated 43 times in succession in his 1947 recording 'Jet Propulsion'. He also had a high billing on Norman Granz's Jazz At The Philharmonic package

tours, which for several years provided a public arena for duelling tenors and other high-adrenaline saxophone encounters.

Arnett Cobb, who succeeded to Jacquet's place in the Hampton court, marked his arrival with a vigorously revised 'Flying Home' (1944) that would be as influential as its predecessor. Like Jacquet, Cobb (1918-89) grew up in Houston. Later, together with his contemporary Buddy Tate, he would be enrolled by historians into the Texas Tenor school of burly, bluesy blowing. "He blew the kind of fast extrovert tenor, complete with gag quotes, for which Jacquet and JATP created a vogue," noted Stanley Dance. "With his small group, he indulged in the kind of showmanship practised by Hampton, marching off stage, up and down theatre aisles, while still playing his horn."

The braying call-and-response figures of his 'Go, Red, Go' (a title taken,

King Curtis, master of the short, groovy solo on numerous R&B classics, and Earl Bostic, the king of alto melodrama.

most appropriately, from a pep-squad cheer heard at Cornell football games) were popular with tenor-players; Red Prysock re-recorded the tune with the Tiny Bradshaw band, retitled 'Free For All', as much as six years later. The 1947 original was made for Apollo, a label whose office was down the street from the famous Harlem theatre of the same name, where Cobb and his confrères regularly blew the dust off the rafters. Apollo made rather a thing of R&B tenor players, including on its roster Willis "Gator Tail" Jackson and – another Hampton alumnus – the young King Curtis (1934-71).

As Bob Porter has observed, Jacquet and Curtis neatly bracket the golden age of R&B tenor. "It can be argued," he says, "that Jacquet was the first to demonstrate the potential and that King Curtis was the last of the great tenor stylists of that era." In fact the true heyday of the honk was the decade or so from 1945 to the arrival of rock'n'roll.

The tenor was not immediately eclipsed by the young men from Sun Records; if there was little evidence of it on the records of Elvis Presley or Jerry Lee Lewis, it was intrinsic to the northern rock'n'roll of Bill Haley, and Curtis's own voluminous contributions to what are now regarded as classic rock'n'roll and soul records continued well into the 1960s. But it was inevitable that the more immediate, and whiter, sexual lure of rock'n'roll guitar and its players would drive the front-of-stage honker back to his place in the band.

But for those ten years (or so) there was a splendid parade of blowers whose names and hit records evoke an entertainment scene with a pronounced if today almost alien character: Hal "Cornbread" Singer, Big Jay McNeely with 'The Deacon's Hop', Eddie Chamblee and his 'Lima Beans', Jimmy Forrest's

'Night Train', Al Sears with 'Castle Rock', Sam "The Man" Taylor, Wild Bill Moore (another Houstonian), Jack McVea, Paul Bascomb, Red Prysock, Joe Morris, Sil Austin, Lee Allen, Joe Houston and a hundred others.

Almost to a man (they seem nearly always to have been men) they had put in some time with "name" bandleaders. Forrest (1920-80) had been with Jay McShann, where he sat alongside Charlie Parker, and with Andy Kirk; Sears with Ellington; Taylor with Millinder and Cab Calloway; McVea and Morris with Hampton (McVea between Jacquet and Cobb); Bascomb with Erskine Hawkins and Basie; Prysock and Austin with Tiny Bradshaw; Singer (like Buddy Tate) with the unrecorded but influential Nat Towles.

Most of them, too, were young men, passing through their 20s in the 1940s, but otherwise they were a mixed bunch whose abilities might range, as Porter put it, "from reed-biting squealers to honkers just slightly less creative than, say, Lester Young". Many were good second-class jazz musicians who didn't disdain playing more simply: "robust, a big tone, always a swinger," as Clark Terry said of Forrest. Others had more limited technique and were lucky to be around at a time when, thanks to that great leveller the jukebox, you could parlay a rasping up-tempo blues into a hit.

Or a furry slow one, or a hypnotic medium-paced shuffle. R&B was not all supercharged. Annotating a Jimmy Forrest CD, the historian Frank Driggs was moved to remember the jukebox favourites in late-night bars of the 1950s: "Tough finger-popping items like 'Soft' by Tiny Bradshaw [with Red Prysock on tenor], 'Honky Tonk' by Bill Doggett, 'Steamwhistle Jump' by Earl Bostic, 'Smooth Sailing' by Arnett Cobb and 'Night Train' by Jimmy Forrest." Scarcely any of them are rave-ups in the mould of Jacquet's 'Jet Propulsion', and probably the biggest seller of them all, Forrest's 'Night Train' (1951), was a zonked-out slow blues so suggestive in its execution that it could have been subtitled '(For Strippers Only)'.

A huge proportion of the R&B sax repertoire was blues. This is easy to say, so let us inspect a couple of modern CD anthologies that were compiled with documentary purpose rather than to throw together a mess of blues. Delmark's *Honkers & Bar Walkers Volume 1* is drawn from the Chicago labels United and States and features, among others, Forrest, Bascomb, Fats Noel and the altoist Tab Smith; Westside's *Groove Station* is taken from the King label-group and offers Sears, Wild Bill Moore, the altoist Preston Love, Jesse Powell and Noel again. The former's 22 tracks include 11 blues, and the latter's 23 ten, quotas that are likely to be typical. Given that kind of weighting, it is only to be expected that some of the blues will be slow ones and, given the genre's love of bold contrasts, some very slow; and so it proves.

Typically, an R&B single – and at the time we are dealing with, singles were virtually the only game in town – would couple a fast blues with a slow ballad, or an uppish shuffle with a slow blues. Constrained to mask this reliance on one form, musicians – or, more probably, their record companies – became fluent in the invention of unrevealing but evocative titles like 'Applejack', 'Hot Box', 'Rear Bumper', 'Rocket Flight' or 'High Tide'. Often a blues would be named for a disc jockey in the hope that he would use it as his signature tune, such as Teddy Brannon's 'Mixin' With Dixon' (Ray Abrams, tenor) for the Philadelphia DJ Randy Dixon, or Big Jay McNeely's 'Willie The Cool Cat' for the bandleader-turned-jock Willie Bryant. Numerous tunes, not only blues, were dedicated by Jacquet, Cobb and others to New York's most famous jazz DJ, "Symphony Sid" Torin.

Big Jay McNeely (b.1927) was about a decade younger than most of the roster assembled above, and was an exponent of musical athletics which distant critics like McCarthy would certainly have found challenging if they had witnessed them. He would fall on his knees, lie on his back, go on a walkabout through an audience, march out the club into the street, playing all the while.

"We used to have Battles Of The Saxes," McNeely recalls. "Myself, [Vido] Musso, Chuck Higgins, Joe Houston… all those guys. That was like a constant happening when the sax was the thing before the guitar took over. They'd be advertised like a boxing show. I'd created a lot of excitement by lying on the floor and stuff and other saxophonists began to copy my act. There were dozens of 'em doing it. I thought, 'I'm gonna have to come up with something a little different.' I was in an after-hours club, The Nitecap; they had a striptease show and one girl came out. They turned off all the lights. She just had panties on and they were fluorescent. I thought, 'That's what I'll do.' I stripped the horn, painted it with gold leaf, and put on the vivid transparent

Big Jay McNeely: luminous paint and "the joy of meaningless sax".

paint. When the lights go out, it just glows, all you see is the horn moving."

McNeely's horn moved pretty energetically on records, too, communicating the joy of meaningless sax in tunes like 'Jaysfrantic' and 'Real Crazy Cool': "honking," as Bill Millar describes it, "at its most mantra-like... midway between a desperate, chaotic mess and a marvellously invigorating noise." 'Let's Split' was recorded, like those two, in 1950, and gave rise to one of the most bizarre claims of melodic genealogy ever asserted when McNeely maintained that it was based on the English music-hall song 'One Of The Ruins That Cromwell Knocked About A Bit'. One can confidently say that without this revelation, his secret would have been safe. (Actually, and hardly less surprisingly, the latter part of 'Let's Split' is the even older hoe-down tune 'Turkey In The Straw'.)

But while the honkers surely owed little to Marie Lloyd, some of them when they wrapped themselves around a ballad displayed a sentimentality that would not have been wholly out of place in the Victorian halls. As Robert B Parker's private investigator Spenser likes to say, "It takes a tough man to cook a tender chicken," and when Fats Noel turns from the riot-act-reading of 'Duck Soup' to caress the melody of 'You Belong To Me', or Tab Smith plays 'Because Of You', they seem to be yearning for the ineffable with the same naked emotion as the black balladeers of the day like Al Hibbler and Pha Terrell or the doowop groups like The Platters and Sonny Til's Orioles.

"Mantra-like", Millar's well-chosen phrase for Jay McNeely's music, incidentally suggests something important about R&B that many critics at the time might not have recognised. The honkers were given to repetition not (or not necessarily) because they were inept or unimaginative but because emphatic reiteration is an emotive device intrinsic to African-American musical expression – from ring shout to sermon, from boogie woogie to Bo Diddley. The point is not expand the senses by melodic narrative or developing improvisation but to focus them by repetition into a state of trance. McCarthy hinted at that, perhaps unwittingly, when he referred to "sledgehammer blows driving [the listener] into a sort of hypnotic fascination" ("or," he added, "a splitting headache").

The comment appeared in a long discourse about a musician who seemed to the critic to exemplify the new trend especially vividly, the altoist Earl Bostic (1913-65). Born in Tulsa, Oklahoma, Bostic worked for several Midwestern bands before moving to New York and joining Lionel Hampton. By 1944 he was well enough placed to form his own small group, though he also played on sessions under other leaders.

Recordings with Hot Lips Page such as 'Good For Stompin' and 'Fish For Supper' (both 1944) reveal Bostic's speed and technique while suggesting a predilection for slightly freakish effects – a tiny earnest of the surprise he would unveil a few years later when he did a thorough makeover on his style. Moving largely in the lower register, so that he sounded more like the tenor men of the day, he applied a sandpaper-coated rasp and wide vibrato – both emphasised by King Records' studio engineers – to a series of standards like 'Temptation', 'Roses Of Picardy', and 'Flamingo' (a gigantic hit in 1951).

It was a path that narrowly skirted the marshlands of melodrama and vulgarity, and sometimes Bostic did not escape with his boots dry. The combination of mannered but essentially melodic playing and stark echo – "so full of sand and sex," said Arnold Shaw – seemed to jazz critics of the time rather unsubtle. Victor Schonfield, writing in *Jazz Journal International* more

Sharp and witty Louis Jordan – good times at the Saturday Night Fish Fry.

than 30 years later, was still striking out against the current of mainstream opinion when he commended the altoist's "real taste and artistry" and roundly described him as "surely the most swinging and exciting altoist jazz has ever known". Concluding his remarkable reassessment, Schonfield said: "Bostic not only did all the things 'pure' jazz musicians try and do, but by and large he did them better… the bottom line when it comes to music must be its power to move people, and this Earl Bostic had to the highest degree."

At this point it seems appropriate to double back chronologically and consider another altoist who, though he had little in common with most of the players mentioned above, contributed prodigally to the general R&B scene in which they operated. A near contemporary of Bostic, Louis Jordan (1908-75) made his name in the late 1930s with Chick Webb before forming The Tympany Five, or rather the first of many line-ups (not always quintets) with that billing.

Bebop aside, Jordan's Tympany Five was the most influential small band of its era. What made it so was primarily Jordan's sharp, witty material, songs like 'Saturday Night Fish Fry' and 'Ain't Nobody Here But Us Chickens', delivered with knowing bonhomie, that drew their listeners into a communal celebration of the brighter corners of African-American life. Consequently Jordan's upbeat but even-tempered blowing, generally on alto but not infrequently on tenor and occasionally on baritone, has tended to be undervalued, though not always by other musicians: Sonny Rollins stands in the forefront of his admirers. Louis Jordan's idiom marked one of the two chief directions in which R&B saxophone would move. In his wake came the "jump jazz" of Roy Milton, Joe Liggins, Jack McVea and their contemporaries. They filled the space recently vacated by the big-bands, which had been priced out of existence, by artfully arranging for six- to eight-piece groups so that they sounded like big-bands in miniature. That so few of them have any reputation today beyond the circles of R&B enthusiasts is an oblique testimonial to the vastly superior quality of Jordan's material: thanks to stage shows and periodic revivals of his kind of music, pieces like 'Let The Good Times Roll' have acquired the patina of popular standards.

Many of the more exuberant tenor-men, however, opted for the minimalist setting of the trio with tenor and Hammond organ. For a decade or more this was a sound – indeed, it might almost be called a genre – which, though rarely acknowledged by jazz critics, filled countless neighbourhood bars in cities throughout the United States (see also chapter 13). In this setting the primacy

of the blues was expanded to virtual dominion, and the no-frills honking that took flight with 'Flying Home' was left to spiral down to almost comically rudimentary manifestations like The Champs's 'Tequila' or Boots Randolph's 'Yakety Sax'. Fortunately for admirers of the protean form, a good many of its pioneers survived to re-enact its excitement for new generations.

What is impossible to recreate is the social and cultural milieu from which the honking tenor drew part of its meaning. When McCarthy approvingly contrasts the "almost indecent vitality" of R&B with the "lifelessness" of 1950s society and "the zombie-like music of the cool musicians" ("better the fiftieth repetitive honk than the hypodermic!") he evokes a time long past and attitudes long changed; his schoolmasterly tone is likely to seem quaintly inappropriate today. Yet his address would be echoed in an unexpected quarter. "The point [of repetitive riffs] was to spend oneself with as much attention as possible, and also to make the instrument sound as unmusical, or as non-Western, as possible," wrote the black jazz critic and polemicist LeRoi Jones. "It was almost as if the blues people were reacting against the softness and 'legitimacy' that had crept into black instrumental music with swing."

In the long view, then, the acrobatic screamer was responding to the post-war frustration of black America, to the segregated audiences, the ever-closed doors in radio and recording studios, the whole blackout curtain of racism, with a revolutionary act, making music that disobeyed the rules and dissed the rituals of white popular song.

RICHARD PALMER   SONNY ROLLINS

*FEW WOULD QUARREL WITH THE PROPOSITION THAT THEODORE
"SONNY" ROLLINS IS THE GREATEST TENORIST LEFT ALIVE,
AND NOT MANY MORE WOULD RAISE AN EYEBROW AT THE
CONTENTION THAT HE IS ONE OF THE MOST IMPORTANT
SAXOPHONISTS IN JAZZ HISTORY.*

Before one listens to even a single note blown during a career that now spans
over half a century, there are two things about Sonny Rollins (b. 1929) that
make him a singular figure. First, he was never completely sure he wanted to
be a musician. He had considerable talent as a painter, and right up to his
recording debut in 1948 he does not appear to have had a vocational
determination to carve out a career in jazz. By his own account, Rollins's
decision to pursue such a course had little to do with a belief in his own
artistry, and more with the realisation that his first bosses, Bud Powell and J
J Johnson, had a liking for him personally. This implies an engaging but not
always felicitous diffidence.

Second, Rollins is the only significant hornman of his era who did not
attend any of the leading schools for jazz musicians: the big-bands. To this
day his only recorded performances with a large jazz outfit are four tunes that
appear on *Trio/Brass* (1958). In this he was unfortunate rather than perverse:
by the time he decided that his future lay in music, almost all the big-bands
had folded, and opportunities for such an education were scarce.

It would be wrong to suggest that this proved a problem or points to any
shortcoming. On the contrary, Rollins's craft and technical mastery have
always been bywords; saxophonist Steve Lacy once remarked that he has
"never seen anyone in love with the tenor saxophone the way Sonny is". But
it did mean that Rollins learnt through solitude, which may partly explain his
subsequent periods of woodshedding.

Rollins's initial inspiration was Coleman Hawkins, who lived in the same
neighbourhood in New York. What began as hero-worship (the youngster
would hang around just to get a glimpse of the great man) developed into an
abiding musical influence. But there were other energising sources, subtler but
just as important. One of Rollins's earliest enthusiasms was for Louis Jordan,
whose jump band of the 1930s and '40s was highly successful. Jordan's outfit
epitomised impeccably precise, good-time music – virtues always central to
Rollins, no matter how demanding his work may also be. Furthermore, his
fondness for Jordan's lissom swing touches on an aspect of Rollins's playing
that has not been sufficiently addressed: his kinship with Lester Young.

Much has, rightly, been written about Young's tone; yet his rhythmic
conception was even more significant, for it influenced jazz musicians of all
kinds, not just saxophonists. The ferocity which his tone precluded was
replaced by a gymnastic suppleness. Young was as natural a swinger as jazz
will see, but he seemed to dance rather than stomp: he caressed the beat
rather than drove it. His lithely fluent lines opened up a new territory,
ushering in the seminal achievements of Parker and Gillespie. And from the

Saxophone Colossus: Sonny Rollins's tenor has been one of the great individual voices of jazz for almost half a century.

outset it was evident that Rollins had embraced Young's initiatives. On 'Bouncing With Bud' (1949) in a group led by pianist Bud Powell, Rollins plays "against" Roy Haynes's drums as well as feeding off them, creating a complexity absent even in Powell's brilliant outing. To hear such Young-inspired virtuosity in a player whose attacking sound is so clearly founded on Hawkins is to be aware of an excitingly fertile synthesis.

'Bouncing With Bud' also illustrates Rollins's precocious sense of form. His solo, delivered with satisfying raspingness, is a series of long, primarily legato lines (another link with Young) in which he dismantles normal rhythmic conventions, creating an organic, extended structure rather than a mere succession of blowing choruses. Several critics highlighted such properties in their ecstatic response to Rollins's *Saxophone Colossus* album seven years later – but they were there from the beginning, fundamental to his art.

Rollins capitalised on this auspicious start, working and recording with Art Blakey, Tadd Dameron, The Modern Jazz Quartet and Miles Davis. In this writer's view he is the star of *Collector's Item* (1953) – no mean

Each step in Rollins's career has been marked by key albums like these. Others include Newk's Time, The Sound Of Sonny, *and* The Cutting Edge.

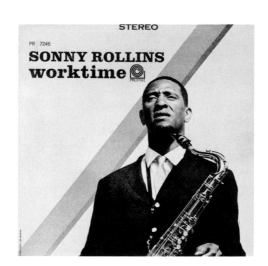

achievement given that the other horns were Davis and Parker – and he is no less splendid on Davis's *Bags' Groove* made a year later, a date additionally notable for premiering three Rollins compositions that have become jazz standards: 'Oleo', 'Doxy' and 'Airegin'. The same year also saw his first collaboration with Thelonious Monk on *Work*; Monk's oblique, harmonically quirky approach suited him perfectly.

Yet despite such successes there were signs that Rollins was far from serene. By now he was in the grip of drug abuse; enervating enough in itself, that seems also to have created frustration and doubt. His first collaborations with Davis convinced him of the need to study more, and although he was not entirely absent from the music scene, he recorded nothing in 1952. Three years later he went further, taking most of 1955 off. These woodshedding periods certainly bore fruit, but they also connote a diffidence remarkable in one who had achieved so much so fast. That syndrome would recur (even more mystifyingly) at the end of the decade; however, 1955 had a happy ending for the tenorist. Harold Land left the prestigious Clifford Brown-Max Roach quintet and Rollins was asked to replace him, setting up the most important influence of his musical and personal life.

It is clear that Clifford Brown was not just a creative artist of the first order, but that he was a wholly admirable man. In Rollins's words: "Clifford was so together as a person you wouldn't have believed it. For a guy that plays that much to be so humble and beautiful, it was just amazing. So I tried to be nice after that." Brown was decisive in helping Rollins to kick his drug habit. His bubbling humour was also edifying. And it is hard to over-estimate the musical benefits that the trumpeter afforded him. It was the only time in Rollins's career when he worked regularly with a frontline partner who was not only his equal but perhaps his superior.

Tragically, this on-the-road symbiosis lasted for only eight months. Brown was killed in a car smash on June 26th 1956. We are fortunate that a large number of recordings preserve the group's work, the best probably being Brown's last recording date, *Sonny Rollins Plus Four* (1956). This is hard bop of the highest quality, characterised by a sublime sense of untapped resources even when the heat is at its fiercest. Both 'Valse Hot' and 'Pent-Up House' offer further evidence of Rollins's compositional gifts, and his playing throughout is as assured as Brown's. That renewed confidence illuminated his work away from the quintet, culminating in the album recorded just four days

*In early 1962, The Bridge (above) was the
album that marked Rollins's return from
retirement. The later 1960s found him
touring widely: this shot (left) was taken
in Berlin in 1966.*

before Brown's death which put all the tenorist's previous work in the shade –
and, arguably, most of his subsequent work too.

Commentary on *Saxophone Colossus* (1956), especially its final piece 'Blue
Seven', has been definitive and exhaustive, but perhaps too much can be
made of that one number, for the other performances are just as fine. Indeed,
some would say that 'St Thomas' is the masterpiece. Not many things in jazz
are perfect, but Rollins's definitive calypso is one of them. Hardly less
impressive are 'Strode Rode' with its dazzling array of stop-choruses, the
wittily trenchant 'Moritat', and the impassioned 'You Don't Know What
Love Is', among the tenorist's greatest ballad readings. One should also stress
that the musicians' rapport is staggering for a pick-up group. Drummer Max
Roach was a regular confrère, but bassist Doug Watkins and the estimable
pianist Tommy Flanagan were drafted in on a one-off basis.

During the next two years Rollins put together a corpus of work that
would be remarkable in any circumstances, but is the more so when one
reflects how hard he was hit by Brown's death. Perhaps it was a sense of his
own good fortune (he had been travelling in the car behind) that impelled him
to make the most of the gifts which the trumpeter had done so much to

Rollins relaxes in Oslo, 1971.

nourish. Maybe it was the instinct to lose himself in work, a familiar recourse in the event of bereavement.

Whatever the motivation, 1956-58 was the apex of Rollins's career. Virtually everything he touched turned to gold, and his range of idiom was just as remarkable. In Blue Note's studios he cut another classic quartet date, *Newk's Time* (1957), with Wynton Kelly, Doug Watkins and Philly Joe Jones. He partnered Dizzy Gillespie and Sonny Stitt in an exuberant mainstream session that includes one of the greatest tenor solos extant, his opening choruses on 'I Know That You Know' from Gillespie's *Sonny Side Up* (1957). At the same time he was experimenting with pianoless groups: two of the finest results are *Way Out West* (1957) with Ray Brown and Shelly Manne and *The Freedom Suite* (1958) with Max Roach and Oscar Pettiford. And then there's the aforementioned *Trio/Brass* (1958) where he fronts a big-band, playing as if born to do so.

These records are essentially a personal selection from the cornucopia that was Rollins on record during this period; another commentator might quite justifiably cite five alternative nominations. Such divergences of taste signify little. The real point is that in 1959, at the absolute height of his powers, Rollins suddenly embarked on a sabbatical that lasted over two years. Why?

Any number of answers have been advanced over the years. Some are more plausible than others, but it is beyond dispute that by now Rollins was seriously bothered by the advent of the "new music" of Ornette Coleman, Cecil Taylor and, especially, John Coltrane. Forgetting what he himself could do so superlatively, Rollins was looking ever more anxiously over his shoulder.

No matter that he had been Miles Davis's first choice for the trumpeter's seminal mid-1950s quintet – Rollins had not thought himself "ready", so Coltrane got the tenor chair instead. No matter, either, that in their famous *Tenor Madness* "battle" in 1956 Rollins exuded assurance and warmth, improvising with a controlled swagger that made his partner's lines frenetic and awkward by comparison. "You were just playing with me," Coltrane is reputed to have said afterwards. The salient point is that, despite overwhelming evidence to the contrary, Rollins himself no longer felt

Rollins puts phenomenal energy into his performances, so much so that he now will not play concerts on consecutive nights.

confident of producing the goods. This time his woodshedding was born of depression and angst.

And this time it didn't work, for two main reasons. First, his withdrawal had been unwise, or else he was just unlucky. Events had conspired to leave him behind. As he had foreseen, Coltrane and Ornette Coleman were about to occupy the centre stage – and so was fellow tenorist Stan Getz, in a way that nobody could have predicted. The colossal success of Getz's samba records was disparaged by some purists, but it established him in the jazz public's mind as the only serious rival to Coltrane. Moreover, just around the corner were Archie Shepp and his acolytes, ready to launch "Black Power Jazz", somewhat analogous to Coltrane's work but with an aggressive political agenda all their own. If critic James Lincoln Collier's judgement that Rollins "had come back too late" is over-simplified, the sad fact is that in these turbulent times his return was far less notable than might have been expected.

The second problem was the music itself. Rollins had landed a six-album contract with RCA worth $80,000 (about £53,000), a prodigious sum in those days, especially for a jazz musician. The results had – and still do have – a mixed press. Some welcomed this "new" Rollins unreservedly, applauding his synthesis of the avant-garde and more traditional virtues, but others found it muted and strangely indeterminate.

He had altered his tone, eschewing that voluptuous jauntiness of the 1950s in favour of a more insistent reediness. While its buzziness was undoubtedly arresting, many of his admirers did not consider it an advance. Moreover, far from curing his uncertainty, Rollins's sabbatical seemed to have increased it. He appears to have had no truly coherent idea of what he wanted to play or with whom he wanted to play it.

The RCA albums (1962-64) document all these properties, and are indeed a weirdly disparate lot. They are replete with interest – Rollins has never been other than a great player – but the unity and assurance that characterise the records made between 1956 and 1958 have gone. In their place is a near-obsessive desire to explore as many directions as possible: samba, avant-garde, the Hawkins legacy, and so on. Such a catholic approach might be considered admirable, but so many and so frequent are the changes of personnel and conceptual focus that it smacks of restlessness, even dilettantism.

In 1965 Rollins switched to the Impulse label, cutting four albums which by common consent are more satisfying than the RCA records. Some hold the view that *On Impulse!* (1965), which restored him to the classic quartet context, was his last great record. Yet by 1967 Rollins had become disenchanted once more, and while he continued gigging, he recorded nothing for five years. This latest withdrawal was partly motivated by frustration at the current state of jazz, which by now was in a very bad way. But it is hard not to see it also as tacit acknowledgement that all was not well with his own art. He had met with neither triumph nor disaster; his return had instead been largely inconsequential, and it was time for another re-think.

When in 1972 producer Orrin Keepnews persuaded him to record for Milestone (with whom Rollins has been ever since) the early results were auspicious. Not all would share the author's view of *The Cutting Edge* (1974) as the finest latter-day Rollins available on record, but that and contemporaneous sessions such as *Next Album* (1972) and *Horn Culture* (1973) displayed a vigour and focus reminiscent of his 1950s grandeur. Alas, it was not sustained. It is difficult to cite a Rollins record since the mid 1970s that one could term essential, and most of his studio work since then has been perilously close to routine.

There is a very good reason for that: Rollins's increasing aversion to the ambience of the studio and the whole business of recording. No one, including the tenorist himself, seems to be sure quite when it started, but by the mid 1960s such commentators as Ira Gitler and Martin Williams had begun to notice a significant disparity between Rollins in concert and Rollins on record, and many other observers came to endorse that perception. For a while the picture was somewhat blurred in that he allowed himself to be recorded live – *The Cutting Edge* was taped at the Montreux Jazz festival – with suitably thrilling results. But the phobia grew, and despite the efforts of Keepnews and other would-be persuaders, it has been a long time since a Rollins concert was preserved for posterity.

That is a shame of near-tragic proportions. A Rollins concert is invariably a momentous occasion: in Britain, people still talk about the tenorist's 1993 concert at London's Drury Lane Theatre, and his 1998 visit to The Barbican was comparably sublime. The wonderful music made on those occasions and others will, however, exist only in the inevitably fading memories of those who were there. Conversely, when Rollins is assessed as an artist by future generations, the last 20 years or so of his career are likely to be judged a period of sad decline – for those appraisers will have only lacklustre albums like *No Problem* (1982) and *Here's To The People* (1991) to go on. The majesty of Rollins deconstructing and reassembling a tune for 20 minutes-plus will be known to them only through yellowed press cuttings.

It would be wrong, however, to conclude on such a note of regret. Instead, this account ends with a celebration of Rollins's most enduring strengths: his innovative repertoire and his all-informing Romanticism.

Rollins has always been a marvellous blues player; his investigations of Kern, Rodgers and other doyens of the American popular song never fail to edify. He responds to hard-bop originals with no less relish, and few if any have surpassed his interpretations of Monk's music. But his definitive repertory characteristics are a love of the calypso and a predilection for oddball tunes. The former both reflects his West Indian heritage and embodies a paradox inherent in his musical nature. Ostensibly spontaneous and light-hearted, the calypso is the result of evolutionary refinement and epitomises an entire culture. As such, it is both highly organised and supremely elastic. Its natural bounce speaks deeply to Rollins's taste for dance rhythms (the Louis Jordan influence), his instinctive swing and his fondness for accessible melodies. On the other hand, its formal properties facilitate some of his most penetrating improvisations. If 'St Thomas' on *Colossus* comes most immediately to mind, 'Hold 'Em Joe' from *On Impulse!* and his perennial concert favourite 'Don't Stop The Carnival' follow close behind.

Rollins's liking for unusual material emerged early on. His work contains a string of titles which no other jazzman has recorded or, probably, ever thought of playing: 'There's No Business Like Show Business' (1956), 'If You Were The Only Girl In The World' (1958), or 'Swing Low, Sweet Chariot' (1974). It has sometimes been supposed that such choices indicate a desire to sneer at tin-pan-alley and its devotees, but that is at odds with the tenorist's gentle nature and cultivated aesthetic grasp. More important, it does not explain why his treatment of these tunes is so joyous. There is a degree of lampoon, yes, but it is underscored by a respect for the songs' ethos.

That is especially evident on 'Toot Toot Tootsie' on *The Sound Of Sonny* (1957). The song was made famous by Al Jolson, and one might assume that the singer's blacked-up antics would offend Rollins at a fundamental level. Yet it should be remembered that Jolson was a Jew, and one can infer from his knowing humour a sardonic awareness of the prejudice all minorities attract. That would have appealed to Rollins's political ideas as well as his angular wit, and his reading of the song abounds in virile good spirits – typically so, too. It is no accident that on all these tunes Rollins swings with a force unusual even for him. Humour and the pleasure principle have always brought out the very best in him.

The Romanticism which distinguishes Rollins's art has both an aesthetic and a spiritual dimension. The synthesis in his work of the old and the new, the traditional and the radical, is one fundamental to the original Romantic movement which also characterised the approach of two of his chief mentors, Parker and Young. And the political idealism that is most obviously present in *The Freedom Suite* has been a lifelong commitment. If its latest incarnation has a green hue, indicated by his most recent album title, *Global Warming* (1998), then that is of a piece with remarks he made long ago. "Jazz was not just a music," Rollins told Ira Gitler, "it was a social force in this country, and it was talking about freedom and people enjoying things for what they are and not having to worry about whether they were supposed to be black, white and all that stuff. Jazz has always been a music that had that kind of spirit. A lot of times, jazz means no barriers."

No other tenor saxophonist sounds remotely like Sonny Rollins, and his concentration on standard American songs for the bulk of his material now sets him apart from the contemporary mainstream.

There is, finally, a third aspect to his Romanticism, albeit a poignant one. It is that, like so many associated with that movement, Rollins can be seen as an artist who did nearly all his best work early on. His many avid concertgoers of the last two decades may not agree; neither will those who think his 1960s work a genuine advance rather than a disappointment. And in view of his talent, which has not waned at all in half a century, and his still-awesome stamina, that judgement could appear inaccurate and quite unjust. But the fact that ten of his 13 records recommended at the back of this book were made before 1960 may yet prove eloquent.

RONALD ATKINS # THE HARDBOPPERS

AS SAXOPHONISTS EMERGED FROM CHARLIE PARKER'S SHADOW
THEY PLAYED HARD BOP – DERIVED FROM BOP, BUT AT SOME
REMOVE – BEFORE THEY FOUND AN ALTERNATIVE FIGUREHEAD
TO PUSH THEM ALL IN THE SAME DIRECTION.

Hank Mobley, the "Middleweight
Champion" of hard-bop tenor.

The Bud Powell quintet was perhaps the official precursor of hard bop. Between the outfit's recording for Blue Note in August 1949 and Parker's death in March 1955, jazz changed. Aspiring saxophonists in the 1940s played Parker's tunes and tried to ape his style. Ten years after the revolution, their successors of the early 1950s were choosing models from a wider sample.

As a result, where bebop referred originally to a particular two-note phrase, and cool stands for an attitude to music, what followed cannot be categorised so precisely. Whoever coined "hard bop" intended the term to illustrate a contrast with cool jazz: a move toward more outgoing, emotional sounds as part of an attempt to promote a consciously racial perspective. "White" jazz was represented as being rather bloodless, while "black" jazz overdosed on passion – a distinction that hasn't stood the test of time.

The increasingly common formula of trumpet and tenor plus rhythm section underlined the tenor saxophone's tendency to dominate over the alto – a change from Parker's rule in the 1940s. But even that is relative. When Art Blakey, whose Jazz Messengers were the template hard bop group, needed to replace Hank Mobley, he looked no further than altoist Jackie McLean.

Sonny Rollins, covered in the previous chapter, had played on the Powell tracks and, if you discount the cool tenors, became the first significant post-bop saxophonist. As an influence, he was soon overtaken by John Coltrane, so fans today may not realise how much Rollins stood out. In terms of his style being picked up by others, it was the early, comparatively immature work, up to 1954 and the first of his many sabbaticals, that initially made an impact. Whether Rollins ever directly influenced Hank Mobley (1930-86), who was

Hank Mobley was essentially a Lester Young follower, a cool, balanced, melodic soloist with a light, warm tone.

three months older, is debatable, but Mobley's style had similar characteristics. Owing little to the breathy Hawkins tradition, his cloudy, somewhat plaintive tone was closer to Lester Young's, with a clean edge in the high registers as favoured by the likes of Stan Getz and Zoot Sims. While the phrasing reflects the wider harmonic vocabulary and the more flexible rhythmic underpinning introduced by bebop, there's none of the concentrated intensity associated in particular with Parker.

As a saxophonist regularly backed by Art Blakey during the period when the drummer was at his most volatile – prodding the soloists through a series of accents that fell like thunderclaps, and suspending the time through belligerent drum rolls that might cut off the unwary in their tracks – Mobley learned to turn such accompaniment to his advantage. Compared to the imperious mid-1950s Rollins, there may be a hint of diffidence in his phrasing, but whereas Blakey flailing in the background would give many cool saxophonists nightmares, Mobley thrives.

His solo on the old Benny Goodman tune 'Soft Winds' with The Jazz Messengers, recorded at the Cafe Bohemia in 1955 and one of the finest live jazz performances, begins by riding over a barrage of counter-melodies from Horace Silver's piano which riffs away in the manner of a big-band. Further in, Mobley effortlessly slips back into the original tempo while Blakey is doubling-up behind him. The same knack of exploiting musical ambiguities crops up on 'Camouflage', a piece with breaks built into the structure, recorded the following year by the Horace Silver quintet that grew out of the Messengers. The quartet on Mobley's most acclaimed album, *Soul Station*

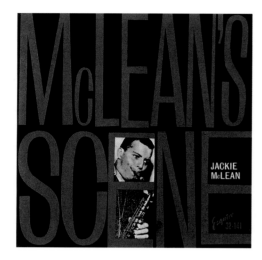

An intense and passionate player, Jackie
McLean (right) investigated free jazz
during the 1960s, but returned to his basic
hard-bop roots thereafter.

(1960), included Blakey. By now the drummer's aggression had become more
obviously controlled in line with current orthodoxy, exemplified by the Miles
Davis rhythm section that included Paul Chambers on bass and Wynton
Kelly on piano, both alongside Blakey here. Mobley, who would himself join
Davis not long afterwards, plays with effortless invention. Compared to earlier
performances his tone has hardened, but not by much. After *Soul Station* and
the stint with Davis, who said later that Mobley's playing failed to ignite him,
Mobley made several excellent albums before his career petered out in the
1970s. Among his few ventures abroad was a gig at Ronnie Scott's London
club in 1968 where, introduced to his British accompanists immediately before
the opening set, he ended up sounding as good as ever.

Judged purely by affiliations, Mobley deserves his status as the original
hard bop tenorist, but there were links both stylistic and emotional with the
cool school. One is reminded of the analogy, attributed to Dexter Gordon,
that if saxophonists were ranked as in boxing, Hank Mobley would be
middleweight champion. The same hardly applies to Johnny Griffin, especially
to his form on the records that made his name. Touring with Lionel

Hampton's band as a teenager, Griffin (b. 1928) experienced musical extroversion at first hand. After re-emerging from his native Chicago during the 1950s he hit the spotlight through gigs with the Jazz Messengers and Thelonious Monk, and through a series of albums for Blue Note and Riverside.

The solos identified most closely with Griffin are fast-fingered affairs taken at ferocious tempos. Even with the notes raining down, his tone had body, and every so often he did something winningly eccentric – maybe some excessive high-register vibrato, or sequences cut off with a squawk. There was the same kind of invention at speed that you get from Charlie Parker and, though the phrasing was more predictable, the same kind of rhythmic drive.

For an example, 'The Way You Look Tonight' from his Blue Note album *A Blowing Session* (1957) sees him, in terms of confrontation, wipe the floor with both Mobley and John Coltrane. Admittedly, Griffin is on home territory, having selected tune and tempo and being backed by Art Blakey again, whose style would not really suit Coltrane. After the others have struggled, he roars back as if to imply, "Can't you do better than that!" while there's a moment during the exchanges when he cheekily halves the tempo.

Griffin had a stimulating on-off partnership with Eddie "Lockjaw" Davis that kept up the tradition of contrasting tenors in tandem, where a beefy sound is pitted against a bit of flash. Since the early 1960s he has been based largely in Europe, which may have contributed to a mellowing of style, the tone now warmer, and greater emphasis placed on a genuine skill at unfolding slow ballads. While establishing a reputation through his early vigour, he has spread his wings and, as an all-round saxophonist, is seriously underrated.

After Griffin, the next tenor to spend time with The Jazz Messengers came from a very different musical lineage. Benny Golson (b. 1929) had already built a reputation as a composer of tunes likely to become jazz standards, and the Messengers benefited by 'Along Came Betty', 'Blues March', one of their biggest hits, and 'Are You Real?' (all 1958). His writing rather overshadowed his saxophone playing, an unusual mix of Don Byas and John Coltrane that seems smoother and better integrated in his more recent work.

Golson's successor Wayne Shorter (b. 1933) is today linked with both Miles Davis and Weather Report, and with a number of tunes other people queue up to play. When part of the Messengers, his solos might be said to have uniquely realised the ideal of hard bop: in texture, the tone was harder than most, and he blended the vertical, many-noted approach of Coltrane with the compositional touch of the mature Sonny Rollins, latching on to phrases he

Harold Land's tenor style has evolved over the years, from something rather like Hank Mobley's to a harder and more aggressive approach. Like Dexter Gordon, Johnny Griffin enjoyed a second career in Europe.

then elaborated (rather than, as Rollins did, improvising around a given theme). Examples are strewn over albums by the Messengers on Blue Note and Riverside, but one of the more remarkable appears on almost his first recording with the group. The version of his classic 'Lester Left Town', performed at a 1959 Paris concert and released originally on French RCA, unwinds rather like the game of a chess master who plans many moves ahead.

The simulated rivalry in the 1950s between jazz styles from the East Coast and West Coast of the US, identified by the cities of New York and Los Angeles, tended to place hard bop as an exclusively Eastern phenomenon. In fact, trumpet-tenor quintets in that idiom were common in California, those led by drummer Shelly Manne and bassist Curtis Counce among them. Manne's saxophonist, Richie Kamuca, is normally classed under cool though

Equipped with a phenomenally fast technique and mental processes to match, Johnny Griffin is a musical whirlwind. His duet partnership with Eddie 'Lockjaw' Davis (album above) was a classic pairing. Griffin moved to Europe in the mid 1960s; this shot (right) catches him in Oslo with drummer Art Taylor, bassist Bjorn Pedersen and pianist Kenny Drew.

he fits the hard bop ethos well enough, which shows how elastic the business of labels can be. More obviously suited to the style, Harold Land (b. 1928) came up with a distinctively gruff tone and a faint jerkiness of phrase.

After touring with the Clifford Brown-Max Roach quintet – impeccably hard bop but different, in that Max Roach differs from Art Blakey – Land became part of Counce's quintet and of other Los Angeles bands, often as leader. A regular partnership that has continued on and off was with vibraphonist Bobby Hutcherson. At one point, Land's playing lost some character following the impact of John Coltrane, though over the years he has successfully synthesised new and old elements to revert to his very recognisable self.

One of his successors with Max Roach was Stanley Turrentine (1934-2000) whose early R&B experience helped develop a contemporary style that retained elements of his original influences – Illinois Jacquet, Don Byas and Ben Webster. His breathy vibrato set him apart from many in this chapter, while the stop-start timing faintly resembled that of Lockjaw Davis. He could heighten the tension through excellent control in the high register and he loved to whoop it up when the beat got heavy, as in the 1965 version of 'Stan's Shuffle'. Married for a spell to organist Shirley Scott, Turrentine also slotted naturally into the tenor-organ ethos, appearing on such Jimmy Smith staples as 'Back At The Chicken Shack' (1960).

Even at the start, many albums under Turrentine's name were slanted more toward the soul-funk end of the market. His first company, Blue Note, gradually spotlighted his playing at the head of larger groups, and never involved him with their more avant-garde artists. Such a policy was tailor-made for his next label, CTI, and several albums beginning with *Sugar* (1970) became bestsellers. If anything, Turrentine's sound grew softer and perhaps closer to Ben Webster's, though the approach was otherwise little changed and lost none of its appeal.

Apart from The Jazz Messengers, the working outfit most readily identified as a hard bop quintet was led by Horace Silver, whose first group arose out of the then-current Messengers minus Art Blakey. Hank Mobley's replacement with Silver, Clifford Jordan (1931-93), might have modelled his hard, rounded tone on Coltrane's, though his playing was more austere and economical, something of a cross between Rollins and Dexter Gordon.

Rollins seems the main influence on Junior Cook. who partnered trumpeter Blue Mitchell in the longest-running Silver quintet that produced such albums as *Finger Poppin'* and *Blowin' The Blues Away* (both 1959). Cook (1934-92) had the priceless knack of grabbing attention on the faster or more extrovert numbers – among them 'Mellow D', 'Sister Sadie' and 'Strollin' – through a strong though far from overpowering tone, and by timing his climaxes cleverly. His replacement, Joe Henderson, arrived in time to deliver a perfectly judged solo on 'Song For My Father' (1964), typifying the all-round mastery of Latin tempos common to all phases of his illustrious career.

Never in the limelight for long, Tina Brooks (1932-74) found a style recognisably his own that bypassed the increasingly predominating influence of Coltrane. His light tone, use of the higher registers and slightly off-centre timing may have been inspired by Mobley, and had a similar emotional appeal – a kind of keening melancholia that might seem at odds with any conceivable definition of hard bop. More in that groove, the murky tone and staccato phrasing of the equally undervalued J R Monterose (b. 1927) made him the East Coast counterpart of Harold Land.

John Gilmore (1931-95) spent a year with The Jazz Messengers, but he was indelibly associated with Sun Ra's Arkestra and appeared on albums by Andrew Hill and Paul Bley. Much of the material featured therein falls well outside the scope of this chapter. When in a more orthodox context, the Rollins and Mobley similarities – probably coincidental – were later complemented by echoes of Coltrane.

Tenors from outside the US mostly avoided the brasher side. In Britain, Tubby Hayes (1935-73) grafted an exceptionally fluent technique and a

Benny Golson was responsible for assembling Art Blakey's first Jazz Messengers, as well as playing with the band. Later, he co-led the Jazztet with trumpeter Art Farmer.

Griffin-like momentum onto a lightish tone not far removed from Mobley's. France's Barney Wilen (1937-96) and Belgium's Bobby Jaspar (1926-63) developed from coolish beginnings to more extroverted styles, while Britain's Dick Morrissey (b. 1940) uses a softer version of Stanley Turrentine's vibrato that goes well with his jazz-rock and tenor-organ affiliations.

As jazz moved into the 1950s, Parker's influence on alto saxophonists seemed overwhelming. Absorbing surface characteristics, they failed understandably to get near the sum of the qualities that made Parker a musical genius. What happened subsequently was a kind of specialisation, with saxophonists homing in on certain aspects of his playing.

The passionate, blues-inflected side of Parker has been developed most memorably by Jackie McLean, who grafted on to Parker's clean and vibrato-

John Gilmore solos with the Sun Ra Arkestra (opposite); the other two saxophonists are Marshall Allen (left) and Danny Thompson (right). Junior Cook (this page) played with Horace Silver, Blue Mitchell and Freddie Hubbard in the 1950s and '60s, and also taught at Boston's Berklee School Of Music.

less sound a searing edge much in the way that Dexter Gordon aired out his tone on tenor. Exposure with Miles, Mingus and Blakey helped spread the word: when the 1960s arrived, an increasingly mature McLean (b. 1932) had evolved into something of a leader himself, notably on several Blue Note LPs.

Always retaining the essentials of his style, McLean kept up with happenings elsewhere. Modal improvising – as practised by Miles Davis or by John Coltrane – became commonplace. He was also sympathetic to the so-called new wave as ushered in by Ornette Coleman and Cecil Taylor, though the most audible reflection of this was a strange whistling effect of which he soon grew tired. From the 1970s onwards, he has generally taken a mainstream stance – exemplified by *The Meeting/The Source* (1973) made alongside his first influence, Dexter Gordon – while avoiding obvious bop or hard bop revivals. McLean's phrasing and declamatory tone, the impact of which is often heightened by being presented slightly off-pitch, have inspired countless disciples, from Gary Bartz to Vincent Herring, to the extent that his direct influence over the years probably exceeds that of other altoists.

Charlie Parker's withering up-tempo solos – sweeping ahead irresistibly. accents dropped in unexpected places and phrases beginning or ending between beats – are best seen as expressions of his unique personality. When

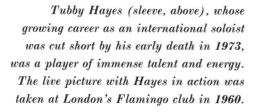

Tubby Hayes (sleeve, above), whose growing career as an international soloist was cut short by his early death in 1973, was a player of immense talent and energy. The live picture with Hayes in action was taken at London's Flamingo club in 1960.

musicians with comparable techniques adapted his attack, the rhythmic accents fell more evenly, which in practice made their solos less nailbitingly intense. Gigi Gryce (1927-83), half-forgotten today but whose engaging tunes did the rounds of hard bop sessions, offered Parker-ish phrases filtered through the intonation of Lee Konitz. From different directions, Phil Woods and "Cannonball" Adderley exemplified the flowing, post-Parker approach.

In the 1950s, Woods (b. 1931) formed a two-alto quintet with Gene Quill (1927-88), a similar stylist but slightly more in thrall to Parker. His tone full and rounded, Woods sweeps along in a jaunty, affable manner closer to a swing-style alto – and when he recorded with Benny Carter on Carter's *Further Definitions* album (1961) the similarities in phrasing stood out. At the head of many invigorating groups in recent years, Woods has expanded along these lines, the basic Parker influence progressively modified.

"Cannonball" Adderley's tone exuded even more in the way of sweetness and bonhomie and, though something of a blues specialist, he seemed further removed from Parker. Consciously or not, the impact of Adderley (1928-75) can be heard today in the playing of Jesse Davis and Wessell Anderson.

Another to exhibit a formidably flowing technique, Britain's Peter King (b. 1940) appeared in bop-revival contexts, even though the work produced under his own name increasingly reflects much more recent developments. Also linked to Parker tributes, Charles McPherson (b. 1939) learnt throughout a long association with Mingus to cope successfully with a spread of styles. There were similar contrasts on America's West Coast. Herb Geller (b. 1928) had a tone somewhat along the lines of Adderley's and, based in Europe for many years, his inherent lyricism has further blossomed.

In sound and style, Joe Maini (1930-64) was more rugged and possibly closest on the Coast to Parker. Somewhere in between, Lennie Niehaus (b. 1929) was a fluent technician who gave up a life of chasing gigs and became better known for film scores, the most notable in a jazz context being *Bird*, Clint Eastwood's 1988 film about Parker.

The prodigious leap in popularity of the soprano saxophone, previously confined to Dixieland ensembles, emanates from a John Coltrane

Phil Woods has been one of the world's leading alto saxophonists since the mid 1950s. He is pictured here with his long-time associate, pianist Gordon Beck.

interpretation of 'My Favorite Things', first recorded by him in 1960, that fits no hard bop definition. Before him, Steve Lacy was already improvising around recognisable tunes and, to that extent, must among his other achievements be regarded as the pioneer post-bop soprano player. Underrated in the 1960s as a tenor saxophonist influenced by Sonny Stitt and Dexter Gordon prior to hearing Coltrane, Nathan Davis (b. 1937) used the soprano to good effect on ballads and blues, his tone rougher than Lacy's and his approach more traditional than Coltrane's.

Another instrument saxophonists tended to double on was the baritone. Its lineage from the mid 1950s up to the growth of free improvising switched between the rugged power of Serge Chaloff and the lighter touch of Gerry Mulligan. Because of their indispensable role as anchor of the big-band saxophone section, with the resultant bonus of regular gigs, many baritone players were given time and opportunity to build solid solo styles. Nick Brignola (b. 1936) emerged as one of the most talented. Before joining Sun Ra in the 1960s, Charles Davis (b. 1933) plied his trade in small groups, most notably with Kenny Dorham, and combined the necessary post-bop mobility with a deep, rounded tone.

Mobility lay behind the success of Pepper Adams (1930-86). His gravelly sound derived from Chaloff rather than Mulligan and, knowing his way round bop harmonies and spitting out notes at speed, he set the pace for mainstream baritones over the coming decades. Co-leader with trumpeter Donald Byrd of an exceptional hard-bop quintet that proved the trumpet-tenor formula was not sacrosanct, Adams later became a cornerstone of the Thad Jones-Mel Lewis Orchestra. An adaptation of his introduction and solo on 'Moanin' by Charles Mingus, among the few classic baritone set-pieces outside Duke Ellington, is heard whenever Ronnie Cuber or Gary Smulyan, latter-day disciples who have extended Adams's approach, tackle 'Moanin' with the Mingus Big Band. Forty years on, the gap between "hard" and "cool" is narrower than pundits made it seem at the time. The music played in both cases conformed to similar rules: the very rules that many who came along in the 1960s would break or ignore.

SOUL SAXOPHONES

BEFORE ITS USE IN THE EARLY SIXTIES AS THE NAME FOR A FRESH BLACK-MUSIC HYBRID, "SOUL" HAD BEEN WORKED TO DEATH IN JAZZ. ADS PROCLAIMED "WE'VE GOT SOUL!" TO SELL NEW RECORDS BY LOCKJAW DAVIS OR CANNONBALL ADDERLEY, HARDLY ENDEARING LABEL OR PLAYER TO JAZZ PURISTS.

The type of saxophone playing associated with tenor-and-organ outings has long been considered something of a peripheral jazz pursuit, given the often formulaic and unadventurous approach to music-making and improvisation, especially at the bargain-basement end of the genre. Yet the best of the players – and the great altoists who also profited by the style – brought a unique personality and viewpoint to the music. Their inventiveness within a narrow ambit was every bit as fresh and commanding as that delivered by the hard boppers of the late 1950s and early 1960s.

Perhaps the opprobrium often directed toward these players is because many – including the very best of the breed – kept one foot in R&B while the other was in jazz. The great tenorists who presaged the movement – Illinois Jacquet, Arnett Cobb, Al Sears, Sam "The Man" Taylor, Eddie "Lockjaw" Davis and Gene Ammons – all spent time in bands that had impeccable swing, jump and R&B credentials, especially Jacquet and Cobb, who helped launch Lionel Hampton's fame as an entertainer who fronted a band with a solid R&B-based backbeat. Many of them had close links with the blues-and-riff-drenched Count Basie band, a catalyst for so much of what was to come. Davis and Jacquet in particular were great Basie stars.

Gene Ammons (1925-74), son of boogie pianist Albert, came out of the bop cradle of the Billy Eckstine band, but from the beginning had deep roots in the swing styles of Lester Young, Coleman Hawkins and Chu Berry. Ammons was only 20 when in 1945 he first made an impression, and became the single most important agent in fermenting the saxophone soul-jazz hybrid that by the end of the 1950s was a staple. Ammons himself was not around much of the time to capitalise on this huge explosion in popularity, for after his seminal ballads and driving blues-based recordings of the 1940s and early '50s he was constantly removed from the scene by a string of narcotics convictions that resulted in lengthy jail terms.

It was no real contradiction that Ammons and the colleagues of his generation – including sometime partner Sonny Stitt – had a good grasp of bop as well as swing. Bop players shared the common heritage of the blues with swing-era musicians. So it's not surprising to find Eddie Lockjaw Davis, standout soloist for the 1950s Basie band, productively paired with Bill Doggett in the late 1940s, or Illinois Jacquet making bestselling small-group records for Norman Granz with Count Basie on organ and enjoying a long association with influential organist Milt Buckner. Jacquet (b. 1922) also made a towering prototypical album in December 1954 with Ben Webster, *The Kid & The Brute*, where both men snarled and hooted good-naturedly at each other across the common ground of the blues.

Eddie "Lockjaw" Davis (left) had his roots equally in bop and R&B. His partnership with fellow-tenorist Gene Ammons made the ideal 'tough tenors' duo. Ammons also worked in a duo with Dexter Gordon (sleeve, above).

But it was Ammons who gave the genre its initial shape and substance by simplifying a bop-based style with roots in Berry and Young, adding an impassioned, caressing approach to ballads which won him a large following almost from the start. This and his penchant for the two-tenor duel so beloved by Lionel Hampton and the Jazz At The Philharmonic aggregations (as well as bop duellists such as Dexter Gordon and Wardell Gray) added up to some very important ground-rules. It even led to his co-fronting a two-tenor band with Sonny Stitt in the early 1950s. Ammons bypassed the hysteria and crudity of the R&B instrumentals where a remorseless shuffle-backbeat drove honking and screaming saxophones to ever more outlandish exhibitionism, and brought style, taste and sophistication to basic musical elements.

However, the impetus toward a definitive genre was provided by organist Ray Charles (b. 1930). His early forays into music lounges and recording studios revealed worthy but hardly inspired imitations of Nat King Cole and his great rival Billy Eckstine. Charles was a pianist of note and a capable alto saxophonist, but it was only when he brought together the previously disparate strands of blues, R&B and gospel, with a sprinkling of jazz's sophistication, that his startling talent emerged and his huge popular influence was felt. Ray Charles habitually ran a big-band which took as its starting point the Count Basie outfit, emulating its riff-based jazz charts and the way it showcased singers such as Joe Williams. He then added his own patent mix of call-and-response gospel hooks, shuffle rhythms and other R&B staples.

With his big, breathy tone in the Ben Webster manner, Ike Quebec made several superb albums for Blue Note in the 1960s. He also acted as the label's talent scout, bringing a number of future stars into the studio for the first time.

Charles's saxophonists, all with jazz roots, soon developed a winning and adaptable shouting style to complement the star's own vocal delivery. Altoist Hank Crawford (b. 1934) and tenorist David "Fathead" Newman (b. 1933) in particular rose to public attention, aided by Charles's own promptings. He also landed them deals with his recording company of the day, Atlantic.

Both men stuck closely to a fairly basic stock of blues-based lines within simple material and concentrated on the depth and expression of their sound (as would King Curtis and Junior Walker in the next decade). They largely shunned developed improvisation in their solos. This disciplined and restricted approach, popular in its own right and giving them successful careers beyond Charles's band, would provide a blueprint for hundreds of later saxophonists, with Stanley Turrentine and Eddie Harris prominent among them.

In the 1950s Charles made a string of purely instrumental albums for Atlantic covering a fair stylistic range, of which *Soul Brothers* and *Soul Meeting* from 1957 and 1958 found him often on alto saxophone and accompanied by Milt Jackson on piano. Charles's stark and impassioned playing reaches back to musicians who influenced Charlie Parker, such as Buster Smith and Lester Young, as well as to jump jazz players like Pete Brown and Louis Jordan.

Before Jimmy Smith's emergence in 1956, jazz organ had not progressed stylistically beyond the phraseology, attack and harmony of the swing era. Smith combined the previously disparate threads of bebop, soul and blues inflections alongside the exploration of the massive sonic and timbral potential of the electric Hammond organ. Working within an organ-guitar-drums trio, he quickly built a solid base of jazz fans, in part due to his brilliant adaptation of Ray Charles's crucial merger of gospel, blues and R&B.

Early on, Smith expanded his working group to include a tenor saxophonist to give him a soul-filled melodic lead in the Charles style. His first choice was John Coltrane. The tenorist had worked with the Johnny Hodges band, which had scored an R&B hit with 'Castle Rock' (1951), and had yet to link up with Miles Davis. But Coltrane stayed only very briefly with Smith, complaining of the organist's volume. Others were less fussy: later partners included first-choice altoist Lou Donaldson and a string of hard-bop tenorists such as Hank Mobley, George Coleman and Tina Brooks.

By 1960 Jackie McLean, Percy France and Ike Quebec were added to this list, although the dream-team pairing of Jimmy Smith with labelmate Stanley Turrentine didn't happen until Smith's very last date for Blue Note, in January 1963 – well into the peak years of soul jazz.

Interestingly enough, of all the saxophonists to have recorded with Smith at Blue Note, only Ike Quebec (1918-63) did not come from a bebop background. (Even Turrentine came direct from the Max Roach quintet where he and his brother Tommy had replaced Booker Little and George Coleman.) Quebec, an older contemporary of Ammons, went on to make a series of highly-rated tenor-and-organ records for Blue Note in the early 1960s before his untimely death from cancer.

Smith's rapid success brought a barrowload of imitators. There was also a rush to apply the same principles of music-making to combinations underpinned by the traditional piano-bass-drums, often with electric guitar as a soulful addition. Many of the musicians caught up in this came from swing, jump and R&B backgrounds, whether they were saxophonists, pianists or guitarists. Prestige Records, then associated mainly with bop, quickly became Blue Note's early rival in the field. Diversifying their range, they began making records with the generation of players who had presaged Parker and his acolytes. By early 1959 Prestige had lost Coltrane and Jackie McLean to other labels and were recording virtually nothing but soul saxophone or organ trio dates.

In 1954 the company had brought Gene Ammons back into the recording studio, and by 1956 had updated his approach to accommodate the emerging style. Two years later Coleman Hawkins made a series of records for Prestige with "Soul" in the album title or song titles. In contrast to the discs he'd made for Verve just the previous year, these emphasised Hawkins's affinity for the blues as well as his giant, roughly affectionate way with a ballad – and there were no organs in sight or within hearing, as Hawk preferred a piano on every session. Soon after this, Eddie Lockjaw Davis (1922-86), a long-time advocate of tenor-and-organ trios, started his fine series of *Cookbook* albums (1958) for Prestige, featuring Shirley Scott on Hammond organ. He also appeared on a classic of the genre, Arnett Cobb's first date for Prestige, *Blow, Arnett, Blow!* (1959).

Under the guidance of producer Esmond Edwards, Prestige even gathered together a whole roomful of talent for *Very Saxy* (1959) featuring Hawkins, Davis, Cobb and Buddy Tate, with Scott pulling it all together at the organ. Even Ben Webster was finally caught up in this late-flowering coupling of swing-era saxophonists with the latest soul-organ craze: he appeared on an early Richard "Groove" Holmes date for Pacific Jazz recorded in spring 1961, sounding perfectly at home at any tempo. Later that year Holmes made a co-led date for Pacific with Gene Ammons, *Groovin' With Jug*, reinforcing the impression of a large stylistic pool of talent which could operate together under the soul-jazz banner. Webster, of course, had already established his down-home credentials many times, especially during the early 1950s when he recorded some truly funky sessions for Mercury with Jay McShann's small group (and the bruising *Kid & The Brute* session mentioned earlier).

Other less prominent saxophonists who signed to Prestige at or around this time included Jimmy Forrest, Hal Singer, King Curtis and Al Sears. Of these, the youngster Curtis (1934-71) was to have the most lasting effect on the development of the saxophone, but his jazz career was truncated and part-time. His records for Prestige (as opposed to those made for 1950s R&B labels) luxuriated in blues made palatable to jazz fans by the presence of an orthodox piano-bass-drums jazz rhythm section, often of considerable sophistication, rather than by his own rather basic improvised patterns.

By October 1959 the versatile young Oliver Nelson (1932-75) had signed to Prestige and would make an important series of albums for them, often with a distinct soul slant, prior to his 1961 classic for Impulse, *The Blues & The Abstract Truth*. Like Curtis, but coming from the opposite extreme, Nelson incorporated soul saxophone elements into his overall musical palette, rather than making them his central point of reference. His later successes as a composer/arranger for a plethora of jazz and non-jazz dates bore out his early Benny Carter-like tendency to cover as many options as possible.

Most importantly for Prestige and for soul saxophone, Willis "Gator" Jackson (1932-87) began a new series of key tenor-and-organ recordings. Jackson had come to prominence with his screaming R&B-style tenor solos on Cootie Williams's 'Gator Tail Pts 1 & 2' (1949) and his own 'Call Of The Gators' (1950), but by 1959 had matured into a complete saxophonist with a natural proclivity for soulful tenor. His working band had on board the young

The organ-and-saxophone combo was one of the most popular forms during the late 1950s and early '60s. Top organist Jimmy Smith (above) included in his combo at various times Lou Donaldson, Stanley Turrentine, Hank Mobley and Ike Quebec.

organist Jack McDuff, who appeared on Jackson's first Prestige date. This session supplied music for a number of Jackson releases, including *Please, Mr Jackson* (1959). The repertoire was the familiar combination of evergreens like 'Angel Eyes', 'Three Little Words', 'The Man I Love', and "originals" (which usually turned out to be head arrangements of the blues).

Jackson stayed a decade with Prestige, sticking to his familiar soul-jazz groove and making a series of sizzling albums for the label. Although he and McDuff parted ways (McDuff was having his own hits and went out with his own combo featuring Harold Vick on tenor), Jackson usually stuck with a Hammond player on his dates, live and in the studio. His accompanists included Freddie Roach, Carl Wilson and Trudy Pitts.

Considering the amount of tenor-and-organ activity in the small clubs and

Eddie Harris scored an early hit with his R&B version of the theme from Exodus. A keen experimenter, Harris invented a number of curious instruments, including what he called a "reed trumpet".

rooms of the urban United States, it was only a matter of time before someone crossed over in a big way. The two most likely contenders to emerge in the early 1960s were Stanley Turrentine, then making headway at Blue Note with his own group after leaving Max Roach, and young Eddie Harris, a player of enormous talent and quixotic musical tendencies.

Turrentine (1934-2000) had in fact played as a teenager alongside Ray Charles in bluesman Lowell Fulson's 1951 band, so he was well aware of the singer's ability to project emotion through music. From the opening notes of *Look Out!*, Turrentine's 1960 debut as a leader, the listener is under no illusion as to what underpins the music: blues, blues and more blues, even with a rhythm section wholly comprising the "modernist" Horace Parlan Trio.

Turrentine's own playing concentrates on a pattern of short phrases and held notes – the musical equivalent of shouts or exclamations – that could have come straight from the saxophonists in the Ray Charles band of the time. Turrentine focusses on his huge, preaching tone and his polished ability to phrase the smallest musical unit in a way that gave it emotional significance. It was on the nurturing of these two gifts that he spent his entire subsequent career – just as Ben Webster and other great swing players honed their own gifts to perfection. By the early part of the 1960s Turrentine was running a tenor-and-organ group with his wife, Shirley Scott, at the keyboard. She had quit Lockjaw Davis in 1960 to go out on her own (and was replaced by Johnny "Hammond" Smith). With Scott signed to Prestige and Turrentine to Blue Note, there are fewer records of them together at this early stage than one would expect from a working group, but *Never Let Me Go* (1963) is an early indication of their fruitful combination.

Turrentine continued to record with the best soul and funk jazz talents signed to Blue Note, and was free to play sessions, including recordings with Les McCann, Grant Green, and The Three Sounds (with Gene Harris on piano). But his early peak was perhaps reached on his wife's 1964 live date for Impulse, *Queen Of The Organ*, recorded at The Front Room, a tiny New Jersey club with a decidedly down-home atmosphere. On this date every element of the developed tenor-and-organ genre is in place and the whole group works seamlessly toward their soulful ends, whether the repertoire comes from Ellington, Lennon-McCartney, Richard Rodgers or the blues. Turrentine would later vary his settings and formats considerably, including a period where he was equally at home with strings as with small combos, sometimes largely abandoning any jazz framework, but his own playing rarely rose above this highpoint. Yet his ability to function as a soul-based player – whatever the musicians and arrangements around him were doing – provided an important example for each new generation of saxophonists who tried to marry art and economics in a satisfactory manner.

Eddie Harris (1934-96) was equally intent on such a marriage, but he rarely touched upon the tenor-and-organ routine. An accomplished musician across a range of instruments, Chicagoan Harris saw it as his business to make music which was popular and tuneful rather than ape any one jazz genre. After a varied apprenticeship, success came suddenly with his very first session as a leader, a jazzed-up version of the theme from 'Exodus', the 1960 movie. Harris's 1961 record for the tiny Vee Jay label sold over a million copies, featuring his featherlight tenor tone amid a medium-tempo beat (reminiscent of Cannonball Adderley's soul successes of the 1960s such as 'Work Song'). Harris's hit contained just one chorus of improvising (where Lester Young and Stan Getz are ever-present) and a tight arrangement of the minor-key theme.

Taking his cue from flautist Herbie Mann, Harris followed up this hit with many tunes based on vamps and strong rhythmic patterns. But his next million-seller, 'Listen Here', didn't hit the stores until early 1968, by which time the soul and blues phrases which were stock-in-trade to many 1960s saxophonists were filling his repertoire. This and a love of bluesy and soulful vamps of the type favoured by his friend Les McCann meant that Harris finished the decade heading away from jazz and toward pure instrumental soul. This was confirmed by the next milestone in his career. Harris's appearance with McCann at Montreux in 1969 was released by Atlantic and spawned another million-seller, 'Compared To What?', as well as a best-selling album *Swiss Movement* and follow-up singles such as 'Cold Duck Time'.

These tunes showed how much could be derived from the soul route being taken concurrently by Cannonball Adderley's band: 'Mercy Mercy Mercy' and other Adderley hits were then important indicators of where jazz had to go for commercial survival. Harris was as comprehensively gifted a player, leader and arranger as Adderley, and wrote good tunes – as the continuing

A founder-member of The Crusaders, Houston-born Wilton Felder is a latter-day representative of the "Texas Tenor" school. His strong, blues-inflected sound has had considerable influence on younger players.

popularity of his 'Freedom Jazz Dance' attests. Yet he was often derided, as Adderley rarely was, for dumbing-down (or "selling out" as it was then called), for playing simplistic clichés when he had so much more to offer.

Harris didn't see his music that way, always protesting that, like Adderley, he played music that interested and stimulated him, and that he had no interest in supplying simply what the critics felt he should. That his talents and interests often led him outside jazz is certain; that he always stretched his talents to the artistic limit is a moot point, especially when his least inspired and most formulaic records are taken into consideration. But Harris remained a fiercely independent and committed player, as well as a tremendously influential one, right up until his death.

The West Coast was not, as we've seen, a particularly fertile breeding ground for soul saxophones, but there were notable exceptions. And none more so than Wilton Felder (b. 1940). Felder had come to LA from Texas with his Houston high-school buddies Stix Hooper, Joe Sample and Wayne Henderson. Their group was titled the Modern Jazz Sextet before becoming The Nitehawks and finally The Jazz Crusaders, just prior to their 1961 recording debut. Felder was, like his Crusaders colleagues, a well-schooled musician equally adept at a range of musical styles. His versatility is well documented on the long sequence of records the band made for Pacific Jazz during the 1960s, but at the core of his playing is a rock-hard tone and a Texas cry as strong and direct as anything from Arnett Cobb, Booker Ervin or his fellow Texas-to-LA tenorist Curtis Amy.

Felder was the star soloist in a band gifted with more than one good composer/arranger. His gritty, blues-drenched phrases were often embellished by snatches of the sort of harmonic questing that John Coltrane was currently popularising among young saxophonists. This is as noticeable on *Freedom Sound* and *Looking Ahead* (both 1961) as on later albums such as *At Newport* (1966). Felder continued to deepen his saxophone message and concentrate increasingly on the bass guitar as The Jazz Crusaders metamorphosed into The Crusaders, moving labels (to Motown), becoming more solidly aligned with the rock side of funk and soul, and even touring widely in the early 1970s as support group for The Rolling Stones. Felder's powerful tenor voice had a less central role to play, but his important jazz work was done, influencing hundreds if not thousands of young players coming up after him who inhabited the fertile worlds of creativity between the jazz and rock forms of soul and funk.

Cannonball Adderley's contribution to jazz lies in more than one area, but his largest audience was the one that responded to his funk and soul-jazz hits. His funk repertoire, often supplied by brother Nat or pianists Bobby Timmons and Joe Zawinul, was adroitly mixed with more imaginative jazz from band members such as Yusef Lateef and Charles Lloyd, enough to keep both his popular and artistic credentials in good order right up to his untimely death in 1975.

By that time the larger part of the soul saxophone movement had withered on the vine, although some late arrivals were still scoring hits in an increasingly disco-oriented genre. Of these, tenor player Houston Person (b. 1934) was perhaps the most talented and charismatic. Debuting on Prestige in the late 1960s when that label began to contract its activities, Person had the big sound and ballad sensibilities of Ammons, Davis, Jackson, Quebec and other forebears. But he was also eager to delve into the crossover between older soul-jazz forms and the various disco rhythms that became such a hypnotic attraction for the commercial end of the jazz market as rock triumphed worldwide. This interest peaked in the first half of the 1970s, but a general move back to more traditional jazz structures and ambiences at the end of the decade led Person – as well as others such as Willis Jackson who in 1977 made the superb *Bar Wars* – back to a more loosely defined soul and organ jazz format. Person made a string of magnificent recordings for Muse during the 1980s and '90s.

The careers of Houston Person and Willis Jackson during these decades reflect the larger changes suffered by many saxophonists who skirted the fringes of popular music while attempting to uphold something of a jazz tradition in their playing. As with any business connected to media and the arts, fashion is ever-changing, style is all. The rapid turnover of popular genres and dance crazes determines a short stay in front of the spotlight and an inevitable return to cult status for all but the most determined and outstanding figures. That players like Person and his peers stuck to their styles in the face of disco and fusion – and every other succeeding musical wave – speaks a great deal for the force and longevity of their original visions, and says much of the inexhaustible roots that the music found in the various blues forms of the mid-century.

BRIAN PRIESTLEY **JOHN COLTRANE**

A TRUE ORIGINAL GENIUS, COLTRANE RECAST THE
VOCABULARY OF JAZZ IN THE EARLY SIXTIES AS RADICALLY
AND COMPLETELY AS ARMSTRONG AND PARKER IN THEIR TIME.
COLTRANE'S INFLUENCE IS STILL CLEARLY IDENTIFIABLE IN
THE PLAYING OF VIRTUALLY EVERY MAJOR SAXOPHONIST
BELOW THE AGE OF FIFTY.

Miles Davis (right). It was as a member
of Davis's quintet that John Coltrane made
his first big impact on the world of jazz.

The importance of John Coltrane to the history of jazz saxophone can hardly be overestimated. Like one of his most famous employers, Miles Davis, he created not only a widely imitated style on his instrument, but several different and separately imitable versions of it. More than that, and again like Miles, he was equally significant as a bandleader, and the sound of his 1960s groups has had a lasting, worldwide influence. Yet until at least his 30th birthday not even a close observer of the jazz scene would have predicted Coltrane's rapidly rising position in the ensuing decade, nor his even greater eminence in the period since his premature death at the age of 40.

The concept of the late-starter is relatively common in jazz. But it often has more to do with perception and the particular player's lack of access to a wide audience through recording than with their ability. For instance, Lester Young was clearly a fully formed soloist by the time he finally appeared on disc at the age of 27. The same was true of Eric Dolphy, despite the fact that he had seldom left the West Coast until he was nearly 30. Coltrane at the same age had already played with the best but had failed to impress, partly because the elements of his style were still diffuse and insufficiently organised. Born in 1926, it took until 1957 before he began to sound like John Coltrane.

He was raised in North Carolina. His father, a tailor, played violin and clarinet by ear. John grew up with his father and mother in the home of his maternal grandfather, a minister in the African Methodist Episcopal church. His other grandfather was a minister of the same denomination. John was brought up to take an interest in black history and black artists such as poet Langston Hughes and soprano Marian Anderson. But a warm and close family relationship was suddenly jeopardised when John was 12, as his father and both his maternal grandparents died within a few weeks of one another.

The damage to the family's financial stability was considerable and John's mother now had to work outside the home. So perhaps it was fortunate that, just at this time, he started to become involved in playing music. In the local community wind-band he was first given an alto-horn but later asked to try

the clarinet. He stayed on that instrument when, a while later, his high-school also started its own band.

Three early Coltrane classics: Blue Train (1957), Miles Davis's epoch-making Kind Of Blue (1959), and Giant Steps (1959), still one of his most admired albums.

He immediately fell in love with the clarinet and began to practise diligently. But as he listened to dance-bands on the radio – and sometimes went to see touring bands live, in the company of his cousin – he was drawn to the sound of the saxophone. When he succeeded in borrowing an underused alto from a local restaurant-owner, he was on his way.

Pretty soon, his mother moved to Philadelphia and later to Atlantic City, in search of better-paid work. After graduating from high school in 1943, John joined his mother up north. He found himself in a large metropolis whose black ghetto area was a hotbed of music. When his mother bought him a secondhand alto of his own, he took lessons in saxophone and theory at a local music school and made connections with a very fertile jazz scene. Soon he began attending jam sessions and playing in small groups, and he was both impressed and thrilled by the new bebop style when he witnessed the 1945 Philadelphia appearance of Dizzy Gillespie's quintet featuring the then little-known Charlie Parker.

Coltrane immediately set to work emulating Parker, but his musical odyssey proceeded in fits and starts for a whole decade. He was drafted into the Navy for a year, playing in both military bands and small groups, getting a taste for life as a professional musician. Back home from summer 1946 and already known as Trane (or Train), he became acquainted with Philadelphia-based jazzmen such as Benny Golson, "Philly Joe" Jones and Jimmy and Percy Heath. He also briefly joined various touring R&B bands, the most

famous of which were those of fellow saxophonists Eddie "Cleanhead" Vinson (during 1948-49) and Earl Bostic (in 1952). A happy consequence was that Vinson, having no space for another altoist, bought Coltrane his first tenor saxophone. In between these two affiliations, he spent 18 months with Dizzy Gillespie, in the big-band and then a sextet, enabling him to record a handful of brief solos and to play on several broadcasts.

The surviving evidence shows his playing to be a somewhat ungainly mix of Parker, Lester Young, Don Byas, Dexter Gordon and possibly Paul Gonsalves (a colleague in the Gillespie big-band). One of the facts of life in the bebop world was the availability of hard drugs and, like so many of his peers, Trane became hooked for several years. This hardly helped his career. (Even Parker, the Pied Piper of Heroin, said, "I may have thought I was playing better but, listening to some of the records, I know I wasn't.") The drugs led directly to Coltrane's dismissal by Dizzy.

During the first half of the 1950s bebop had lost most of its audience to R&B, and some of Coltrane's run-of-the-mill jobs back in Philadelphia required the tenorist to "walk the bar" while playing rabble-rousing solos. So it was a distinct step up in the world when in 1954 he joined Johnny Hodges, whose band's small-group swing was one of the sources of R&B. Coltrane later described Hodges as "the world's greatest saxophone player".

Unfortunately Hodges too fired Trane for his drug use, so he once again spent a year gigging with locals, including organists Shirley Scott and Jimmy Smith. It was while working with Smith that Coltrane was plucked from obscurity by none other than Miles Davis. In autumn 1955 Davis, on a comeback after kicking his own drug addiction, was putting together his first regular quintet. Initially he had hoped to get Sonny Rollins, with whom he had performed in public and on record, but was thwarted by Rollins taking a drug-rehabilitation sabbatical. Miles was alerted to Trane by two musicians he'd already hired, pianist Red Garland and drummer Philly Joe Jones.

Davis's use of Coltrane was not only unexpected, but unwelcome to some of the trumpeter's fans. In an uncanny repetition of the contrast ten years earlier between Parker and the more tentative Miles. the now masterful Davis had as his foil a tenor whose music was interesting and exploratory, yet not totally together. Trane even said subsequently, "I had all kinds of technical problems – for example, I didn't have the right mouthpiece – and I hadn't the necessary harmonic understanding. I am quite ashamed of those early records I made with Miles. Why he picked me, I don't know. Maybe he saw something in my playing that he hoped would grow." If so, Davis was eminently clear-sighted. Later, Miles's own more succinct verdict about the quintet was that: "The group I had with Coltrane made me and him a legend."

Certainly the six albums made by the quintet during 1955 and 1956 are still impressive, especially for Miles and the dynamic rhythm section. Trane's frequently exciting performance is more variable. Among his highspots are the contributions to *Round About Midnight*, including the solos on the title track and 'Dear Old Stockholm'. Both are highly atmospheric pieces in a minor key, and they point forward to some of the tenor player's 1960s work.

Coltrane's sudden visibility as a member of the leading small group of the day coincided with the boom in releases of the then-new 12-inch LP. It led to a considerable amount of freelance recording for Coltrane and, starting in 1957, to albums made under his own name, including the excellent *Blue Train* (1957). Before that, however, there had been another hiatus as Davis fired, re-

Coltrane (opposite) added the soprano saxophone to his customary tenor in the early 1960s. Its sound was well suited to the Eastern-influenced modal music he was exploring. Later he complained that switching from tenor to soprano and back again during a single concert posed severe technical problems.

hired and then re-fired Coltrane, once again because of his drug habit. This time, Trane's return to Philadelphia was different, for he decided to end his addiction once and for all.

At the same time as joining Miles 18 months earlier, he had married a serious and sober young woman, Juanita Austin, whose religious leanings were toward Islam. (Indeed her Muslim name, Naima, became the title of a particularly lovely Coltrane ballad, first recorded in 1959 on *Giant Steps*.) In early 1957 he elicited her moral support as he cured himself by total drug abstinence – the "cold turkey" method used by Miles a few years before. As Coltrane described it, "I experienced by the grace of god a spiritual awakening which was to lead me to a richer, fuller, more productive life. At that time, in gratitude, I humbly asked to be given the means and privilege to make others

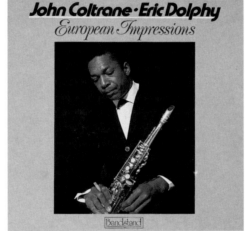

Eddie "Cleanhead" Vinson, blues singer and alto saxophonist, was one of Coltrane's early employers. Eric Dolphy joined John Coltrane's quintet for a European tour in 1961. Coltrane's European tours of the early 1960s, first with Miles Davis and then as leader, were widely recorded by radio stations. These recordings were later issued on disc.

happy through music." The immediate consequence was a six-month playing engagement with Thelonious Monk, who was undergoing a renewal of public interest. Now pushing 31, Trane was finally able to bring together the various elements of his stylistic amalgam. This included not only the influence of contrasting major figures of the past, but also his attraction to complex harmonic substitutions (which later bore fruit in *Giant Steps*).

Rather than being tentative and therefore sometimes unrhythmic, Coltrane's music was now markedly rhythmic – but didn't swing in the traditional sense. Instead, it surged forward like waves on a shore, with all manner of contradictory currents and eddies. This immediately caught the attention of fellow musicians, including some previous doubters. It then reached the ears of a wider audience as he rejoined Miles, in a new sextet featuring "Cannonball" Adderley and with Red Garland soon to be replaced by pianist Bill Evans.

If the previous quintet had been excellent, Davis's 1958-59 sextet was remarkable in harnessing disparate elements such as the bluesy undertow of Adderley's alto and the probing quality of Trane's urgent tenor. There were classic albums: *Milestones* (1958; still with Red Garland), *Jazz Track* (1958) and *Kind Of Blue* (1959; with Bill Evans helping Miles to assemble some of the material). These records were hugely influential in turning other players away from post-bop chord sequences toward the looser frameworks of modal and free jazz. Coltrane had already been moving in this direction, and soon began working on vastly extended improvisation on a single scale, typical of Indian classical music. This caused some bemusement for Davis, and possibly self-consciousness on the part of Trane. Once, when a stick accidentally flew out of drummer Jimmy Cobb's hand and narrowly missed the saxophonist, he said, "I thought you finally threw something at me for playing so long."

When Coltrane left Davis of his own accord in spring 1960 to form a new group, he relished the freedom to solo at greater length (and with less harmonic variety in the backing) than any of his predecessors. This required great stamina, not only from himself but his sidemen. The young pianist McCoy Tyner had to create textural variety from essentially static chords, while the driving drummer Elvin Jones played a wealth of cross-rhythms to sustain Coltrane floating aloft. Finding a bassist who could keep the whole enterprise spiritually grounded proved more difficult. But after stints by Steve Davis and Reggie Workman, Jimmy Garrison – raised like his predecessors in Philadelphia – fitted the bill. Untypically for most jazz groups of the 1960s, work was plentiful enough to enable each of these key quartet members to stay with Trane for more than five years.

During the autumn and winter of 1960-61 the group was augmented by the adventurous playing of multi-reedman Eric Dolphy and, much more briefly, by the straightahead guitarist Wes Montgomery. Ultimately, however, Trane was already providing his own contrasts, since he had been interested for a while in the sound of the soprano sax and now began to feature it in public. Partly this was in order to extend his upper register in a more natural way than the strained high notes he used on the tenor, and partly it reflected his growing interest in the wind instruments of Indian and North African music. Coltrane created a classic definition of how this music could influence jazz, achieving a considerable jukebox hit in inner-city black bars with 'My Favorite Things' (1960). Follow-up versions of the pop tunes 'Inchworm' and 'Chim Chim Cheree' plus ancient modal folk-songs like 'Greensleeves' and 'El Vito' (which he renamed 'Olé') exploited the same catchy waltz-time feeling.

Elvin Jones, powerhouse of the classic John Coltrane Quartet of the early 1960s.

However, at the same time as he was espousing this second major style, Coltrane was happy to revert to the harmonically-based approach associated with his first stay in Miles's band and his Monk period. Especially in albums he made for the Impulse label such as *Ballads* (1961) and *Duke Ellington And John Coltrane* (1962) – and even, for the sake of contrast, during live gigs too – his readings of standards were, perhaps revealingly, usually done on tenor rather than soprano. As a spin-off, he also introduced a new twist to such slow, lyrical and meditative playing by creating original material that, while clearly related to the jazz-ballad tradition, was done entirely out-of-tempo. Examples are the gentle 'After The Rain' (1963) and the less-celebrated but beautiful opening and closing sections of 'Wise One' (1964), another composition which was reportedly dedicated to Naima.

A contrast certainly existed between the stately and poignant sounds Trane produced in such contexts and the demanding nature of his up-tempo work, which often burst the barriers of conventional saxophone pitch and of formerly acceptable tone-quality. His R&B experience helped here but, in contrast to the pleasure principle of that music, what he was now producing was thought-provoking and inspirational.

The spiritual aspect of his searching melodies and his questing multi-noted improvisation was brought to fruition in late 1964 on *A Love Supreme*, which was played entirely on tenor. An avowedly religious work, it includes a passage of chanting by two voices (which I believe to be Coltrane himself, overdubbed) and, in the last section, an out-of-tempo ballad that is, in fact,

John Coltrane backstage (right) at a Paris concert in 1965. Pianist Alice Coltrane (née McLeod), Coltrane's second wife and collaborator in his later projects, is pictured in London in 1987 (below).

the saxophone "reading" of a poem published on the album's sleeve. Through its unique style and the strength of the group's playing it became one of the best-selling jazz records ever.

It was typical of Trane that, having achieved what he must have known was a highpoint of his music, he then headed off toward new pastures. The first half of the 1960s had been marked on the one hand by the breakthroughs of Ornette Coleman and pianist Cecil Taylor in revitalising the energy of jazz without using chorus structures and harmonic sequences, and on the other by the growth of the black civil rights movement (soon to be imitated by a white counter-culture opposed to America's war in Vietnam).

Coltrane was not the person to make any public comment on politics, but he was well aware of what was going on in music. Younger and more extreme tenor players emerged, such as Albert Ayler and Archie Shepp who both made their US debut albums in 1964. Shepp's record was in fact facilitated by Trane, and he was now alerted to his position as the figurehead of a new generation of musicians.

As a result, he began inviting some of them to join in his public appearances, helping them to gain recognition from listeners and critics. In June 1965 he went into the studio with an 11-piece ensemble featuring his quartet plus a second bassist, two altoists, two trumpeters and two extra tenormen (Shepp and Pharoah Sanders, who was soon to join Coltrane's touring group). The resulting album, *Ascension*, was a single performance lasting nearly 40 minutes and consisting of a series of turbulent solos backed by the rhythm section, introduced and separated by lengthy tracts of collective improvisation by all the musicians simultaneously. Compared to the fierce glow of *A Love Supreme*, done only six months earlier, this was an unstoppable flow of molten lava.

Though it lost him much of his previously wide audience, the new direction of Trane's music was something he felt compelled to pursue. Many of his subsequent live performances were with quintet, sextet or septet line-ups, plus added saxophone, added bass or, for a period in late 1965, a second drummer. Inevitably this led to the break-up of the fixed quartet personnel: McCoy Tyner found it harder to focus on his role (and harder to hear his acoustic piano) while Elvin Jones complained that the freely rhythmic style of the new percussionist, Rashied Ali, wouldn't work alongside his own drumming. As a result, Ali wound up as the sole drummer. The new pianist in

the group was equally different: Alice Coltrane was the woman for whom Trane had left Naima in 1963 (and who in the following three years bore him three children). Coltrane's new group recorded prolifically, especially so as his contract allowed him to organise his own sessions – only some of which came out, and those that did were issued on Impulse alongside material done with the label's in-house producer Bob Thiele. Much of it, however, remained to be released posthumously. To the consternation of everyone involved in jazz, Coltrane succumbed to liver cancer and died in July 1967. Performers, listeners and commentators realised that they were mourning a major innovator, while the avant-garde movement of younger players proceeded to recast elements of his work into various movements such as fusion, soul jazz and European "improvised music".

According to that most perceptive biographer, Lewis Porter, "There is absolute consensus about three things. First, Coltrane was a sweet, quiet man, a man of few words... Second, he had a dry sense of humour if you caught him in the right mood. Third, he practised constantly and obsessively." Whether or not he burned himself out trying to perfect his instrumental control, and trying to fulfil what he saw as his destiny, is pure speculation. Trane said in 1962, "It's [the] universal aspect of music that interests me and attracts me; that's what I'm aiming for."

Measured in terms of his influence on thousands of saxophonists from Pharoah Sanders to Michael Brecker, and of his ability to touch millions of listeners worldwide, Coltrane's success is greater than he could have imagined.

Three albums are pictured here from Coltrane's great early-1960s period. Africa/Brass features the Quartet backed by a large orchestra; A Love Supreme is widely regarded as his masterpiece; and Ascension marked the saxophonist's move into free-jazz territory.

THE MODALISTS

UNTIL THE LATE FIFTIES IMPROVISATION WAS BASED ON RESOLVING HARMONIES, OR CHORD CHANGES – WHICH HAD GROWN MORE COMPLEX AND FAST-MOVING, POSING GREATER CHALLENGES TO PLAYERS. MODAL JAZZ REPLACED THIS WITH HARMONIES THAT WERE STATIC OR MOVED VERY RARELY.

The first classic example of modal jazz is generally acknowledged to be Miles Davis's *Kind Of Blue* (1959), which also featured the saxophones of John Coltrane and Cannonball Adderley. Davis brought his formidable synthesising powers and single-mindedness to bear on modal theory and how best to incorporate it into modern mainstream jazz. But he wasn't the first.

The man who spent many years studying modes and their application to contemporary music-making was George Russell. His theories, expressed in his book *The Lydian Chromatic Concept Of Tonal Organization In Improvisation* (1959), were not widely dispersed or understood until the late 1960s and early 1970s. But Gil Evans, Charles Mingus, Miles Davis and other progressive musicians of the 1950s were aware of his ideas and of his compositions written in their wake. Coltrane played on one of Russell's records in the late 1950s, but it was Davis who found a way of presenting modal improvisation in the most favourable light.

For Davis, a supreme master of melody and economy, modality was a phase in his development. For Coltrane, it was the starting point for a consuming passion which would occupy his musical quests until his death in 1967. The other saxophonist in Miles's band, Julian "Cannonball" Adderley (1928-75), quickly absorbed modality's implications and, like Davis, found a way of assimilating its principal traits into an already mature hybrid style.

Florida-born Adderley was possessed of a beautifully rich alto tone with more than a hint of Benny Carter about it. In addition he had the harmonic and rhythmic sophistication brought to jazz by Charlie Parker, as well as a good helping of southern soul. This was also present in the playing and compositions of his cornettist brother Nat, some of whose pieces – 'Work Song' included – helped make the Adderley brothers' band one of the top-billing groups in jazz for over a decade.

This fame and success led to accusations of a sell-out and of pandering to the funk market, but a set from the Adderley band was never stylistically monochrome. What's more, the very catholic tastes of the leader allowed him to hire intelligent and experimental sidemen such as Yusef Lateef and, later, Charles Lloyd, while his own recording career included albums made with Bill Evans, Milt Jackson, Miles Davis, Wes Montgomery (whom he discovered), Victor Feldman and vocalist Nancy Wilson. Later sidemen included keyboardists Joe Zawinul and George Cables, both of whom proved to be innovators in the 1970s.

Like Duke Ellington, Adderley was adept at keeping up a supply of successful singles – whether from brother Nat's pen or from pianists Bobby Timmons and Joe Zawinul – while still giving 100 per cent of his improvising

skills in live performance. On a string of mid- and late-1960s Capitol albums there would be hits such as 'Mercy Mercy Mercy' and 'Little Boy With The Sad Eyes', but also serious workouts. 'Rumplestiltskin' was one, a modal piece with Cannonball using the Varitone octave divider on his alto to deliver one of his fieriest solos; another was 'Sweet Georgia Bright', where the altoist fully utilises the lessons learned from Evans, Coltrane and Davis while employing a plethora of substitutions and more exotic, vocalised devices to create a highly charged atmosphere.

A contemporary of Adderley with strong connections to other schools of jazz is altoist Jackie McLean (b. 1932). Often thought of as an acolyte of Charlie Parker, McLean by the late 1950s was a regular with the Charles Mingus workshop and a willing participant in that leader's experiments with longer form, improvisations over ostinato patterns or held chords and scales, and collective interplay.

By the early 1960s McLean, a gifted composer as well as instrumentalist, was sufficiently enthused by the probings of Coltrane, Ornette Coleman and others to make a series of records using the newer musical ideas of the day, including intensive use of modes. This is especially apparent on *One Step Beyond* (1963) and subsequent albums for Blue Note where McLean deploys scales very much in the manner of Coltrane, whether on a ballad or an up-tempo piece. This part of McLean's long and successful career was relatively brief, lasting some half a decade or so, but it was influential in its own right and contributed a number of jazz classics to the music's recorded legacy. McLean's intensely human "cry", his sheer intensity and his questing nature served as a model for younger altoists looking for ways of marrying the legacies of Coltrane and Parker in particular. Some of the more prominent altoists to benefit to a greater or lesser extent from his example were Gary Bartz, James Spaulding, Eric Kloss, Marion Brown, Sonny Fortune and Robin Kenyatta. But despite this, and reflecting the overwhelming influence of John

The Adderley brothers, Nat (cornet) and Julian "Cannonball" (alto saxophone). Their quintet was one of the most popular jazz outfits of the early 1960s.

Coltrane on every generation of saxophonists to arise since the late 1950s, the impact of modal schemes is most extensively found among tenor and soprano players. Wayne Shorter's hours of practice and study alongside Coltrane in the latter's Manhattan apartment, going through huge lexicons of scales, is a story often recounted in interviews, articles and books.

Shorter (b. 1933) showed little sign of this during his first years on the New York scene, but by the end of his tenure with Art Blakey's Jazz Messengers both his playing and writing showed a musical intelligence straining at the leash of Blakey's hard bop formulas.

Shorter's personal release was found in the ranks of Miles Davis's quintet between 1965 and the end of that decade, as well as on a raft of albums made for Blue Note both as leader and as sideman. The way in which Tony

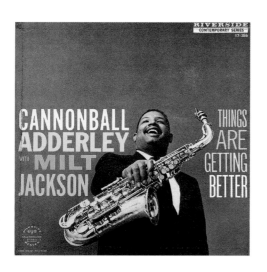
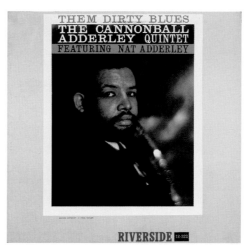

Cannonball Adderley's popular success did wonders for the fortunes of the independent Riverside label. Booker Ervin first came to prominence with Charles Mingus. His early death, at age 39, cut short a hugely promising career.

Williams used him alongside fellow tenor player Sam Rivers on the drummer's *Spring* (1965), for example, demonstrates Shorter's formidable command and oblique use of harmony.

With Davis's band Shorter offered intense, closely-argued solos, mostly of a brevity astonishing by the long-winded saxophone standards of the day, and also displayed a burgeoning talent for composition. Only in the Davis quintet's live recordings does Shorter respond to the challenge of the Williams-driven rhythm section and cut loose at length. Even then, his solos are not gargantuan, either in length or conception. Here and on other appearances as a sideman – Grachan Moncur lll's *Some Other Stuff* (1964) is a notable occasion – Shorter shows a marked reluctance to adopt the heroic soloist role brought into vogue by the genius of Coltrane and Sonny Rollins, both of whom could (and did) regularly improvise for between 30 and 50 minutes on a single theme. Shorter preferred even then to look for colour and mood, drama and contrast, often displaying his knowledge of uncommon scales in the most tangential, unobvious ways.

By the end of the 1960s Shorter, like Davis, Williams and others of the Miles circle, was experimenting with electric (and, later, electronic) instruments and with rock and Latin-based rhythms. His last albums for Blue Note, including classics like *Super Nova* (1969) and *Moto Grosso Feio* (1970), amply display this new fascination as well as his continuing use of drones, slow-moving harmonic patterns and other open-ended improvising and composing vehicles. They show why Shorter moved from Davis to Weather Report and, perhaps, why he latterly neglected the tenor saxophone in favour of the soprano. He preferred its relative lack of jazz pedigree, and its ability to lead an ensemble line or play at the top of a series of chord patterns, rather than the middle intervals and less brilliant range of the tenor.

The music – progressively more heavily arranged and orchestrated, albeit for small ensembles – now demanded the full flowering of Shorter's own improvisatory inclinations toward brevity and dramatic effect. In the 1970s he embraced Latin influences, confirming this love of colour and pastiche. His excursions with VSOP and later acoustic all-star groups only emphasise the ground he abandoned when Miles Davis and all the members of his great 1960s quintet dropped acoustic abstraction and adopted the mixed blessings of electrification. Tenorist Joe Henderson (b. 1937) spent just two weeks in the Miles Davis quintet, but he trod a similar path to Shorter's through the 1960s.

Charles Lloyd is pictured recording a TV show in London during 1965. Lloyd's band had great success during this period, and also introduced pianist Keith Jarrett to a worldwide audience.

The hugely influential Wayne Shorter was an important member of the bands of Art Blakey and Miles Davis, as well as being a founder-member of Weather Report. Shorter is also a leading jazz composer.

Henderson began his New York career with a long series of solid hard-bop sessions for Blue Note, notable among them being Grant Green's 1963 album *Idle Moments*. He also made spirited contributions to Horace Silver's quintet, in which he replaced the long-serving Junior Cook, but soon shifted toward the siren call of Coltrane's methodology on his own dates.

Henderson was a key sideman on records that by Blue Note standards were experimental: Andrew Hill's *Black Fire* (1963) and *Point Of Departure* (1964), Pete La Roca's *Basra* (1965), Larry Young's *Unity* (1965) and McCoy Tyner's *The Real McCoy* (1967).

Henderson had a thorough and sophisticated grounding in the art of negotiating chord changes at speed. He combined the gruffness of Rollins's middle and bottom register with Coltrane's upper-register cry, and had the musical inquisitiveness and passion to match fire with fire – even when soloing over Elvin Jones at his most possessed. This made him more than simply a modal player (quite frankly, anybody any good at jazz is "more than just a modal player") at a time when many more limited musicians were carving a career out of such severe restrictions. He was also one who could successfully combat the economic slump that jazz suffered in the late 1960s. Like Shorter, Henderson experimented with electric instruments at the close of the 1960s and the start of the 1970s, and also dabbled in Brazilian ideas and personnel. Unlike Shorter, Henderson stuck just to the tenor, and delighted in taking extended solos, both live and on record. This in itself led him eventually back to orthodox acoustic jazz performances as his preferred setting. His rhythmic thrust, dark tone and ability to shape even the longer flights into satisfying musical shapes meant he rarely fell below very high standards of musicianship and interest, even when the setting may have been less than ideal.

When the setting is spot-on the playing has overwhelming impact and imagination, as with the early Blue Note album *Inner Urge* (1964) which is the Coltrane quartet with Henderson subbing for the great man. Henderson has not substantially changed his style since the early 1960s, preferring to refine and simplify rather than abandon his methods. This led to a renascence in his popular fortunes in the 1980s (as heard on *The State Of The Tenor* for Blue Note, 1985) and in the early 1990s (epitomised by the great popular and critical reception accorded his restrained, tautly eloquent tribute albums for Miles Davis and Billy Strayhorn).

The man who was slated to appear instead of Henderson on Andrew Hill's *Point Of Departure* in 1964 was Charles Lloyd (b. 1938), but label boss Alfred Lion insisted on the switch to his own Blue Note artist. Lloyd is the quintessential 1960s modalist. He displays an eager adaptation of the Evans-Davis-Coltrane brand of modal theory, but developed into a personal and readily identifiable sound and approach.

Memphis-born Lloyd was a contemporary of Booker Little and George Coleman. He spent his university days in LA where he met Eric Dolphy and Ornette Coleman, among others, and the LA connection led eventually to Lloyd joining the Chico Hamilton Quintet in 1961. Soon composing and arranging for the group, Lloyd (doubling liberally on flute) applied his own ideas within its unique "chamber jazz" sound. Finding a natural foil in Hungarian guitarist Gabor Szabo, Lloyd wrote a number of open-ended modal pieces which moved through a succession of moods and rhythmic patterns. These were the prototype for his phenomenal success just four years later.

After a stint with Cannonball Adderley (replacing Yusef Lateef) where Lloyd once again arranged for the band and had a significant number of his pieces played, he started his own quartet, with Keith Jarrett, Jack DeJohnette and, initially, Cecil McBee (soon replaced by Ron McClure). This young and gifted quartet came up with a remarkable mix of contemporary jazz elements which found instant success, at first with jazz-festival audiences, and later among the burgeoning acid and psychedelic rock scene.

Lloyd was using simple harmonic underpinning for clever compositional constructs which told lucid musical stories. He also allowed his group to develop a taste for rhythms which were, at the time, exotic for instrumental jazz, and even occasionally crossed over into blues and rock beats. But knitting it all together was Lloyd's gift for melody, colour and drama.

These attributes came together successfully at the 1966 Monterey Jazz Festival. A new performance of 'Forest Flower' (which Lloyd had recorded in 1963 with Hamilton) floored the crowd and, when released on an Atlantic album of the same name, sold over a million copies worldwide. Also in 1966 the Lloyd quartet began a season of appearances at Bill Graham's Fillmore West venue in San Francisco (later documented on two separate Atlantic albums) and consolidated their appeal among the young hippies who were as happy to lie around listening to Lloyd's group as they were to the Grateful

Dead, Frank Zappa or other local favourites. Lloyd's success was not limited to the US, but was international in its scope. Like Dave Brubeck – and unlike many other top jazzmen – he was invited to tour in a huge range of countries, including the Soviet Union, the Near East and Japan. Remarkably, Lloyd's phenomenal success was generated by his exciting, hard-driving, modal jazz. His supercharged, melodic style appealed to an untutored, un-ghettoised audience in much the same way as Coltrane's *A Love Supreme* or 'My Favorite Things'. Lloyd may often have had intonation problems, and his flute playing may have lacked technical surety. But his ebullience and desire to communicate, along with the brilliance of the rest of the band (Jarrett in particular was a perfect foil), kept Lloyd at the forefront of jazz until the group's demise in late 1968.

At this point the saxophonist toyed with a variety of ensembles and ideas, and lost much of his impetus. The 1970s found him exploring areas outside jazz, some of which in the 1980s would be developed by others and re-branded as new age. By then Lloyd himself had come full circle, forming another power-packed quartet featuring the brilliant pianist Michel Petrucciani but, wisely, not re-treading the old musical territory of his 1960s triumphs. His recent career has been every bit as successful musically as that of his youth, but the musical canvas has been mostly outside strict modality.

Altoist John Handy (b. 1933) had a similar impact to Lloyd at the Monterey festival, but a year earlier. Handy was a Texan with West Coast musical roots, and had made a considerable name for himself at the turn of the 1960s during a short New York tenure with Charles Mingus. But it was not until 1965 that he formed a group that accurately reflected his musical intentions. Handy's group dispensed with piano, instead using guitarist Jerry Hahn and violinist Michael White as frontline partners.

At Monterey '65, with Handy resplendent in a quasi-maharajah outfit, their set was built on ostinato rhythmic and riff patterns, on recurrent chord cycles and long musical vehicles moving through a number of moods and sections. This abandonment of the bop and hard-bop routine of theme-solos-theme allowed the musicians space to create elaborate musical narratives over simple modalities. There was also room to exploit the considerable exoticism inherent to the group's line-up. Handy's beautiful, ringing alto sound and well-developed cry, as well as his considerable lyricism, served as an ideal focal point for the music.

The group's string of hit albums for Columbia which followed on from that initial Monterey triumph have remained enormously influential among other musicians, even if their popularity has not been so well sustained among the general public. Handy remained vigorously active during the 1960s, forming a new group with Bobby Hutcherson on vibes after White and Hahn left in 1967. But the economic difficulties afflicting jazz caught up with him, and by the early 1970s Handy was playing a type of music closer to that of Donald Byrd, Grover Washington and the funk instrumentalists than to jazz, whether it be modal or non-modal. To be fair, few escaped this fate – even Jackie McLean made an ill-judged funk/disco album for RCA in 1979 – but Handy has rarely been glimpsed since in a jazz setting.

Another altoist treading a not dissimilar path for at least part of this time was Marion Brown (b. 1935). He was a well-respected member of the New York avant-garde, having appeared on Coltrane's *Ascension*, and possessed a full and attractive alto tone as well as a penchant for melodic arabesques over

Joe Henderson (above) qualified as a teacher before turning professional as a jazz musician. He continues to teach and advise young players.

a static chord pattern – as his two ESP-Disk records of the 1960s show. An interest in non-jazz improvisatory methods and other musical disciplines led Brown into some fascinating if obscure musical waters as the 1970s opened, but by 1974 he was sufficiently sated with this to produce a minor (and generally overlooked) masterpiece for the Impulse label, *Vista*. Featuring Stanley Cowell and Anthony Davis on electric piano, the record revisits many of the themes of his ESP-Disk dates, but in a much more spare and focused manner. It even includes a moving version of Stevie Wonder's 'Visions' sung by Allen Murphy, while the presence of minimalist composer Harold Budd on his own composition 'Bismillahi Rrahmani Rrahim' perfectly marries modal jazz with the harmonically static landscape of minimalism. Unfortunately, Brown has not followed this line of endeavour since.

Booker Ervin (1930-70) was a "Texas Tenor", and shared not only his home state with Handy; he, too, spent time with Mingus in New York before going out on his own. But he had none of the breaks of Handy's career, and died during jazz's deepest economic doldrums as the 1960s came to a close. Ervin would perhaps have been bemused by his inclusion in this chapter, but his forward-looking style, full of Texas keening and advanced harmony applied to a raft of original and standard material, is even less at home with hard bop and other less adventurous post-war offshoots. Ervin made many fine albums for Prestige, especially between 1963 and 1965, but none is better than *The Freedom Book* (1964) with the magical rhythm section of Jaki Byard, Richard Davis and Alan Dawson.

There are many other saxophonists who felt the winds of modality blow in their direction during this period. Harold Land, a solid hard-bopper from LA who, by the end of the 1960s, had absorbed much of Coltrane's later legacy, is an example. There are also literally thousands of players who emerged within ten years of Coltrane's death in 1967 and began to apply textbook principles to copying his work. The best of these, like David Liebman, Azar Lawrence, Sonny Fortune, Bill Evans and Michael Brecker, went on to establish an identity of their own, but the majority stayed put in modal mysticism and mere copying, eventually giving modal playing a bad name, just as bop suffered in the immediate aftermath of Charlie Parker's death. With increasingly vapid and repetitive, quasi-ritualistic 1970s performances and recordings from many previously cutting-edge players, running the modes had become a tedious pastime long before new age inhabited the area in the 1980s.

Three of the best albums of Joe Henderson's long career: The Kicker (1967), Power To The People (1969) and his reworking of the themes from Porgy & Bess (1997).

R O N A L D   A T K I N S   **POST-BOP INDIVIDUALISTS**

FREE FORMS AND OPEN INSTRUMENTAL EXPRESSIVENESS
AFFECTED MUSICIANS OF VARIOUS STYLES AND BACKGROUNDS.
MANY FOUND THEIR OWN METHODS FOR FITTING THE NEW
SOUNDS WITHIN RULES THAT IMPOSED STRUCTURE – EVEN
WHEN HARMONIC IMPROVISING WAS JETTISONED.

Around 1960, two years after Ornette Coleman recorded *Something Else!*, the floodgates of free improvisation opened. Critics, whether they loved it or loathed it, judged everything in terms of freedom. Supporters recoiled from the merest hint of advance preparation, just as opponents welcomed the slightest chance to connect tunes and routines with the past. The decade that followed ushered in the accoutrements of electric funk and rock, dividing pundits still further, while making jazz-type improvisation accessible to a wider audience.

Musicians covered in this chapter cannot be pigeonholed, whether stylistically or in terms of the people they make music with. In their different ways, Arthur Blythe, Chico Freeman and Sam Rivers branched out from what might be called the freedom camp. During his brief period in the spotlight, Eric Dolphy switched between freedom and familiar tunes. And nobody can contain Roland Kirk within one or two categories. Problems of categorisation extend to the instruments themselves. Saxophonists had already taken to doubling on the likes of the flute, and spreading their wings in this manner became increasingly prevalent during the 1960s and 1970s. So where critiques of each musician covered in earlier chapters can reasonably be limited to a saxophone or two, such restrictions make less sense here.

Many outsiders have a visual image of Eric Dolphy as the intense young flautist captured with Chico Hamilton's quintet in *Jazz On A Summer's Day*, filmed at the 1958 Newport Festival. Growing up in Los Angeles, Dolphy (1928-64) was destined for a career in European music before he discovered jazz. From the start, he practised and studied obsessively to the extent that, at the age of just 20, he was put in charge of the saxophone section in bandleader-drummer Roy Porter's band, the kind of straw-boss job reserved as a rule for experienced disciplinarians.

Instead of hustling hard for gigs, Dolphy carried on practising and then spent a couple of years with Hamilton without making much national impact, perhaps because the group's tight approach, at least on record, allowed little space for individualism. But by the time he left them and settled in New York City his reputation, at least among the cognoscenti, had rocketed.

The first of a series of albums for Prestige under his name, *Outward Bound*, was recorded in April 1960 and presented as a contribution to progress. "This is right out of the Coleman dynasty, this is the sound of tomorrow," enthuses the sleevenote writer, pointing out that Dolphy had met Ornette Coleman in Los Angeles six years earlier. Later in 1960, Coleman recorded his trailblazing *Free Jazz* album with the so-called "double quartet" (see the next chapter) in which the additional frontline roles were filled by Dolphy and Freddie

Arthur Blythe playing at The Tin Palace in New York, 1979, with Bob Stewart (tuba) and James Blood Ulmer (guitar).

Hubbard, Dolphy's trumpet partner on *Outward Bound*. Charles Mingus, at his highest point of both critical acclaim and public acceptance, knew Dolphy from Los Angeles and brought him into the fold. Mingus toured Europe in the summer of 1960 and his quintet was recorded in July at the Antibes festival.

Later that year, Dolphy recorded some classic tracks with Mingus, including a Johnny-Hodges-on-acid ballad version of 'Stormy Weather'. During 1961 he often worked with John Coltrane, touring Europe and appearing on several albums.

Saxophonists doubling instruments is nothing new, but Dolphy uniquely achieved major status on three: alto saxophone, bass clarinet and flute. On alto he captured more of Charlie Parker's headlong drive and cumulative rhythmic intensity than anyone else had, though his sound was more pliable and closer to Ornette Coleman's. At times, Dolphy would break the flow by playing passages across the beat, but the crux of his inventive armoury was the ability to zigzag the widest intervals at speed, bolstered by a belief that any note could fit any underlying chord.

The technical backup, the fruit of all those years in the practice room, was massive: another innovator, Evan Parker, has described Dolphy's music as "very much about the whole saxophone all at once, about access to any part of an extended range at any moment". Dolphy got the flute to talk in the same way, if less abrasively, the wide intervals in particular effective on an instrument that does not share the saxophone's capacity for tonal variation. He was once quoted as being fond of twittering on the flute to the songs of birds, and while he probably did not take the bass clarinet on similar field trips, an aural link exists between some of his sounds and what one imagines deranged flocks of geese, emus and the like might produce. The bass clarinet had rarely been played in jazz except to add mellow orchestral colour, but under Dolphy's fingers often spouted a torrent of grunts and squawks in all registers, dashed off with his usual commanding brilliance. Though he was responsible for its surge in popularity, his many successors have concentrated

Chico Freeman, son of saxophonist Von Freeman, has a wide-ranging style, taking in the electric band Brainstorm and straightahead contemporary acoustic jazz.

largely on expanding the bass clarinet's more house-trained sounds. Dolphy's four years in the spotlight included a brief but rewarding partnership with Booker Little that ended when the young trumpeter died in 1961. They appeared on each other's albums and much of their appeal was down to the fact that, filtered through comparable technical and all-round musical skills, the emotional buttons they pushed were complementary. Where Dolphy wildly galumphed, Little had a plangent, yearning tone and a hesitant way of phrasing that could seemingly transform the most elementary rhythmic pulse into multiples of 5/4.

Max Roach's 'Tender Warriors' from 1960 exploits this contrast superbly. Among many pieces around that time inspired by racial upheavals in the US, Roach programmed it to confront the rightness of the cause, the "tenderness", with the need for militant reactions. For the melancholy theme, the drummer chose Dolphy to present it on flute. Little's beautifully poised flights elaborate the mood of the theme before, in one of the great opening statements, Dolphy's bass clarinet thrashes about like a rampaging elephant.

Dolphy's biggest success with critics, *Out To Lunch* (1964), harnessed his energy within a fairly tight yet semi-abstract format to produce his most disciplined work, notably on bass clarinet. How far this represented the way he might have gone is unknown: in the weeks before his death, he performed in Europe with various expatriates and local musicians, roaring ahead on a mixture of jazz standards and his own tunes. His influence is heard today in the work of saxophonists as different as Arthur Blythe and Michael Hashim. More than 30 years on, the mix of extraordinary musicianship and sheer

Eric Dolphy, a genuine multi-instrumentalist, evolved distinctive approaches to the flute and bass clarinet, as well as alto saxophone. Out To Lunch is his finest studio-recorded album.

vitality makes Dolphy's finest recordings as potent as ever. The same qualities apply to Rahsaan Roland Kirk (1936-77); indeed, such words as "extraordinary" and "vitality" barely do him justice. Blind from an early age, he showed the same dedication over mastering instruments. A tenor saxophonist and flautist, he had a vision of playing three saxophones at the same time. This led him, with the help of a friendly shopkeeper, to a couple of hybrid instruments, possibly of Spanish origin and apparently known as the stritch and the manzello. Straight and very long, the stritch sounds more like an alto than does the shorter and curved-bell manzello, whose sound comes close to the soprano's.

Having made them a physical fit with the tenor saxophone and devised all manner of false fingerings to produce three-part harmony, Kirk could sound like a one-man saxophone section. He continued to play the flute, adding a nose-flute at some point, and he loved to interject the whistling sound of a siren: later, he hung a toy xylophone from his neck and kept an enormous gong within arm's reach.

His solos on tenor saxophone, manzello and stritch tended to occur in that order of frequency, the stritch being the most difficult to project because the sound aimed straight at the floor. They were backed by an occasional riff from the other instruments, all three of which could be used for theme-statements and for riffing behind other musicians. He could drone on one saxophone while improvising at speed on another. During the 'Pedal Up' routine on his *Bright Moments* album (1973) he plays a tune and simultaneously fills in behind. If he suddenly felt the urge to interrupt a solo by riffing for a few bars or by blowing the whistle, nobody could stop him. A flute passage might, or might not, be backed by vocal noises – the result could evoke anything from the splutter of a Hammond organ to the grinding of an amplified violin. Kirk might associate a particular instrument with a particular tune, but he was perfectly free to change his mind on the spot. Add the occasional songs and outbursts of verse, and you had performances that were wholly unpredictable.

When one ignores the impact overall and concentrates on what he did on each instrument, a virtuoso musician emerges. As a tenor saxophonist, Kirk did not invent a style that inspired a flood of disciples, but a combination of technique, including circular breathing, and good ears enabled him to reproduce in his own manner anything he heard, from swing-style rhapsodies to the rasps and high harmonics of the avant-garde. His sound was difficult to

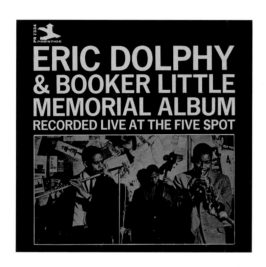

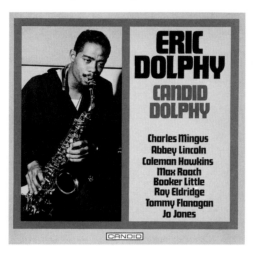

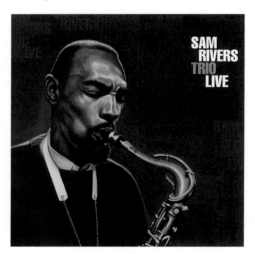

During his short life Eric Dolphy managed to play and record with an astonishing variety of leading jazz artists. Sam Rivers has been a jazz innovator since the 1950s.

classify, perhaps somewhere between Gene Ammons and Sonny Stitt but eminently pliable.

John Coltrane's music undoubtedly affected him: on the *We Free Kings* album of August 1961 the title track recalls Coltrane's treatments of 'My Favorite Things' and 'Greensleeves', though the former had been recorded within the year, the latter just four months previously and possibly was not even released yet. Direct references of this kind tended to be a fleeting part of an infinitely varied programme. A vibrant and compelling performer before audiences, Kirk kept them in the palm of his hand whether playing, singing, talking, haranguing or asking them to participate. Rarely heard other than as leader, he contributed crucially to the original version of Charles Mingus's 'Ecclusiastics' (1961), most noble of jazz-gospel pieces, building to the moment when all his saxophones suddenly erupt.

His amazing musicianship was underlined when he suffered a stroke that almost paralysed his right arm and restricted him to the use of five fingers. Far from being put out of action, Kirk merely cut down to two saxophones, twisted the body of the flute so that all keys were vertical, added a couple of background musicians, and carried on as usual.

Just as some alto saxophonists focused on Charlie Parker's approach to the blues, so did the Texas-born tenor Booker Ervin (1930-70) take the declamatory tonal projection of Coltrane's late-1950s playing for a model. The outcome was a blistering but concentrated attack that Mingus, with whom he worked on and off for several years from 1958, exploited readily, often toward the end of a piece to create a suitable climax, as on 'Wednesday Night Prayer

Meeting' (first recorded 1959). Another saxophonist with Mingus associations, George Adams was part of the bassist's quintet in the mid 1970s and later co-led a group with Mingus's pianist Don Pullen. He also played in the Gil Evans orchestra that included Arthur Blythe. Born in Georgia, Adams (1940-92) doubled on flute and tenor. His essentially vertical style on tenor was tinged with post-Coltrane sophistication and post-Ayler cries. Excellent examples of his playing can be found on record with Evans, Mingus and Pullen.

Born in Oklahoma into a very musical family, Sam Rivers studied at the Boston Conservatory and became part of the 1950s Boston scene. One of his groups included drummer Tony Williams, then a teenager, who subsequently recommended Rivers to Miles Davis for a Japanese tour and probably helped persuade Blue Note to record him. Rivers (b. 1923) had already latched on to

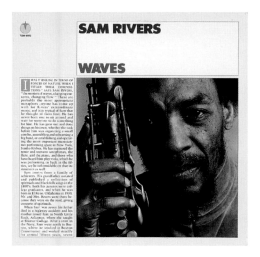

freer developments; most of his albums in the 1960s – those under his own name and those led by Williams, pianist Andrew Hill and vibraphonist Bobby Hutcherson – fall under that category. During the 1970s he collaborated fruitfully on several occasions with bassist Dave Holland.

In much the same way as George Adams, Rivers harnesses florid improvising and a somewhat bruising tone on tenor saxophone, qualities first identified with Coleman Hawkins, to the cries, overtones and other expressive devices introduced in the 1960s. A multi-instrumentalist who plays most of the reeds, he gets a grittier sound from the soprano than do those who follow Wayne Shorter, while his flute takes off in the manner of Dolphy.

A leader for at least 30 years – though he was happy to join one of Dizzy Gillespie's last touring orchestras and has played with the saxophone tribute-band Roots – Rivers ranks high among those creating music at the junction where freedom meets preset structures. For example, in a rehearsal orchestra he runs that plays his compositions, solos are surrounded by all manner of riffs and counter-melodies – even if you could never confuse the results with the average Count Basie score. Many of the younger forward-looking musicians who revere him play in this orchestra, which is named after the Studio Rivbea that Rivers, long a byword for self-help, set up with his wife as a venue where musicians could perform and study.

The careers of Chico Freeman and Arthur Blythe often cross, not least in all-star groups such as The Leaders and Roots. Some would say they both inched toward the centre from a revolutionary start, though that is borne out as much by association as by what they actually play. Freeman's father Von

Waves (1978, above) finds Sam Rivers (also pictured left) teamed with bassist Dave Holland.

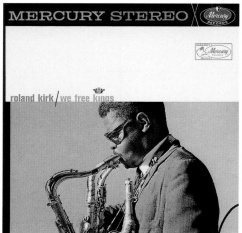

The unique and utterly overwhelming Rahsaan Roland Kirk could play three saxophones at once. He also invented a totally new way of playing the flute. Only those who personally saw him in action ever fully experienced the impact of this extraordinary artist.

Freeman, relatively unsung because he doesn't join name bands and rarely leaves the Windy City, represents the cream of the tenor saxophonists linked to Chicago, along with Gene Ammons and Johnny Griffin.

The musical background of Chico Freeman (b. 1949) includes a period studying under Muhal Richard Abrams, as well as gigging with other members of the Chicago-based Association for the Advancement of Creative Musicians (AACM) and with Sun Ra. That suggests at least a toehold in the avant-garde, but he has always used recognisable structures. On tenor Freeman's tone, rounded and flecked with fur, has a lightness of touch that hardly fits the progressive stereotype. A liking for the higher registers probably derives from a youthful admiration for John Coltrane, but the actual sound produced veers more toward that of mid-period Stan Getz. One can describe his approach very loosely as combining the Getz tone with Dexter Gordon's phrasing.

Whether or not The Leaders began in the mid 1980s as a concept band to please some promoter, it lasted for several years, long enough to develop a repertory of its own. Freeman, who usually shared frontline duties with Blythe and trumpeter Lester Bowie, decided to cut down the multi-instruments that had been a feature of his earlier groups, putting the tenor out front followed by the soprano, from which he gets a pure, pellucid sound.

Other instruments, including alto saxophone, bass clarinet and flute, turn up more often in Brainstorm, the fusion group in which Freeman experiments with the latest electronic gear, sometimes modulating the performance from a central control. Saxmen often whoop it up in such a context, but Freeman's tone retains its roundness and there's scarcely a rasp heard. He is also a member of Sam Rivers' Rivbea All-Star Orchestra, and is on their two albums.

Arthur Blythe (b. 1940) is from the West Coast, a native of Los Angeles. Before moving East he worked with pianist Horace Tapscott, the leading exponent around LA of the newer jazz forms. On Tapscott's 'The Giant Is Awakened', recorded in 1969, the high-register cries from Blythe's alto saxophone are definitely post-Albert Ayler, though his tone already had a distinctively keening edge that would become pronounced under more orthodox conditions, simply because one expects it less. By the time he recorded under his own name in 1977 he was already a member of a Gil Evans orchestra that, with David Sanborn also on hand, offered two of the most striking alto sounds in the business.

Some of Blythe's finest albums, currently unobtainable, were recorded for the Columbia label, beginning with *Lenox Avenue Breakdown* (1979). It may have been under pressure from Columbia that for a time he gradually moved toward a more commercial approach, perhaps with a view to becoming that label's Sanborn. His sound is creamy, more Johnny Hodges than Charlie Parker, but with the occasional gritty edge and with a piercing cry at the top end. The way it sings and sweeps has attracted violinist Regina Carter, who regards Blythe as a modern counterpart to Ben Webster and Paul Gonsalves, the saxophone players whose soulfulness, she says, particularly influenced her approach. Blythe can negotiate the kind of intervals Eric Dolphy introduced on the alto, though the tone is shriller. A reason why he and Chico Freeman make so compelling a team may, in fact, be the sense of contrast, with Freeman more relaxed and always prepared to underplay.

Few have developed so consistently with the times as Charlie Mariano (b. 1923). He began in the 1950s as a Parker-inspired altoist, putting over Parker's more passionate phrases with a slightly sweeter tone. By the time he starred on Mingus's *Black Saint And The Sinner Lady* (1963) the Parker influence had been thoroughly assimilated and bebop left well behind. Since then, Mariano has added the soprano and worked with musicians in Europe and Asia, being one of the first to bring different musical traditions together. Whatever the context, his passionate commitment always shines through.

James Spaulding (b. 1937) has stayed in demand as a sideman through his versatile professionalism as an alto saxophonist doubling on flute. He appeared on several Blue Note albums in the 1960s and has been part of David Murray's various projects, including the big-band. Spaulding is of the post-Parker generation and plays long lines with a slightly rough-edged sound in a manner that sometimes recalls Dolphy.

Greatly admired by his peers, Joe Henderson (b. 1937) finally got to a wider public when his album of Billy Strayhorn tunes *Lush Life* (1992) topped *Billboard*'s jazz chart and the unaccompanied title tune won a Grammy. It is a rare example of a concept album that draws the best out of the performer. Henderson's lyrical side has rarely been so well presented; when his tenor eases into 'Blood Count' at the top of the range, it could almost be a soprano.

While Henderson, Eric Dolphy and, in his own way, Roland Kirk stand out among the saxophonists in this chapter as stylists leaving identifiable imprints on those who came after, most of the others have contributed significantly as leaders of groups ranging from free to fusion.

In addition to saxophones and flute, Kirk carried on stage a selection of whistles, sirens and the like. Sometimes he would pass these out among the audience and invite people to join in.

ORNETTE COLEMAN

*ORNETTE COLEMAN BROUGHT ABOUT A REVOLUTIONARY
CHANGE IN JAZZ BY ABANDONING THE FIXED ELEMENTS OF
HARMONY, PITCH AND FORM WHICH EVEN HIS MOST RADICAL
PREDECESSORS HAD ACCEPTED AS VITAL. HIS EXAMPLE
HELPED LAUNCH THE ENTIRE FREE-JAZZ MOVEMENT.*

*Dewey Redman (left, on tenor) and
Ornette Coleman (alto) on stage at the
Newport Jazz festival, 1971.*

From the time he founded his revolutionary quartet in the late 1950s, Ornette
Coleman had an irreversible effect on jazz and on saxophone playing. He was
not only a prolific composer. He also introduced improvisation without chord
changes, and solos in which the length of his melodic material, and the pitch
at which it was played, could be changed on the spur of the moment.

Although much of his music was erroneously dubbed free jazz after the
title of his controversial 1960 double-quartet album, Ornette Coleman's work
of that time was far less "free" than the "new thing" movement of the mid
1960s that followed it. Both in his early quartet that included bassist Charlie
Haden and drummer Billy Higgins and his later recordings with his fusion
group, known as Prime Time, Coleman never abandoned the related ideas of

metre and of playing in time. Nor did he abandon clear, hummable melodies, which he is capable of producing in profusion. Despite the apparent chaos of the simultaneous playing of the eight musicians on *Free Jazz*, there is still a discernible theme, solos that emerge from the ensemble, walking basslines, and a clear sense of beat in the drumming.

From the time of that album and in almost all his work since, Coleman's changes to jazz, both practical and theoretical, revolve around the idea of setting aside a conventional harmonic framework, and replacing it with something else. Because of this, many of his early colleagues, such as pianist Paul Bley with whom he played in 1959, have identified Coleman as the missing link between bebop and the totally free improvisation of new-thing players like Archie Shepp and Albert Ayler. In the list of jazz innovators, he

belongs somewhere alongside Louis Armstrong, Charlie Parker, Miles Davis and John Coltrane. The world has been both slow and reluctant to recognise this, as it was not until the 1990s that he received most of his crop of honorary degrees and the MacArthur Foundation "genius" award. Yet since the mid 1950s Coleman has been changing the way we listen to jazz and redefining collective improvisation. Nevertheless, because of his radicalism he divides listeners into staunch enthusiasts and equally trenchant opponents.

John McDonough summed up 30-odd years of hostile criticism in *Down Beat* in 1992 by describing Coleman's music (and that of those who followed him) as "a counterculture, separate and apart from the main body of jazz activity.... Free jazz, with its ideological subtexts of black liberation, third-world primitivism, and spiritualism, continues to exist in the outer world of 20th century eccentrics."

Turn that apparently negative criticism on its head, and it neatly encapsulates several things that are key to Coleman's art.

First, his music grew out of his experiences in his hometown of Fort Worth, a cattle-producing centre amid the deeply segregated society of 1940s Texas, where he had been born on March 9th 1930. In high school he played with several musicians who later became long-term associates, including saxophonist Dewey Redman and drummer Charles Moffett. With them he discovered jazz – from the swing era to the first bebop discs by Charlie Parker, whose work Coleman admired.

But his earliest professional jobs were performing the dominant popular music of the day in his part of the South: R&B. He played this earthy dance

Ornette Coleman's early records kick-started the free-jazz movement and, in the words of the 1959 album title, set the shape of jazz to come.

music over a solid backbeat in bands such as those of Pee Wee Crayton, Silas Green and Clarence Samuels; it provided one of the few escape routes open to African-Americans who aspired beyond Southern poverty and manual labour. Such music became a potent symbol of the black liberation movement so derided by McDonough. Coleman's playing has always remained charged with the intensity of the blues he played in his formative years, overcoming the deep-rooted racial divide of his home state.

Second, Coleman's preoccupation with aspects of African music and spiritual qualities drew him in 1973 to Morocco, where he recorded with The Master Musicians Of Joujouka, a Sufi-influenced community of former court musicians whose trance-like sounds of drums and shawms directly influenced Coleman's fusion band Prime Time.

Coleman's third and fourth albums (1959-1960), recorded for the Atlantic label.

Third, despite outward appearances of eccentricity, Coleman has from his early bearded appearance to his later self-designed clothes and hats rationalised his music into an impressive – if daunting – intellectual framework which he calls "harmolodics". He chooses to express some of these ideas in an elliptical, often allegorical, manner, but it would be a mistake to see his metaphorical descriptions of his art as mere eccentricity, as they often contain profound insights.

Starting with the writings of Gunther Schuller, who began analysing Coleman's work shortly after meeting him at the 1959 Lenox Summer School of Music in Massachusetts, he has always attracted champions every bit as defensive as McDonough is critical. Yet, even for his apologists, Coleman's music presents problems. It is not easy to analyse it in the normal way. Melodic phrases change length within performances and underlying harmonies shift erratically. With typical candour, Coleman himself once said: "I would prefer it if musicians would play my tunes with different changes as they take a new chorus, so there'd be all the more variety in the performance."

This readiness to accept almost instant change, and a commitment to improvisation over composition, has been a consistent part of Coleman's musical philosophy since he worked out his own approach to music in 1950s Los Angeles.

The legend – enhanced by the fact that, like Bob Dylan, Coleman has told his story in various slightly different versions as the years have gone by – is that he taught himself to read music and to finger the saxophone, and in doing so incorporated some basic errors into his understanding of musical

Ornette Coleman's long-term musical partner Don Cherry, seen here playing the strange "pocket trumpet" which he preferred. The sound is the same as that of a conventional trumpet.

theory. He believed that A, rather than C, was the home note of the basic scale, relying for guidance on the alphabet rather than the piano keyboard, and the habits he learned then stayed with him.

Playing in those R&B bands on the road from the late 1940s onward did not make great demands on his theoretical knowledge, although as he was interested in bebop, and heard things in his head in terms of his own ideas of scales and harmony, his occasional opportunities to improvise a chorus or two produced some strange results. He was more than once restrained from playing his wild variety of solos. His long-haired, bearded appearance – a hippie before his time – did not win him friends in the segregated South either, and at one point he was badly beaten up in Louisiana while on tour. In due course he settled in Los Angeles, working as a lift operator among other things, and developed his own approach to music.

"After three years or so in Los Angeles, learning how to play bebop," he told me, "I realised I didn't have to transpose to be with the piano. I found I could use notes in a way that was equal to using chords, but if I used notes as chords without them being chords, I was no longer restricted to doing sequences.... I write music that sounds like inspirational ideas. A melody may have structures that express themselves at other levels, not just a single line of music – but I also express a musical philosophy that if I'm playing with someone else and they can do better, they have the right to change it." The underlying point is central to Coleman's importance to jazz improvisation. If you abandon chord sequences as the basis for improvising and use melodic fragments instead, and if you play those fragments at whatever length and speed feel right, even if the underlying pulse never changes, you have the essence of what Coleman began to explore in earnest in the mid 1950s in Los Angeles with trumpeter Don Cherry, drummer Billy Higgins, pianist Walter Norris and bassist Don Payne.

When The Modern Jazz Quartet's pianist John Lewis heard them, he knew that their 1958 debut recording *Something Else!* was taking jazz in a new direction. He encouraged Coleman and Cherry to come to the Lenox school, and soon afterwards along with Higgins and their new bassist Charlie Haden they moved East and played for some time at a club on the edge of the seedy Bowery area in New York, The Five Spot. Their legendary residency there, plus the albums they recorded for Atlantic like *The Shape Of Jazz To Come* (1959/60), suddenly propelled Coleman into the limelight at the age of 29.

Between 1959 and 1962 Coleman's quartet recorded numerous albums, appeared frequently in New York, and created definitive versions of several of his compositions including the plaintive 'Lonely Woman', the bluesy 'Ramblin'', the Latin dance 'Una Muy Bonita' and the lyrical 'Peace'. Integral to the group's discs was the telepathic interplay between Coleman's alto and Don Cherry's pocket cornet, and the equally close-knit partnership between Haden and Higgins (and then, after Higgins had his cabaret card revoked for drug offences, between Haden and Ed Blackwell). Toward the end of the Atlantic sequence, Coleman also recorded on tenor saxophone, the instrument that had been the mainstay of his shortlived R&B career.

Whether he was using alto or tenor, his 1959-62 work with his quartet is unlike that of any previous saxophonist in jazz. Most noticeable about Coleman's own playing from this period is that although he clearly adopted some aspects of Charlie Parker's playing – impressive speed, complex linear phrasing and a trenchant, bluesy tone – he added ingredients of his own. These included the introduction of microtonality (playing on pitches that lie between the conventional notes of the scale or keys of a piano) and long, wailing, vocalised phrases that seem to come direct from the plantation ring-shouts of the earliest African-Americans. Sometimes the debt to Parker was explicit, as in the piece called 'Bird Food' from *Change Of The Century* (1959), about which Coleman wrote at the time: "Bird would have understood us. He would have approved our aspiring beyond what we inherited."

Not everyone who heard the quartet understood it. Pianist Paul Bley told me that the group's unorthodoxy, underlined by the fact that it opened at the Five Spot opposite the very conventional Jazztet of Benny Golson and Art Farmer, "struck fear into the heart of the average world-famous jazz musician walking the streets of New York". Confronted by this quartet that had failed to pay its dues on the New York scene, and which had turned up from the West bristling with new ideas, musicians from Miles Davis to Charles Mingus decried the music, while the older generation like Roy Eldridge came to listen and went away shaking their heads.

Nevertheless, the band, however revolutionary, did not, as one might have expected, appeal to the young black audiences of Harlem so much as to a white intellectual elite. Figures like the conductor and composer Leonard Bernstein were regulars in Coleman's audiences. As they went on to appear at other Manhattan venues like The Village Vanguard and The Village Gate, Coleman's quartet drew further admirers from the classical world, including Virgil Thomson and Marc Blitzstein. The critical controversy stirred up by the band ultimately became a dialogue between warring critical factions, with

Composer-conductor-critic Gunther Schuller (above) composed 'Abstractions' for Ornette Coleman and string quartet.

opponents like *Down Beat*'s John McDonough ranged against supporters such as Nat Hentoff and Martin Williams.

Those who did understand what Coleman was getting at found his music challenging. Gunther Schuller, for example, wrote one of his classical-meets-jazz "third stream" compositions, 'Abstractions', for Coleman and a string quartet. In it, Coleman's unusual pitching and off-centre phrasing was backed by a harshly atonal score. Just as Bley and his colleagues had seen Coleman as the missing link between bebop and free jazz, Schuller saw him as a means of combining classical avant-garde techniques with imaginative improvisation. Coleman himself recognised the possibilities for developing such ideas, and after briefly taking lessons from Schuller has consistently produced symphonic and chamber-music compositions.

A combination of drug problems and lack of consistent well-paid work led Coleman's quartet to go through some personnel changes in 1962, and the group ended up as a trio with drummer Charles Moffett and bassist David Izenzon toward the end of the year. Despite an enforced lay-off from late 1962 until the spring of 1965, when Coleman's insistence only to play for a much higher fee backfired and left him without work, this trio was equally as creative as the quartet with Cherry, Haden and Higgins.

During his lay-off, Coleman taught himself to play violin and trumpet, and his mixture of intuition and autodidactism led to a highly original and innovative approach to both instruments. Nevertheless, he continued to specialise mainly on alto saxophone, and on writing. With Izenzon's virtuoso bass, played both arco and pizzicato, and Moffett's abstract, colouristic drumming, the trio achieved some extraordinary textures in its work, beautifully exemplified by its extended series of sets that were recorded for Blue Note at Stockholm's Golden Circle club in late 1965. These typified Coleman's mixture of ballads, memorable original themes and aggressive, energetic soloing on his new instruments.

In the mid 1960s Coleman based himself in a building on Prince Street in lower Manhattan called the Artists' House where he could combine rehearsal, recording and performance with a creative workshop atmosphere, within the tradition of "loft jazz" that was being established at the time. Problems with the neighbourhood, the authorities and finances led him to give up the attempt in due course, but he later re-established his studio and headquarters in a similar community setting in the centre of Harlem, near 125th Street Station, where it has continued into the 21st century.

However, during the first Artists' House period his band mutated again – first when he brought his nine-year-old son Denardo into the studio to record with himself and Charlie Haden, and then in 1968 when he briefly drew into the line-up drummer Elvin Jones and bassist Jimmy Garrison (who had briefly worked with Coleman before). These two musicians had worked with John Coltrane until a year or so before Coltrane's death in 1967, and together with saxophonist Dewey Redman they made up one of Coleman's more impressive recording bands, producing such classics as 'Broadway Blues' and 'Round Trip' (both on *New York Is Now*, 1968).

The 1960s also saw Coleman trying his hand at different types of composition, including a piece for wind quintet first performed in Britain, and subsequently his full orchestral suite *Skies Of America* which he recorded in 1972 with the London Symphony Orchestra. This last piece brought together his melodic talent with a compositional style that created textures by

Ornette Coleman (opposite) continues to be an active and progressive force in jazz after four decades of innovation.

juxtaposing blocks of thematic material for each section of the orchestra in different keys or pitches, mixed with his own passionate improvisation. Similar thinking lay behind the creation of his rock fusion band Prime Time in the 1970s, where the trance-like repetitive rhythms of Joujouka underpinned some of the pieces by this unconventional group with two guitars and two drummers. *Dancing In Your Head* (recorded 1973-76), one of the first recordings by Prime Time, takes a movement called 'The Good Life' from *Skies Of America* and re-works it into the new instrumentation and setting as 'Theme From A Symphony'. Coleman did much the same kind of thing on his 1987 recording *In All Languages* on which the title track is interpreted both by Prime Time and by his original quartet with Haden, Cherry and Higgins.

From the time of his late-1950s work with Paul Bley, Coleman had seldom played with a pianist. The initial response of many critics was to point out that having no chordal instrument made Coleman's rejection of conventional harmonic sequences much easier, but these critics were confounded: first, by the way he used other instruments – from the bass of David Izenzon to full string sections, and from the guitars of Charles Ellerbee and Bern Nix to the Grateful Dead's Jerry Garcia – to substitute for the piano's harmonic function; and second, when he introduced pianist Dave Bryant into the line-up of his electric band Prime Time.

Coleman's collaboration with Pat Metheny on the 1985 album *Song X* mixed some anarchic tracks with others in which Metheny's guitar lines are strongly harmonic. In the 1990s, pianist Geri Allen joined the acoustic quartet he put together with bassist Charnette Moffett (son of Charles) and his son Denardo on drums; Allen has produced the most testing exploration so far of how to integrate the chordal and harmonic functions of the piano with linear improvisations that pick up Coleman's own melodic lines. His most vital work of the very late 1990s was a duo with yet another pianist, Joachim Kuhn, who has subsequently continued to develop Allen's pioneering work of creating a role for the piano in Coleman's regular quartet.

Coleman's own reasons for using the piano sparingly over the years are very simple. "Most jazz pianists play in a 'pop' style," he says. "That's to say they play chords as you would do for a singer. And, without sounding degrading, they're always put in the situation to be support. None of the pianists I use play like that. Dave Bryant plays the way he conceives harmolodic music, fitting in with two guitars, two basses and two drummers. And Joachim Kuhn plays in a style that's almost orchestral in the way he improvises. With him the chordal structure is there, but much freer than in a set sequence – it's almost a new format."

On their duo album *Colors*, recorded in Leipzig, Coleman and Kuhn meet as equals. Kuhn is representative of a European tradition of radical improvisation, while Coleman takes on something of a symbolic role as the man to whom many East German musicians like Kuhn looked to typify concepts of freedom during the Cold War. Kuhn once said to me that he thought that life itself was an improvisation – and this is a sentiment with which Coleman heartily agrees.

"The word improvise is supposed to mean something that's not there that you bring there," he says. "In jazz, it's when a person can change his will and thought at the moment he wants to do it. The same 12 notes support all kinds of different performances. There must be something in those 12 notes that lets each individual be free."

STEVE DAY FREE JAZZ

FREE JAZZ IS AN INTERNATIONAL PHENOMENON, WITH MANY LANGUAGES AND DIALECTS. IT IS ALSO A COMMUNAL MUSIC, DEPENDING AS IT DOES ON SHARED SENSIBILITY AND THE CLOSE INTERPLAY OF SEVERAL INDIVIDUALS. FREE JAZZ HAS ITS GREAT NAMES AND INFLUENTIAL FIGURES, BUT IT IS CONSTANTLY CHANGING.

Free Jazz (1960) threw down a challenge to established ideas of form in jazz.

They fished him out from the New York Hudson River on November 25th 1970, dead and waterlogged. As far as anybody can really ascertain, he could have been in the cold, dank, muddy water for almost a month. Did he jump or was he pushed? No one is quite certain how Albert Ayler came to end up in the river at the age of 33. He had his problems like anybody else – or maybe not like anybody else.

Many people have tried to predict the death of jazz. Albert Ayler, the man who personified a new-found freedom for the tenor saxophone, died a short time prior to November 25th, but the music did not. Both the manner of Ayler's death and the surrounding circumstances speak volumes about how far jazz had come in the 50 years since someone, somewhere decided to put a label on this "race" music. Here's the obituary: "Albert Ayler, an early exponent of 'free' jazz."

Freedom has a cost. These facts still remain hazy, like the dawn over Brooklyn. One way or another, Ayler paid the ultimate price.

The meaning of the phrase "free jazz" has often been defined on the basis of conjecture and disinformation, mixed within the socio-political struggle of African-Americans. How to catch a promise of equality from a country that spoke of fulfilling dreams yet dished up nightmares in the shape of the pointed hats of the Ku-Klux Klan? Even worse, in the 1960s came the outright censorship of black America. Think about it. Malcolm X. Know the name? But what did he say? In the so-called land of the free, free jazz was as much about connecting jazz to a people's demand for civil rights as any accurate translation of the music. Just as the words of the old spiritual declare "let my people go", so the musicians of the barely defined "free jazz scene" in the post-Kennedy US were also blowing out a sound that said "let our music go".

Ornette Coleman, composer and alto saxophone player extraordinaire, recorded his double-quartet session entitled *Free Jazz* for Atlantic Records just before Christmas 1960. Whether Coleman actually wanted to hang his music on the title "free jazz" is a moot point. Whichever way it was, those two words struck a chord with the times. After Coleman came Albert Ayler, Jimmy Lyons, Dewey Redman, Frank Lowe, David S Ware, Charles Gayle: the tip of the lip of a long, glorious list of American saxophone players who were to redefine the art of jazz improvisation by getting "outside" the rules of music. Currently in Europe, in different ways, the saxophones of Paul Dunmall and John Butcher are doing much the same thing.

Ornette Coleman and Albert Ayler: it's like the splitting of an atom. Coleman came from Fort Worth, Texas, born in 1930. There was little cash but his mother still bought him a saxophone at a time when the sensible thing

The music of Albert Ayler (left) drew on many non-jazz influences, including folk and brass bands. His album Spiritual Unity (1964) contains a particularly attractive melody, entitled 'Ghosts'.

to do would have been to buy something sensible. There was no one in Coleman's immediate family who knew much about saxophones except his cousin James Jordan, and he was not immediately available. So Ornette learnt things his own way, the hard way.

The jazz came literally free of theory. Initially the young experimenter did not transpose keys, but instead followed a melodic line "dancing in his head" and took it to wherever it felt right (or left) to take it. Replace conventional harmony with a clash of colours and that comes close to the spot where Coleman went, to the very point where "clash" becomes its own harmony. He was later to refer to this process as "harmolodics". Part of the genius was in preserving initial playing methods and not simply throwing them out as soon as right and wrong were pointed out as roadsigns.

Ayler was six years younger than his kindred spirit in Texas. His father, Edward Ayler of Cleveland, Ohio, was a man with a musical bent, his principal instruments sax and violin. He encouraged both his sons to play saxophone. Don Ayler later switched to trumpet at his brother's request.

The transfigurations of Ornette and Albert have a lot in common. As young men, both were involved in the early shakedown on R&B. Although they each abandoned the confines of conventional musical theory, they nonetheless quite individually bit on melody. Listen to Coleman's 'Lonely Woman' (1959) and 'Long Time No See' (1970): here is a musician grafting alto sax improvisations from out of the line of the melody as if touching the tip of a tail that can simply flick between all possibilities. As the music modulates, so too does the mind. The same can be said for Albert Ayler. Try

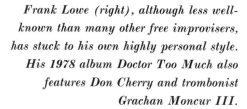

Frank Lowe (right), although less well-known than many other free improvisers, has stuck to his own highly personal style. His 1978 album Doctor Too Much also features Don Cherry and trombonist Grachan Moncur III.

Ayler's best-known composition, the declamatory 'Ghosts', based on a hint of nursery rhyme. It does not stay still, nor does it remain fixed in key. There is a switch from innocent simplicity to a blistering spontaneous study that is only possible from one who has lived and breathed beyond adolescence. In 1881 the Norwegian dramatist Henrich Ibsen wrote a play also entitled *Ghosts*, exploring similar ideas of knowledge over innocence.

Ayler's 'Ghosts' is stripped-down danger. He recorded the theme a number of times, but the key version is the one from 1964 on *Spiritual Unity*. At this time both Ayler and Coleman were working in trio settings, the saxophone perched on the top of a triangle, underpinned by double bass and drums. In each case the triangle can suddenly turn, to leave one of the other musicians at the top of things. 'Ghosts' is like the sound of a sob, so far down it is like listening to a man climbing back inside himself. I do not understand why John Coltrane's 'A Love Supreme' has taken on classic status while 'Ghosts' is left in the margins of this music. Gary Peacock's double bass is free of any central tonality, constantly circling the horn and catching the movement rather than the note. Strange how things work out. Since the early 1980s Peacock has been bassist with pianist Keith Jarrett's "Standards Trio". In jazz terms, Jarrett's outfit is about as far away from the A For Ayler band as it is possible to get, yet inasmuch as they are both trios it is possible to draw some comparisons. Not right here; there is more in this than meets the ear.

American names: Sam Rivers (b. 1930) was, and is, one of the most adventurous pioneers of free-jazz saxophone and flute. He was also important because in 1970 he became one of the first musicians to open a New York loft, Studio Rivbea. A loft was a space, used for concerts, rehearsals, recording and domestic life. Here were musicians taking charge of their own destiny.

It is easy for individual stories to get hidden in their own headlines. Archie Shepp's tenor saxophone is often pegged to the legend of John Coltrane, particularly the *Ascension* session (1965). Shepp's story, though, goes way beyond even that intoxicating heart-of-darkness date. Shepp (b. 1937) also plunged his depth-charge tenor into Cecil Taylor's 1960/61 recordings. There is a fragile kind of thunder on the various versions of the track 'Air', a performance that even now sounds like a very deep breath. He also formed the New York Contemporary Five with Ornette Coleman's trumpet partner Don Cherry and alto and tenor ace John Tchicai.

David Murray (b. 1955) is the man most commentators would identify as the saxophonist who picked up a tenor and blew a legacy for Albert Ayler.

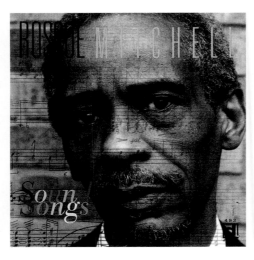

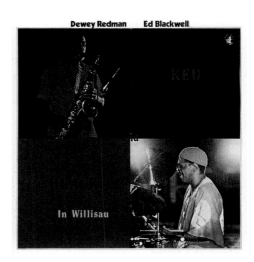

His music at this point inhabits a broad church – a long way from the river and the ghosts of *Spiritual Unity*. Murray's saxophone has been through a number of styles over the years, from funk to Duke Ellington to freedom. This is music that needs to travel a distance.

One name from somewhere else: Joe Harriott (1928-73) was born in Kingston, Jamaica. He arrived in London, England, in the late 1950s with alto saxophone ready for some action. He is often referred to as a "free" player. As the 1960s started swinging Harriott did something different: he produced two recordings, *Free Form* (1960) and *Abstract* (1961) which, despite the titles, contained very technically tight music. Harriott was an experimenter with structure as well as being an agile soloist. Listening to his music now is like hearing seeds being sown. The tragedy is that he rarely got the chance to develop his ideas. He shared little in common with Albert Ayler except for the fact that his death in 1973 came way too early. As with Ayler, there were not enough people listening.

Take from the shelf any book about the history of jazz and there is a myriad of names: individuals who, at different stages in the jazz continuum, have seemingly moved the music on. This chapter is no different. Free jazz too has famous names. But there is something else taking place.

Free jazz is also communal. Perhaps unlike any other strand of the music, the response from the free scene has been to divide up into collectives. There is a clear parallel here with early jazz groups led by people like King Oliver and Kid Ory where improvisation emerged out of the ensemble rather than from the playing of a soloist. The music becomes a family affair, interactive with a measure of equality and, like any family, argument.

As free jazz became a loose concept for creative musicians in America in the 1960s, important group projects were formed: the Association for the Advancement of Creative Musicians (AACM) in Chicago; Black Artists Group (BAG) in St Louis; Jazz Composers Orchestra Association in New York.

During the same period, across the Atlantic, a number of flexible groupings emerged in Europe. In England the Spontaneous Music Ensemble was based at the Little Theatre Club, London. It was not so much a band as a co-operative, albeit at first centred on drummer John Stevens, alto saxophone maestro Trevor Watts and trombonist Paul Rutherford. In Holland the Instant Composers Pool came together, involving a wide-ranging set of individuals including Han Bennink (drums), Misha Mengelberg (piano) and Willem Breuker (tenor saxophone). A German scene also developed, fuelled in

Three contemporary saxophone leaders: Dewey Redman, Roscoe Mitchell and Britain's Paul Dunmall.

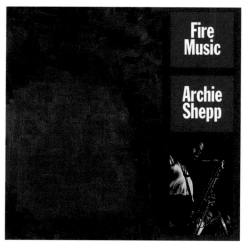

*Fire Music was an apt description of the
youthful work of Archie Shepp (right).
He went on to explore other areas of the
jazz tradition, including the blues.*

part by the formation in 1966 of the Globe Unity Orchestra to play the Berlin Jazztage, then nurtured by Jost Gebers' FMP Records and the Total Music Meeting concert series.

From out of these events tenor saxophonist Peter Brötzmann (b. 1941) came to prominence. In 1968 he recorded his seminal small-group blow-out, *Machine Gun*. Twelve months later rock guitarist Jimi Hendrix was to lacerate a live recording at the Fillmore East, New York, with the same title. Though the two pieces have nothing to do with each other, they share a need to break from performance expectations. Where Hendrix had his sights still fixed on a form of space-age blues, Brötzmann's line of enquiry had already shaken off every vestige of Americana. (Albert Ayler would have recognised a connection, but now there was nothing left of his spiritual concerns, nor anything of the old street fighting blues. Peter Brötzmann would later record a tribute to Ayler titled *Die Like A Dog* in 1993. Sad but true.) I have never felt comfortable with the Brötzmann *Machine Gun*. We were never supposed too. The fact remains that Brötzmann took the saxophone to a new place with that recording, and there is never any going back.

Around the same time as things in Europe were hotting up, a number of the new breed of free players in sweet home Chicago were itching to travel. Roscoe Mitchell had already met another reeds player, Joseph Jarman, who shared his passion for multiple horns. The free scene in Chicago had been invigorated by the formation of the AACM under the direction of Muhal Richard Abrams. Mitchell and Jarman made a couple of classic individual recordings under their own names (try *Sound* and *Song For* respectively – both 1966) before coming together as The Art Ensemble with trumpeter extraordinaire Lester Bowie, bassist Malachi Favors and original drummer Phillip Wilson. By the time they made their sojourn to Paris in 1969 Wilson had left, to be replaced the following year by Famoudou Don Moye, who was also over in France sampling what the old world knew about new things. They added "Of Chicago" to their collective name, and the rest is history.

Roscoe Mitchell (b. 1940) is a consummate player of saxophones of all types and sizes. In 1997 he produced a double-CD solo session, *Sound Songs*, which brought together every shape, colour and contrast that had been found in his playing in the preceding 30 years. It uses overdubbing on about half the tracks, with 'Let's Get Ready To Rumble' opening the event like a grand excursion into pure sound becoming song. It is a different kind of beauty and, as Ornette Coleman once said, "Beauty is a rare thing."

Joseph Jarman (b. 1937) also continues to crease up the detail of music. In 1999 he recorded with violinist Leroy Jenkins, another former AACM compatriot, and the New York-based pianist Myra Melford. The result, *Equal Interest*, has an extremely wide range of musical influences. Jarman gets to play flute and double-reed oboe as well as alto. On the track 'B'Pale Night' his alto seemingly moves across the scored motif as if proposing a new composition, floating off on a line that circles the violin like a bird in flight.

Two other exceptional saxophone players who left the United States for foreign shores around the same time as the Art Ensemble were Anthony Braxton and Steve Lacy. Braxton (b. 1945) had been a member of the AACM in Chicago. He had already recorded the session *For Alto* (1968), a magnificent, hungry solo discourse drawing on ideas initially laid down by Eric Dolphy, who five years previously had produced smaller-scale, solo alto improvisations built on standard song forms such as 'God Bless The Child'.

Braxton, however, was a marathon man. *For Alto* went the full distance and beyond. Unlike the Art Ensemble Of Chicago, Braxton's initial stay in Europe was not long, but it set the stage for repeat visits. In 1974 he recorded a stark live session with British guitarist Derek Bailey, *First Duo Concert*. By some mere oversight on the part of the general worldwide music press, absolute classic status has not been accorded this meeting of very different minds. I assume it is only a matter of time. Over the years Braxton has gone on to structure his playing way beyond the confines of freedom. Yet here is a radical dialogue between him and an Englishman who has completely detuned his guitar and himself into a left-field position that no longer recognises jazz, free or otherwise. Here can be heard a master musician still trailing all the colours of the jazz continuum. In the end it is not something that can be described. Hear it! Anthony Braxton is beyond my pocket. He has an output faster than fireworks. I keep trying to catch up with him. It does not matter. All I know is that his recent Braxton House recordings remain provocative territory; music that is free not because it comes un-preconceived but because it is played by a musician who has invented a personal vocabulary of his own.

Steve Lacy (b. 1934) was different. Born in New York, he went to Rome and then Paris at the same time as the others. He stayed. His sole saxophone was the straight horn, the soprano. Sidney Bechet had been the original exponent of the instrument and Lacy's own first jazz gigs had been with

Joe Harriott, the great Jamaican innovator, with drummer Bobby Orr at the Richmond jazz festival in 1963.

EVAN PARKER
saxophone solos

Two giants of the west-European free music scene: Britain's Evan Parker (sleeve, above) and Germany's Peter Brötzmann (right).

Dixieland-style bands. Lacy then flipped. In 1957 he started playing with Cecil Taylor, the pianist who literally tore up tradition and fed it back through a new vision that few others could see at the time.

Lacy went on to blow with Thelonious Monk, and also played a short gig with Ornette Coleman in a double quartet that was never recorded. Lacy and Braxton share a lot in common. Both have discographies longer than this chapter. Both are meticulous in detail, having reputations for writing complex formal scores. And, of course, both can apply an individual, phenomenal technical conception to the art of working a saxophone without preconceived structures. Quite independently of one another, they have experienced the need to play totally spontaneous free saxophone improvisations with Evan Parker (b. 1944), arguably the greatest living exponent of the form.

Lacy and Parker recorded as a duo on a session entitled *Chirps* in 1985. They followed this up with a trio recording for the same label in 1994 on which they were joined by a genuine English eccentric, Lol Coxhill (b. 1932), a soprano player of enormous resources whose generous, positive sound is so often under-reported. So I report: the trio date is called *Three Blokes*, a terrible title for a beautifully-recorded, unadorned three-soprano encounter

Soprano saxophonist Steve Lacy (left) in London, 1973, and the eclectic John Zorn (above) in concert, 1990.

that has vision and virtuosity in abundance. Perhaps the deliberate down-play of the title leaves the music to gain its own equilibrium. Parker defines the territory; Lacy adjusts the angles; Coxhill is, for once, the straightman, asking the questions and then often going on to provide his own bitter-sweet answers.

Parker gained his reputation as a master of both tenor and soprano largely on the basis of his solo recitals, awesome displays where he advanced on a muse and expanded all the possibilities. His two ongoing trio projects, the Schlippenbach Trio and Evan Parker/Barry Guy/Paul Lytton, oscillate between personal expression and sound sculpture. This is free jazz. This is what I now understand by those two four-letter words.

In 1999 I stood beside the New York swirling river and remembered Albert Ayler. In the evening, down on the Lower Eastside, I heard Ayler's old compatriot, the master drummer Milford Graves, placing the heat under John Zorn's alto saxophone in an hour-long extemporised performance of creative music. It was the last year of the 20th century; nine months later Zorn arrived in London with his band Masada. Whether they played "free" or "jazz" does not matter. In my view they are not so far from the river bank, whichever way you want to hear it.

MARK GILBERT

MICHAEL BRECKER

TO SOME, BRECKER'S APPEARANCE ON HUNDREDS OF POP ALBUMS IS INSTANT SELF-INCRIMINATION. YET WHAT QUALITATIVE EFFECT – BEYOND ENHANCING HIS TECHNIQUE – CAN THIS HAVE HAD ON HIS INNOVATIVE FUSION IN THE BRECKER BROTHERS OR HIS STRAIGHTAHEAD WORK WITH HORACE SILVER AND CHICK COREA?

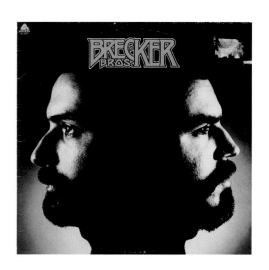  

Three top albums by the Brecker Brothers: their debut album (1975); a live set, Heavy Metal Be-Bop (1978); and their 1992 reunion album, revealing the influence of African music.

In the 1970s, few listeners were imagining much for the tenor saxophone (or even for jazz) beyond that achieved by Coltrane and his apostles. But by the mid 1980s many young listeners and players were talking of a successor to Coltrane, of a player with such a surgically precise technique, such stamina and such mastery of solo geometry that tenor saxophone playing seemed to be entering a new era. At the other pole were critics, perhaps with a longer view of saxophone history, perhaps too with a slender grasp of the contemporary scene, who dismissed the same figure as a session cipher.

Michael Brecker's influence was as prodigious as his studio career. Discounting the non-tonal avant-garde, with which he barely shares a common yardstick, and the tweedy new mainstream contingent, in the mid 1980s it was unusual to hear three new young saxophonists in a row without hearing something of Brecker's sound or phrasing. By the late 1990s that had changed, perhaps through Brecker-fatigue, as fashion continued to prefer the "authenticity" of the acoustic environment, and new tenor styles emerged from Chris Potter and others. Furthermore, by this time ever more sophisticated jazz education meant that Brecker-like technique was becoming a commonplace, and Brecker's own return to straightahead playing in the mid 1990s led, surprisingly, to his becoming absorbed into the generality. By the late 1990s, after three straightahead albums, he'd gone full circle, back to a style that would have fitted perfectly with Horace Silver in 1972.

Nevertheless, there remain those who maintain that Brecker has pushed the envelope that bit further. Perhaps nobody has a better insight into this than the man who has put in the hours behind the horn. Brecker, as mild and

Michael and Randy Brecker play London, 1992. Michael had recently returned from working with Paul Simon in Africa.

unassuming a character as his mentor Coltrane is said to have been, is convinced of his unworthiness in the face of Coltrane's achievements. "I'm definitely Coltrane-influenced, but he was light years ahead. Trust me. I'm not even comfortable, to be honest, with mentioning me and him in the same sentence. I think he reached a level that was extraordinary – intellectually, rhythmically, harmonically, spiritually and emotionally."

The maximum satisfaction he will allow himself is that he stumbled on a serendipitous crossroad in the mid 1970s. "I came to New York at a time when the boundaries between jazz, R&B and rock were starting to mix," he told me, "and it was a very exciting and creative period. There was a lot of freedom, particularly in saxophone playing, because all of a sudden I could take what I knew, what I had learned harmonically from the great players I'd studied, and apply it in an R&B format, and it was something that hadn't been done so much. It was a way of taking modal playing and applying it over a different rhythm, and I found I could come up with some things that were somewhat original – although they came from other sources. In that context, the stuff took a different twist."

Michael Brecker was born into the right environment in Philadelphia on March 29th 1949. His father, Bobby Brecker – immortalised in an appearance on Randy Brecker's delightfully embittered 'Hottest Man In Town' on his 1996 album *Into The Sun* – was an attorney, a pianist and a passionate jazz fan who gave his children every musical encouragement. Michael said: "I grew up thinking that everybody was a musician because there were always musicians at the house, every weekend. My brother Randy began playing

trumpet at about six and my sister played piano at five. My earliest memories are of Miles Davis and Clifford Brown, Dave Brubeck and Charlie Parker.

"I played clarinet first, and then drums, and eventually around junior high I switched to saxophone. We weren't pushed into music, but all of us were bitten by it. By the time I had to decide what to do with my life, I was already playing professionally. I made a brief attempt to go into pre-med, but by the time I had hit college I was already pretty much too taken with music to consider anything else." Randy moved to New York in 1966 and two years later Michael followed, having stopped off, like Randy, at Indiana University.

Michael made his professional debut at 19 with Edwin Birdsong, but his first major gig in New York was more propitious. In 1968 he teamed up Randy, drummer Billy Cobham, guitarist Jeff Kent and bassist Doug Lubahn

 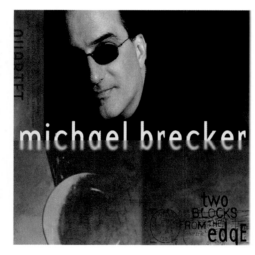

Michael Brecker (opposite) at The Barbican, London, 1995. Two acclaimed solo albums (above): Don't Try This At Home (1988); and Two Blocks From The Edge (1997).

to form Dreams. The band also featured at various times Bob Mann, John Abercrombie, Barry Rogers, Don Grolnick and Will Lee, and made two Columbia albums. The jazz-fusion gospel according to Miles Davis was on the way, two years ahead, but Dreams caught advance notice of the possibilities.

The distinguishing characteristic of Dreams was its use of horns – the same characteristic which would later set The Brecker Brothers apart from guitar- and keyboard-focused jazz-rock bands, and keep the Breckers closer to jazz. Their prowess in Dreams was also their passport to the studio life. "We were one of the first jazz-rock horn bands," Michael said. "We borrowed a lot from R&B and from jazz and mixed it together before there was that commercialised term 'fusion'. We did two records for Columbia: after that we got known as a horn section around town, and got hired for other people's dates. It set off a chain reaction, and it was a good way to make ends meet."

Ironically, despite being branded as a studio player, Brecker notes that he never really qualified. "I was always a sort of renegade. I never really doubled. I played tenor saxophone and could add a little bit of flute, but to really be a studio musician you had to play all the woodwinds, including bass clarinet, bassoon, ocarina and piccolo. It was always kind of funny to me, because the actual studio musicians never considered me to be one of them."

After Dreams dissolved around 1972 he spent some time with Horace Silver. Randy had been in Silver's band as early as 1967, but the two appeared together on the pianist's 1972 Blue Note album *In Pursuit Of The 27th Man*. As his negotiation of Silver's 'Gregory Is Here' shows, Michael had no shortage of the supreme chops one would expect of the studio player. He is far from being the harmonic monochrome associated with much early jazz-rock, proving perfectly fluent on the changes. He noted in the early 1990s that Silver had calmed him down a bit, but that must have come later: his playing here is very excitable but with some crafty rhythmic intelligence.

"Horace Silver was a good guide," Brecker said. "He kind of showed me how to build a solo, how to say more in a short time – probably something I need to incorporate now!" In fact, his magisterial control of pace and drama was well established by the early 1980s, when he produced numerous solos that began in reflection before building with tantalising circumlocution to roaring climaxes – as for example on 'Pools' from the Steps Ahead band's eponymous 1983 album. In the end, that formula became a cliché, but in its day it invariably did the trick.

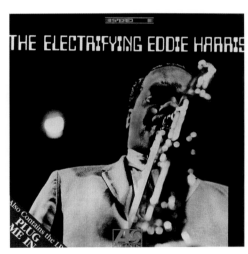

Steps Ahead's 1983 album and Eddie Harris, a pioneer of the electronic treatment of saxophone sound.

In the late 1960s, before jazz-rock and The Brecker Brothers came to the fore, Michael and Randy revealed a dimension in their music not well known to those who denigrate them as shallow fusioneers. In what is sometimes loosely described as the white Jewish New York school of saxophone, alongside Bob Berg, Bob Mintzer, Steve Grossman, David Liebman and Jerry Bergonzi, Brecker had his time as a free player. David Liebman recalls that in the late 1960s this circle of musicians played what they called "Coltrane's little toe". They accepted that playing more of any part of Coltrane's musical anatomy than that would always be difficult, but the particular toe in question was Trane's very freely improvised *Ascension* style. Liebman says: "I have tapes of me and Michael Brecker, Steve Grossman, Randy Brecker and Bob Berg where you can't tell who's playing what. Speed, volume and intensity were a big part of it, with no semblance of a theme."

This approach stood in direct contrast to the highly organised, carefully-crafted charts that Randy Brecker began to devise for The Brecker Brothers band in 1974. Somehow, Randy managed to retain the amiable funk and R&B grooves he drew from Herbie Hancock and others while laying across them wonderfully juicy polytonal harmonies. The result was a new sub-genre, a musical signature often imitated but immediately recognisable as Randy's.

Randy said, "The original concept was like a bebop-funk band. I remember thinking of Herbie's band at the time, and Sly & The Family Stone, but I also enjoyed groups like Cream, so there was a hint of that in some of the tunes. A lot of that stuff was written by just fooling around on the piano till I found something I liked. There's a lot of obvious polytonality – a triad over a root that's a half step above or below the triad. Hornwise there were quite a lot of fourths, something that I think started in Dreams, where we had three horns, with Barry Rogers. Also there was the minor-second to major-third voicing, which Horace Silver used a lot." Of course, as many critics have fairly noted, there was a good deal of less substantial material. Like Chet Baker whose singing he admires, Randy was given to some curious, slightly hip vocals, but the irremovable stain on the Breckers' character comes in such froth as 'Sneakin' Up Behind You' (1975) and 'Finger Lickin' Good' (1977).

Michael said: "We try to forget that stuff. There was some pressure from the record company to make something that would sell, which we really didn't know how to do." Happily, taking the group's albums as a whole, the good easily outweighs the bad. Aside from some extraordinary writing and superb

Brecker admired Chet Baker's singing style and played on this 1971 album (far left). Chick Corea's Three Quartets (1981, near left) includes a tribute to Coltrane, featuring Brecker.

ensemble playing, the soloing of both brothers is well exposed. Michael's early solo work with the Brothers, rather like that with Horace Silver, is a trifle shrill and histrionic at times, but by 1978 and the recording of the live tour-de-force *Heavy Metal Bebop* he had developed the greater range and more relaxed authority of tone and conception that were the hallmarks of his peak years in the 1980s. Perhaps his most successful appearance here is in his extended a cappella coda on his own 'Funky Sea, Funky Dew'. Aided by pitch-shifter and wah-wah, he wrings out the last drop of cod gospel emotion.

A decade later, following on from the effects of the 1970s, Michael used the EWI (Electronic Wind Instrument) which gave him access to sound worlds only dreamed of by earlier electrically-assisted saxophonists. The EWI, heard on Michael's first solo albums in the late 1980s and in the revived Brecker Brothers of the early 1990s, gave him access to eight octaves rather than the tenor's three, and a chance to give expression to his hobby of synthesiser programming. By driving the synth from the electric horn, Michael was able to combine great musicianship with a certain levity, as he emulated the muted trumpet of Miles Davis or the rock guitar sound of his sideman Mike Stern.

It may be a testimony to his musicianship that, unlike some users of synth drivers, including many guitarists, Brecker was able to avoid anonymity and retain an individual character when playing through the device. However, even at the height of the EWI craze around 1991, he knew the instrument's limitations. "It's a kind of half toy, half real instrument," he explained. "It's not an acoustic instrument and does not and will not replace the saxophone. At the same time it's made the sax feel much fresher." For listeners the EWI provided a fine diversion, but it was always a relief that the superior personal expression of the saxophone was not abandoned.

Like most 1970s fusion bands The Brecker Brothers smouldered to a close in the early 1980s – ironically just as Miles Davis was about to come back for a second round. But by the early 1990s the Breckers were ready for a reunion, this time with the new technology of hip-hop on board in the persons of Maz Kessler and Robbie Kilgore. The material well reflected the post-modern mood of the period. This curious mixture of new and old was typified by the electronic scratch samples and acoustic bass on the bluesy Horace Silver-inspired groove 'On The Backside', on *Return Of The Brecker Brothers* (1992).

By now the relaxed, insouciant timing which Michael Brecker had perfected in the 1980s was second nature. Perhaps the first examples of this mature style were to be found on the classy but overlooked 1981 Chick Corea date *Three Quartets*, especially in 'Quartet No.2, Part 2', dedicated to Coltrane and with Corea sounding like McCoy Tyner and Brecker like the dedicatee (but not the same as). That album and Pat Metheny's *80/81* (1980), with Brecker guesting, jointly marked a turning point in his career. For the first time since Horace Silver, Brecker was lined up with top-level acoustic combos, revealing a more circumspect side after the freneticism of the 1970s, and – as with the Steps Ahead band – expressing the appetite of former fusion players for working in a largely unamplified context. But as sideman, leader and co-leader, Brecker continued through the 1980s to appear in highly electrified settings. In fact Steps Ahead was fully plugged in again by 1986 for the disappointingly mechanical *Magnetic*.

Steps Ahead had been started by vibist Mike Mainieri as a jamming band at Seventh Avenue South, a Manhattan club owned and run by The Brecker Brothers from 1977 to 1985. It was effectively led by Mainieri and in its classic format also featured Brecker, Eliane Elias, Eddie Gomez and Peter Erskine. Before it was swept by commercial pressure toward the glassy electro dance sounds of the mid 1980s, the band accidentally created a minor idiom – a kind of jazz-fusion-unplugged – epitomised by the reading of Don Grolnick's 'Pools' on *Steps Ahead* (1983). This might well be an example of the perfect Brecker solo. It's hard to imagine that it – or indeed the solos by Gomez and Mainieri – could have been improved had they been written out and painstakingly edited by a professor of composition. Brecker's immaculately paced solo describes a compelling drama of tentative explorations, small setbacks, increasing confidences and minor subplots, all the while stepping to higher levels of tension and a long-anticipated resolution.

The excellence of Brecker's performance in this co-operative situation is illuminated by the explanation he gave in 1991 for his late debut as leader. "I had a lot of offers, but I really never felt ready to do it," he said. "Partially I was scared and partially I never had any real strong motivation to do it. That part of me was fulfilled by The Brecker Brothers, and I always felt better working in collaborative situations."

Indeed, Brecker has been more convincing as sideman or co-leader than leader. Aside from the Corea and Metheny sets mentioned above, and among scores of other pick-up dates, he made powerful showings on Chet Baker's 1977 electric set *You Can't Go Home Again* and a little known 1986 session with the Canadian violinist Hugh Marsh, *The Bear Walks*. Furthermore, while writing is a function often associated with bandleading, Michael has done relatively little. His brother Randy, in Gil Goldstein's *Jazz Composer's Companion*, refers to

Michael Brecker was the most influential contemporary saxophonist of the 1980s and the 1990s.

"big arguments" with Michael about the writing process, and seems to imply that his brother has a certain impatience with writing, where Randy sees it as graft – the old formula of one per cent inspiration, 99 per cent perspiration. Michael has produced some effective compositions, but seems to view the solo as the first order of business in jazz.

Perhaps because of such traditional elements as swing, and the presence of Charlie Haden and Jack DeJohnette, Brecker's first albums as leader – *Michael Brecker* (1987) and *Don't Try This At Home* (1989) – were critically well-received, notably by writers who'd hitherto consigned Brecker to the scrap heap of fusion. However, despite their interesting attempts at mixing a wide range of idioms, they were musically less cohesive than two of his 1990s Impulse dates, *Tales From The Hudson* (1996) and *Two Blocks From The Edge* (1998). These were models both of programming and soloing. In the same decade Brecker also recorded with McCoy Tyner, as guest and leader, and with Elvin Jones, who was on his 1999 organ record, *Time Is Of The Essence*.

By the turn of the century, fusion was nowhere in sight on his musical palette: stylistically, he said, his career had evolved from back to front. That's not strictly true, of course. It was more like a movement around a circle, from the influence of Coltrane and his peers – Joe Henderson, Sonny Rollins, Wayne Shorter and others are also in there – through fusion and on to his playing with half of Coltrane's great quartet. These latter appearances, well understood by critics because of their historical resonances, were celebrated and symbolic events for Brecker. But his freshest, most creative and "somewhat original" work had occurred around the middle years – where it was least expected, and least noticed.

MARK GILBERT

FUSION: SWITCHED-ON SAXOPHONES

*INITIALLY DUBBED JAZZ-ROCK, FUSION CRYSTALLISED INTO
AN INDENTIFIABLE STYLE AT THE END OF THE SIXTIES WITH
MILES DAVIS'S ALBUM BITCHES' BREW. AMONG ITS LEADING
EXPONENTS HAVE BEEN SUCH GREAT SAXOPHONISTS AS WAYNE
SHORTER, BILL EVANS AND DAVID SANBORN.*

*Saxophonist David Sanborn has worked in
many contexts, with everyone from Gil
Evans to David Bowie.*

Although the synthesiser and guitar seemed emblematic of the hybrid music known as fusion, there were many saxophone players who didn't want to be left out of the party – and, in some cases, who didn't want to miss out on the profits. At its simplest, fusion saxophone meant playing jazz-flavoured lines over rock or funk rhythms and chord sequences. At the extreme, it involved "modernising" the instrument by physically modifying it or by playing it through electronic processing to make it sound more like a guitar, keyboard... or anything but the crusty old saxophone.

At the more moderate end of the spectrum, it sometimes just involved playing supercharged R&B, as David Sanborn did through the 1970s and 1980s. At the fringe, some jazz players – such as Steve Grossman and David Liebman – were classed inaccurately as fusion players simply because they worked briefly in Miles Davis's jazz-rock bands. Wayne Shorter, Bob Berg, Gary Thomas and others meanwhile moved between idioms, sometimes playing fusion, sometimes straightahead. A number of older-styled players – Lou Donaldson, Stanley Turrentine and the like – looked for their place too in a financially promising market.

For the classical establishment, early jazz saxophonists sullied the pure sound of the instrument with their grunts, pitchbends and other distortions. But in jazz such techniques have long been regarded as important expressive tools. The modifications and alterations practised by fusion players could be seen as extensions of this quest for new expression. Ironically, though, many champions of earlier jazz styles were as sniffy about fusion as classical purists had been about early jazz saxophone. Doubtless some fusion saxophonists made cynical bids for the pop charts, but as many if not more developed the fusion style without such premeditation, in the good name of creativity.

Looking for a starting point for fusion saxophone, we might think of the blues playing of Louis Jordan, Earl Bostic or King Curtis. But the kind of R&B embraced by such players didn't become fusion until it met with the new technology and broad artistic horizons of the 1960s. These all came together in the pioneering work of Eddie Harris (1934-96). He combined the essential ingredients of "fusion" in the late 1960s, predating the actual term which was coined during the following decade.

Pianist Cedar Walton recalls that in the early 1960s Harris indefatigably sought the big break, touring major record company offices in search of a deal. He might thus be accused of calculated commercialism, but along the way Harris devised all manner of novel sounds for the saxophone. Perhaps to sell his music, perhaps through sheer inquisitiveness, Harris took to making hybrid instruments and using electronic processing. Among his inventions were a trumpet and flugelhorn each fitted with saxophone mouthpieces. He was also a keen user of the Varitone device, which duplicated the played pitch at another interval, most often an octave below. Walton also suggests that Harris's distinctive, pinched tone and his interest in electronic support derived from the loss of his teeth through gum disease, and says that as a result Harris was known as "the black Stan Getz". The power of Harris's combination of earthy funk and the Varitone can be well understood from 'Listen Here' on the appropriately titled 1967 album *The Electrifying Eddie Harris*, even if much of the rest is forgettable.

Harris encapsulated the key aspects of fusion saxophone: blues, funk, the use of technology and, in his tune 'Freedom Jazz Dance', harmonic complexity. He had a few parallels among later players: Michael Brecker is

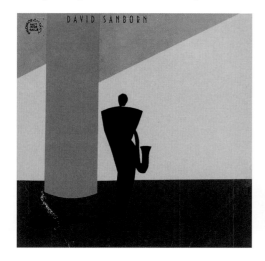

discussed in the preceding chapter, but Gary Thomas, a much later player, also combined these elements to notable effect. It may not be coincidental that, although Thomas (b. 1961) appeared some 20 years after Harris's *Electrifying*, he cited Harris as an influence. Despite an apparent similarity to Coltrane, in 1991 Thomas said: "I never really listened to Trane or Wayne [Shorter] much for solo influence. I listened to Billy Harper, Woody Shaw, Eddie Harris – I listened to a lot of Eddie Harris."

While he was operating in a harmonic environment far more forbidding than Harris's 'Listen Here', the heavily polytonal style that Thomas demonstrated on his *By Any Means Necessary* (1989) was not that far from 'Freedom Jazz Dance'. Despite his impatience with the blues – he said he left Miles Davis's 1980s band because he was tired of playing pentatonic licks all night – his playing is not short of that quality. Note-choice apart, he connects strongly with Harris in his use of the Pitchrider MIDI interface. This was like a distant progeny of the Varitone, enabling him to trigger synthesisers from his horn, thicken his sound and add sinister parallel harmonies. On the other hand, responding perhaps to the jazz-friendly climate of the late 1980s, Thomas appeared on several straightahead records minus Pitchrider, including his own *While The Gate Is Open* (1990).

Thomas was associated with the M-BASE collective of New York, a loose affiliation of players interested in finding a new sound for jazz. Two of M-BASE's players, Steve Coleman and Greg Osby, followed courses similar to Thomas's. Although Osby (b. 1960) subsequently turned to straightahead playing, in the late 1980s he too was a fan of the Pitchrider, using it on his

As We Speak ((1981) and Close Up (1988), two albums on which David Sanborn collaborated with bassist-producer Marcus Miller. Bob Berg's 1987 album Short Stories featured Sanborn as a guest artist.

Stanley Turrentine (right) had numerous
hit albums while retaining his expressive
power as a creative jazz musician.

1991 album *Man-Talk For Moderns Vol X*. Once again the old Harris verities of
the blues, electric hardware and harmonic convolution convene in Osby's
playing from this period.

After playing a row of harmonically tense funk pieces in a set at the Jazz
Café in London in the early 1990s, Osby introduced an unadulterated
rendition of an old soul number, declaring (probably in veiled reference to
Wynton Marsalis's claims for jazz as the only true Afro-American music) that
his band saw no shame in popular black American music.

That sort of soul was always obvious in Osby's playing, but his colleague
Steve Coleman (b. 1956) consciously took a more radical stance, trying to
reconcile electric funk rhythms with an extremely chromatic, unresolved
harmonic universe. Such was the level of tension and absence of resolution in
Coleman's music that, while superficially dramatic, it was often one-
dimensional. Like his namesake Ornette's *Dancing In Your Head* album of
1975, Steve Coleman perhaps stretched the idea of funk-plus-jazz beyond its
limits, to the point where the funk was metamorphosed into something
abstract, and the groove lost.

In between Harris and M-BASE there had been an intermediate
generation of technology, given form in the Lyricon, an early form of wind
synthesiser driver. Two unlikely Lyricon dabblers were Wayne Shorter (for
example on Weather Report's 'Black Market', 1976) and Sonny Rollins (on
'Tai-chi', 1979). But the player most often associated with it is the West-
Coaster Tom Scott (b. 1948). He used it frequently (and also, later, the
Yamaha WX-7 wind controller), but his most expressive work was on the

tenor saxophone, and most of it in The LA Express, formed in 1973 and at various times including Joe Sample and Max Bennett.

The band came about after Sample and Bennett introduced Scott, previously a bebopper, to the soulful funk sound that The Crusaders had developed in the early 1970s. Most of Scott's work on the GRP label in the 1980s and '90s was glossy and formulaic, but his earlier playing in The LA Express and as a sideman with Steely Dan had an authentically gritty blues flavour. One couldn't expect the kind of harmonic surprises that Michael Brecker was springing on the East Coast, but Scott nevertheless played with heart and commitment. A late GRP date, the 1996 *Bluestreak*, reunited him with The LA Express, and brought him closer to his origins. But as with so many GRP albums, even the blues here had a synthetic, cultivated quality.

Scott's rasping, soulful tenor playing provides a link to the R&B-oriented saxophonists whose fusion consisted largely of bluesy licks over funk rhythms. Notable among these, and somewhat influential on Scott, was Wilton Felder (b. 1940) who cultivated a funky yet cool tenor style on the West Coast in the 1960s. Felder is hardly known outside The Crusaders, and it was within this group that he developed an approach which, while apparently unambitious, concealed considerable craft and skill. Often he would play little more than themes, licks and decorations, but their placement, and the use of space around them, was very effective within the constraints of The Crusaders' harmonically uninvolved music. His infrequently exposed voice as a soloist can be heard on 'Hot's It' and 'Soul Caravan' from *Chain Reaction* (1975), although he is typically distant in the mix, underlining his ornamental role. He's more prominent in 'My Mama Told Me So' from *Those Southern Knights* (1975), though without the volubility that had characterised his playing in The Jazz Crusaders, the jazz group from which The Crusaders had evolved.

By contrast, David Sanborn, the best known exponent of saxophone-led electric funk, was centre-stage in the groups he led. His penetrating tone and the barely controlled hysteria of his playing made him popular with audiences and garnered the respect of a wide range of musicians, Gil Evans, Michael Brecker, John Scofield and David Bowie among them. (He is the soloist on Bowie's 1975 hit 'Young Americans'.) By the late 1980s the biting yet tender sound of Sanborn (b. 1945) was probably the most copied alto-saxophone sound in jazz-funk, influencing Nelson Rangell, Art Porter and any number of more ephemeral artists. Creative variations on the blues are at the core of his

Steve Coleman and the free-funk M-BASE concept were early influences on the work of Gary Thomas. Lou Donaldson's live set The Scorpion was recorded in 1970 but not released until the 1990s.

playing, and he's always avoided calling himself a jazz player. But his commitment and passion seem often to have equipped him well for dealing with more demanding musical environments.

When he worked as an essential third of The Brecker Brothers' horn section on 'Rocks' from *The Brecker Brothers* (1975), exchanging licks with Michael Brecker, Sanborn seems driven to pull out harmonic ideas which have a sophistication not heard on his solo albums. In fact, after years of producing unequivocally modern, brassy jazz-funk, in the early 1990s he sensed the need for a change and turned towards more abstract material in the company of such leftfield musicians as Charlie Haden and Bill Frisell.

This may also have been his response to the generally retrospective mood of the time, but whatever the cause, his playing lacked the attack which

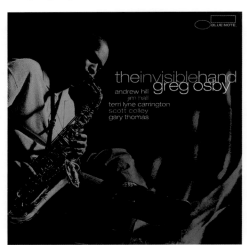

Tom Scott (above) and his 1996 album Bluestreak. Greg Osby (album sleeve, right) is a leading M-BASE artist.

distinguished his earlier, less self-conscious recordings – such as 'Rush Hour' on the 1982 album *As We Speak* where, unusually, he plays soprano saxophone. Perhaps his best work was in the 1980s, when his band featured Marcus Miller playing bass, writing, arranging and producing – just as he had done successfully for Miles Davis in the same period. Pieces such as 'Pyramid' and 'Tough' from *Close-Up* (1988), although now dated by their exaggerated electric drum sounds, show Sanborn in his most incendiary form. The key to the tones he produces in the theme of 'Pyramid' lies partly in the influence of Hank Crawford. But Sanborn added his own particular intensity, which no imitator has managed to reproduce. There may be something in the theory that Sanborn's childhood bout with polio, for which the saxophone was recommended as therapy, fed the passion in his playing.

Another player who brought R&B saxophone into conjunction with the electric rhythm section, this time on tenor, was Ronnie Laws. His *Pressure Sensitive* (1975) was the biggest-selling album on the Blue Note label, and 'Always There' became a jazz-funk anthem, even if little else on that or his later records had much substance. Laws (b. 1950) came from Texas, and his throaty, incisive saxophone voice had its roots in the combative "Texas Tenor" style of Arnett Cobb and Illinois Jacquet. But most of his commercially-targeted work suffered from insipid content and production and featured little saxophone playing beyond themes and simple riffs.

Stanley Turrentine's career might have followed a similar path, but even though he frequently operated in commercially-conscious environments with an R&B flavour, including a spell with the infamous CTI label, Turrentine was able to retain the jazz content and integrity of his saxophone playing in almost all contexts. In his earlier years he played R&B, including a year with Earl Bostic, before moving toward variants of soul jazz in the 1960s. By the 1980s Turrentine (1934-2000) was taking advantage of the technology of the day and had begun playing in more electrified settings, producing for example *Wonderland* (1986), an album of Stevie Wonder covers, and *La Place* (1989), produced and largely written by Bobby Lyle. Whatever the situation, Turrentine produced creative blues playing, adding bebop accents as they seem appropriate.

The story of fusion is, of course, inextricably bound up with Miles Davis, whose bands featured numerous players who later made their own names leading fusion bands. However, this doesn't mean we can automatically dub

The Crusaders' 1975 album Those Southern Knights (left), featuring Wilton Felder. Before becoming a solo artist, Ronnie Laws worked with Quincy Jones and Earth Wind & Fire.

any saxophonist who passed through his 1970s or 1980s bands as a fusion player. His fusion groups, especially those from 1969 to 1975, were so eclectic that electrified funk was only part of the equation. These bands focussed on one-key vamps, and from the improviser's standpoint provided a funky, electrified version of the Coltrane groups of the 1960s. Many of Miles's saxophonists played modal jazz rather than anything clearly distinguishable as fusion, despite the occasional use of electronic processing. The players included David Liebman, Carlos Garnett, Steve Grossman, Gary Bartz, Bill Evans, Bob Berg, Gary Thomas and Kenny Garrett.

The most prominent of Miles's fusion-period saxophonists is Wayne Shorter (b. 1933), and he is a special case. His individual development is so strong and so wide-ranging it seems beyond "fusion". He contributed to it from the outside, but hardly drew from it. For one thing, Shorter played and shaped straightahead jazz for the first quarter of his career, and when he was part of a fusion band – Weather Report – he invariably played and wrote in a jazz style rather than using funky vamps or soul-saxophone clichés. Shorter's extremely individual writing for Blue Note in the early 1960s might have contributed to the decline in functional harmony that characterised fusion, and yet it doesn't sound like fusion. Perhaps the closest Shorter came to playing out-and-out fusion, fully electrified and hi-tech, was in his late-1980s solo albums after the dissolution of Weather Report. The most successful of these is *Atlantis* (1985). Two other saxophonists from Miles's 1980s bands, Bill Evans and Bob Berg, spent substantial amounts of time ploughing and indeed lengthening fusion's furrow. Berg's case is rather like Shorter's in that he played straightahead jazz (with Horace Silver, Cedar Walton, Sam Jones and others) for a long while before he was invited to join Miles Davis in 1984. In Miles's bands, Berg (b. 1951) found himself blowing over high-energy funk vamps, and when he left he carried that mood into his own records and into a group he co-led with guitarist Mike Stern.

Berg hardly, if ever, used electronic variants of the saxophone, focusing instead on using his tenor to play an amalgam of Coltrane, R&B and bebop over the vamps and changes of his and Stern's compositions. Sometimes, in keeping with the mood of the day, the group would play a standard such as 'Autumn Leaves' or 'All The Things You Are'. The Stern-Berg band was clearly a fusion group, and Berg felt it developed a small new direction in the music, but its leaders, most of its rhythm section and its sensibility were jazz-

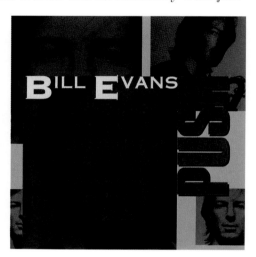

With NTU Troop, Gary Bartz (above) combined bop and soul influences with elements of African music. The 1993 album Push! (right) by Bill Evans, no relation to the pianist of the same name.

oriented. This can be heard clearly in Berg's rocking but chord-rich 'Friday At The Cadillac Club' from *Short Stories* (1987).

In the early 1990s Berg returned with some relief to the straightahead environment. But his predecessor in the Miles Davis band, Bill Evans (no relation to pianist Bill Evans in Davis's late-1950s group), is distinct from other Davis saxophonists both for working almost exclusively in fusion contexts and for proving an able bebop practitioner.

Evans (b. 1958) took lessons with David Liebman, and on Liebman's recommendation was invited to join Miles, returning to public performances in 1980. Evans remained for four years before playing with John McLaughlin's reformed Mahavishnu Orchestra, and began to lead his own groups and record dates – all exclusively electric. His bebop prowess is evident in rare dates as a sideman, and over the changes of 'My Man's Gone Now' from *We Want Miles* (1981). But in 1993 Evans made his most unambivalent fusion statement on *Push*, mixing jazz, funk, hip-hop and rap. Most of his fusion has been good, despite over-indulgences; he may be remembered as the rare jazz-equipped saxophonist who didn't make a straightahead album in the retro 1990s.

Many other saxophonists were involved with fusion to varying degrees, some just by virtue of keeping certain company. Among the latter were Bennie Maupin (with Miles Davis and Herbie Hancock), Bob Mintzer (with The Yellowjackets in the 1990s), Joe Farrell (with Chick Corea), Ernie Watts (with Lee Ritenour), Bob Malach (playing Coltrane-ish tenor on his own R&B records and with Mike Stern) and Steve Tavaglione (with John Patitucci and Frank Gambale). Others played fusion with intent: John Klemmer (whose

Ernie Watts, among the most powerful of contemporary tenor soloists.

1975 album *Touch* followed work at the other extreme with Don Ellis), Jay Beckenstein (Spyro Gyra), Pee Wee Ellis and Maceo Parker (formerly part of James Brown's horn section) and Marc Russo (earlier with The Yellowjackets). In Europe, Elton Dean in Soft Machine, Barbara Thompson in Paraphernalia, Chris Hunter, Bendik Hofseth, Klaus Doldinger and inveterate bebopper Peter King (try *Crusade*, 1989) were among those who widened the web of fusion. Even the free player Peter Brötzmann was heard charging about over funk rhythms on the 1993 German rap album *Expo's Jazz & Joy*.

Fusion became more sophisticated in the 1990s, reincorporating elements of straightahead styles – acoustic instruments playing funk, for example, or double bass used alongside synthesiser. And as a consequence it became increasingly difficult to isolate and, indeed, stigmatise its exponents.

CROSSOVER AND SMOOTH JAZZ

CLEAR JAZZ-INFLECTED MELODIES PLAYED OVER SUBDUED FUNK OR R&B GROOVES BECAME PART OF THE SOUNDTRACK TO URBAN LIVING DURING THE NINETIES. THE GENRE WAS EVENTUALLY DUBBED "SMOOTH JAZZ". IT FILLS THE SAME POPULAR NICHE AS SWING-INFLECTED POPULAR MUSIC OCCUPIED IN THE FIFTIES.

Kenny G – king of the smooth-jazz airwaves – on a 1986 album sleeve.

In the early 1970s, under pressure from record companies to improve sales and increase financial returns, many jazz musicians began to adapt their musical output so it would appeal to a wider audience. Some produced jazz versions of popular hits, while others tried to incorporate the stylistic features of rock and pop into their own music.

Whatever the approach, it was seen as essential for economic success to be able to fuse jazz with more commercial musical genres. The term "crossover" began to be used to refer to the most commercial part of fusion. Also called "smooth jazz" for its easy-listening style, the music combines jazz melody and improvisation with soul, funk and R&B grooves.

One musician often credited as an originator of crossover was saxophonist Grover Washington Jr (1943-99). His *Inner City Blues* (1971) was an electrified version of the soul-jazz that had given artists such as Ramsey Lewis and "Cannonball" Adderley chart hits in the 1960s. The success of the album came as a complete surprise to Washington, who was working at a distribution company at the time packing boxes and had only been called in for the recording at the last minute as a replacement for Hank Crawford. He made more commercially successful albums throughout the 1970s that repeated the soul-jazz formula, notably *Mister Magic* (1974), *Feels So Good* (1975) and *A Secret Place* (1976). In 1980, *Winelight* received two Grammys, one for Best Fusion Recording and the other for Best R&B Song, 'Just The Two Of Us', featuring Bill Withers on vocals.

Despite his smooth-jazz credentials, Washington always had the respect of jazz players. He credited as his influences players like Cannonball Adderley, Stanley Turrentine, Sonny Rollins and Roland Kirk, all of whom had also experimented with merging jazz, soul and R&B. Like them, his saxophone style was unique and instantly recognisable, combining rich tone with melodic soulful improvisation. Like them also, there was a personal intensity that came across in his music, a sense that he was blowing from the heart.

Washington said of his playing, "I've really worked on my sound. I've tried to make it a personal sound. I want it to feel like there's a vocalist in there singing lyrics... . What I strive for in my music is always to tell a story, to portray my inner feelings."

Washington's successful combination of lyrical sax playing and super-funky grooves continued into the 1980s with *Come Morning* (1980) which featured frequent collaborators Richard Tee, Steve Gadd, Eric Gale, Ralph MacDonald and Marcus Miller. Others followed such as *Inside Moves* (1984), *Strawberry Moon* (1987) and the 1988 jazz set *Then And Now*. In the 1990s he remained ubiquitous, recording his own tracks in a variety of styles encompassing jazz, rap, soul and R&B, as well as guesting on sessions for a whole host of artists. In 1999, before his death in December, Washington recorded his last album, a classical set of 12 operatic arias that reflected his ability to adapt to diverse musical settings.

By the late 1970s, inspired by the success of artists like Washington, many other young musicians had begun to find a place for themselves in the crossover market. The saxophone was well represented by players like David Sanborn, Tom Scott, Ronnie Laws, Ernie Watts, Michael Brecker and Eddie Daniels; the instrument's expressive qualities lent it a strong appeal for an audience more used to vocal leads.

The most commercially successful of the new younger generation of saxophone players to emerge in the early 1980s was Kenny G (b. 1959),

Playing tenor, alto and soprano with equal facility, Grover Washington Jr was a primary influence on musicians of many styles, especially R&B and crossover.

originally Kenny Gorelick. Since his first solo album in 1982 he has won a host of awards including a Grammy, and is currently the biggest-selling instrumental artist ever, with over 30 million units to his credit. Despite this commercial success, however, his recordings have received much critical derision over the years, with the attacks mainly aimed at the bland and unchallenging nature of the music.

Originating from Seattle, Kenny G joined the Jeff Lorber Fusion band after leaving college, where he was spotted by Clive Davis, head of Arista Records, and offered a recording deal. His first album *Kenny G* (1982) showcased his talents on all four saxophones, plus flutes, but it was the second album *G Force* (1983) that really launched his career. It sold over 200,000 copies, its success undoubtedly boosted by an up-to-the-minute sound courtesy of top pop and R&B producers.

His playing style is heavily influenced by Washington: he has the earlier player's smooth, mellow tone and uses slick, soulful, fluid melodic lines which he embellishes with flurries of notes and extended pentatonic runs. Although proficient on alto and tenor, perhaps his most individual sound is on soprano, where he often uses circular breathing. He employed this to good effect on the chart hit 'Songbird', from his best-selling album *Duotones* (1986). This chart success continued with *Silhouette* (1988) and *Breathless* (1992), the latter going 15 times platinum and becoming the biggest-selling instrumental album ever.

Some of Kenny G's recent output such as the Christmas-songs album *Miracles* (1994) and *Classics In The Key Of G* (1999), containing a "virtual duet" with Louis Armstrong on 'What A Wonderful World', seem to confirm criticisms of selling-out to major label corporatism. However, there may also be a hint of jealousy in some of the attacks on his playing from those who envy his popularity and financial prosperity.

Whatever the debate over his music, it is true to say that Kenny G's success paved the way for a whole new generation of young saxophonists to emerge and enter the crossover market. By the mid 1980s the demand for

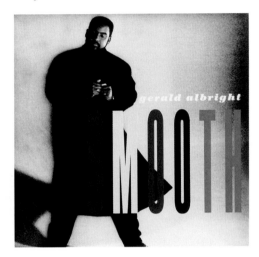

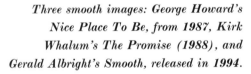

Three smooth images: George Howard's Nice Place To Be, from 1987, Kirk Whalum's The Promise (1988), and Gerald Albright's Smooth, released in 1994.

contemporary soul and pop-influenced jazz was on the increase. Catering for a wide variety of tastes, it was the perfect sound for the growing number of adult-orientated US radio stations, eager to play music that would appeal to a wide audience and fill up schedules.

One of the labels at the forefront of instrumental jazz-fusion in the 1980s and early 1990s was GRP, founded by pianist/composer Dave Grusin and his business partner Larry Rosen. The company built up a huge roster of artists at its peak in the late 1980s, aiming its output at the "adult contemporary" market. As well as established artists, young musicians were given opportunities, including saxophonists Eric Marienthal, Nelson Rangell and George Howard.

Marienthal (b. 1957) first became known as a member of Chick Corea's Elektric Band which he joined in time for their second album *Light Years* in 1986. Concentrating mainly on alto and soprano, Marienthal is a phenomenal technician with an amazing command of the instrument. His sound is centred and his playing style exciting, direct and rhetorical. He alternates rapidly between explosive funky licks, soaring harmonics and complex rhythmic patterns, all executed with perfect timing.

His first solo releases featured him in a variety of funk and fusion settings, but it wasn't until his *Crossroads* album (1990), recorded "live" in the studio, that he was able to blow rather more freely and fully showcase his talents. The follow-up, *Oasis* (1991), is a classic example of Marienthal's style: he alternates between tight funk produced by Jeff Lorber and lyrical, earthy jazz-fusion courtesy of Yellowjackets keyboardist Russell Ferrante. The last

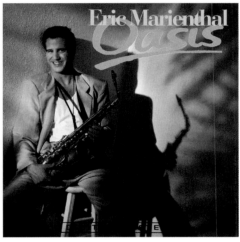

CHAPTER TWENTY-ONE

Eric Marienthal in action (left) during 1994, and his 1991 album Oasis.

track, 'Another Shore', is an up-tempo gospel number that features Marienthal's funky in-your-face alto soaring into the harmonics.

Marienthal continued to release solo albums throughout the 1990s while still recording and touring with Chick Corea and the Elektric Band II – this was a second version of the popular fusion outfit with the addition of a new rhythm section. On his 1998 tribute to Cannonball Adderley, *Walk Tall*, Marienthal returned to his jazz roots and included some straightahead tracks among the funk and fusion pieces.

Another young wind player who made his name through releases on GRP was Nelson Rangell (b. 1961). A native of Denver, Colorado, Rangell is a multi-instrumentalist fluent on tenor, alto and soprano saxophones as well as flute and piccolo. His musical success began in school when in 1979 he won *Down Beat* magazine's Best High School Jazz Soloist competition. In 1984 he moved to New York and soon found himself in demand on pop and jingle sessions. He began recording for GRP in 1989 with *Playing For Keeps* and subsequently released four more successful albums on the label.

Like Kenny G, Rangell has been criticised for being too safe and easy-listening, but this seems a little unfair as his music is much more diverse in style and places more emphasis on improvisation in its content. A good

example of Rangell's versatility can be heard on *Truest Heart* (1993). Starting with the emotive fusion of 'World Traveller' he plays flowing and melodic alto lines with a crying, passionate, Sanborn-influenced sound. He changes to tenor on 'Sierra La Esperanza', blowing with a full and gutsy tone, and then on 'Flight' and the up-samba of 'Regatta De Rio' he demonstrates his superb technique on flute and piccolo.

George Howard (1957-98) also recorded for GRP, and during a 15-year career that produced 14 albums he gathered a huge following and became a firm favourite among contemporary-jazz radio stations. Unusually, Howard's main instrument was the soprano saxophone, on which he recorded almost exclusively for virtually all of his career. Originally hailing from Philadelphia, Howard relocated to California during 1983 and released *Steppin' Out*, an album with a combination of instrumental pop covers, smooth jazz and R&B work-outs. Howard continued with this formula, attaining *Billboard* jazz-chart success with recordings such as *Dancing In The Sun* (1985) and *A Nice Place To Be* (1987), and Grammy nominations for *Reflections* (1988) and *Do I Ever Cross Your Mind?* (1992).

One of the features of the new generation of crossover saxophonists in the 1980s was that many of them did not begin their recording careers playing jazz. Most had studied jazz, but unlike slightly older players such as Washington, Laws, Brecker, Watts and Scott, they had not become established as jazz players first before recording crossover albums, nor did they make straightahead jazz part of their repertoire at all.

Tenor saxophonist Kirk Whalum comes into this category. Although he studied jazz at school and college, Whalum has made recordings firmly centred on crossover, though gravitating toward soul and R&B. His career began in Houston, Texas, where pianist Bob James spotted him after he opened a gig for James's band. Whalum subsequently played on James's album *12* (1984) and then began recording his own series of albums for Columbia, including *Floppy Disk* (1985), *And You Know That* (1988), *The Promise* (1988) and *Cache* (1992).

Whalum is not a brilliant technician; his strength lies in a deep crying tone and a soulful playing style that goes straight for the heart-strings of the listener. On *The Promise*, for example, there are no fast, burning runs or virtuosic crescendos into the harmonics – but everything he plays creates maximum emotional effect. The key to music for Whalum is soul, and not what type of music you play or how fast you can play it. For example, he said of his country-influenced 1995 album *In This Life*, "Soul in my book is what emerges when you're singing or playing with passion. Soul," said Whalum, "has more to do with integrity and colour and depth of feeling than any particular musical idiom."

Whalum's ability to touch an emotional nerve in his audience meant that he was widely sought after as a session musician. His saxophone has been featured on many pop and R&B hits, including albums by other jazz-crossover artists like Larry Carlton, George Benson, and The Rippingtons. However, most people will have heard Whalum as a result of his work on Whitney Houston's smash number-one 'I Will Always Love You' (1992).

One saxophonist who has succeeded in achieving both crossover success and acclaim from jazz critics is Gerald Albright (b. 1957). Albright has recorded a number of crossover soul- and R&B-influenced records as well as several straightahead jazz albums. He originally studied accountancy at

Nelson Rangell's association with the GRP label established his image as a popular crossover artist. Rangell is pictured (opposite) in 1997.

college, but on graduating began to pursue a career as a musician, working as a sideman for artists like The Temptations, Olivia Newton-John and Anita Baker. In 1987 Albright released his first solo album, *Just Between Us*, which featured him on tenor and alto, playing a selection of soul and R&B numbers. Several other crossover albums followed until in 1991 he recorded *Live At Birdland West*, a concert set featuring mainly jazz standards, and with guests Kirk Whalum and Eddie Harris on various tracks.

While the early albums show off Albright's clean sound and soulful improvisations, on *Birdland* he really lets the audience know he can play, with some extended and fiery improvisations. On 'Impressions' Albright's Coltrane influence is clear. However, his main inspiration is Cannonball Adderley, to whom the album is dedicated. On 'C Jamm Blues' and 'Limehouse Blues' Albright plays with the attack and rhythmic confidence of Adderley, combining sweet, soulful riffs and rapid-fire bebop runs. On 'Georgia On My Mind' his sound is personal, clear, clean and driving as he demonstrates his fantastic command of the harmonic register.

As well as the solo successes, Albright has been in demand as a session player on a number of pop and R&B sessions, including work for Quincy Jones, Patrice Rushen, Take 6, The Winans, Phil Collins and Whitney Houston (on 'I'm Your Baby Tonight', 1990). On Albright's 1994 release *Smooth* one can hear why, as his slick funky licks and sweet sound fit effortlessly around the vocals.

Perhaps his best release to date has been *Giving Myself To You* (1995) featuring some great playing on soprano and flute as well as tenor and alto. Although this is an acoustic straightahead jazz set, it is highly soulful, given a contemporary edge by Albright's sparkling arrangements and the talents of players such as George Duke, Stanley Clarke and Harvey Mason. Albright said, "I wanted to satisfy the purists with an acoustic, unplugged feel and at the same time put a 1990s spin on the project, with a variety of rhythmic twists and layering of certain instruments."

In the 1990s other new, even younger saxophonists emerged on to the scene, such as Brandon Fields, Najee, Dave Koz and Everette Harp. All achieved solo success and built their careers playing within the smooth-jazz crossover genre. One player of note among the many was Art Porter (1961-96), a young musician from Little Rock, Arkansas. Tragically, Porter was killed in a boating accident while on tour in Thailand in November 1996, leaving his full musical potential unfulfilled.

During his short career Porter inspired many with his recordings and dynamic performance skills. He had been raised in a jazz household and grew up to the sounds of John Coltrane and Charlie Parker. While still at school he joined his father's jazz trio, a gig that continued until he was barred from playing because he was too young to be in the venues. However, the State's attorney general at the time was sympathetic toward Porter's predicament and pressed for the law to be changed. The attorney was also a famous saxophonist – a certain Bill Clinton – with whom Porter remained in contact throughout his career.

He began playing professionally as a sideman for artists like Pharaoh Sanders and Jack McDuff before signing with Verve and releasing his first solo album, *Pocket City*, in 1992. An energetic funk workout produced by Jeff Lorber, it featured Porter on alto and soprano, showing off his lyrical and energetic playing as well as his songwriting abilities. Other releases followed

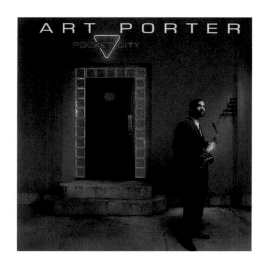

Art Porter's debut album Pocket City was released in 1992 and included Jeff Lorber (keyboards), Buzzy Feiten (bass) and Paulinho da Costa (percussion).

Art Porter's fame was growing fast at the time of his death at the age of 35 in 1996.

such as *Straight To The Point* (1993), *Undercover* (1994) and *Lay Your Hands On Me* (1996), as well as guest spots on keyboardist Jeff Lorber's own projects. All showcase Porter's playing and songwriting, but his all-round enthusiasm and showmanship was most strongly evident at live performances, where he would move through the audience, play two saxes at once, and stride energetically around the stage.

This on-stage energy is captured well on the retrospective tribute album, *For Art's Sake* (1998). In his sleevenote, Verve producer Guy Eckstine recalls Porter as being like a "tightly wrapped package", and combining "great songwriting, mellifluous tone, superior soloing skills, and dynamic live performance". All this is evident on the album. Porter's style mixes the melodic energy of his jazz background with the funky, rhythmically tight licks of the smooth-jazz artist. Eckstine notes that this funk-jazz amalgam once led to Porter being dubbed "Maceo Coltrane" – James Brown's alto player Maceo Parker plus jazz giant John Coltrane.

Despite charges of blandness from critics, crossover has introduced many new listeners to jazz. The players mentioned here have all helped to bring improvised music to a wider audience, as well as to establish and develop the role of the saxophone in popular music as a whole. For this work they more than deserve their places in this collection of jazz saxophone greats.

EUROPEAN VOICES

*JAZZ CEASED TO BE A PURELY AMERICAN MUSIC LONG AGO,
BUT ALMOST EVERYONE CONTINUED TO PLAY IT WITH AN
AMERICAN ACCENT. IT WAS NOT UNTIL THE LATE SIXTIES
THAT A RANGE OF DISTINCTIVELY EUROPEAN JAZZ – OR JAZZ-
TINGED – STYLES BEGAN TO EMERGE.*

*Three albums from the burgeoning
European jazz scene: Bobby Jaspar
(Belgium), Gianluigi Trovesi (Italy) and
Pedro Iturralde (Spain).*

It is within French jazz that one finds some of the earliest evidence of European voices establishing themselves on the saxophone. The contributions which André Ekyan (1907-72) and Alix Combelle (1912-78) made to the musical genius of Django Reinhardt in the late 1930s are clearly informed by their literate enthusiasm for such American masters as Johnny Hodges, Benny Carter and – above all – Coleman Hawkins. One of the indispensable swing recordings – 'Crazy Rhythm' cut by Reinhardt, Carter and Hawkins in Paris in April 1937 – finds altoist Ekyan and tenorist Combelle preparing cultured pathways for the elegance and bite of their American confrères.

A more expansive relation to the American tradition distinguishes the work of the Frenchman Barney Wilen and the Belgian, Bobby Jaspar (1926-63). A key figure in the evolution of European jazz in the 1950s – and one of the finest flautists in jazz – Jaspar dreamed initially of marrying aspects of Warne Marsh and Stan Getz in his work. Following emigration to the US he fell under the spell of Sonny Rollins. As shown on *At Ronnie Scott's* (1962) which he shared with fellow Belgian, guitarist René Thomas, Jaspar's eventual maturity on tenor was such that he could sublimate the rhythmic clout and harmonic acuity of Rollins into lengthy, supple and melodic lines of his own.

Barney Wilen (1937-96) first came to international attention through his playing with Miles Davis on the 1957 *Lift To The Scaffold* film soundtrack recording. A year later he made *Jazz Sur Seine*, a lovely blend of Reinhardt-like swing, blues and New York bop, with Milt Jackson on piano, drummer Kenny Clarke and the Senegalese percussionist Gana M'Bow. After accompanying Davis on an extensive European tour, Wilen appeared at the

Newport festival in 1959. As with Jaspar, the importance of Young and Rollins for Wilen's work of this time is clearly evident. However, Wilen was always a saxophonist in quest of his own voice.

In the late 1960s that quest led Wilen to free jazz and jazz-rock, encounters with Indian music and the making of a cult album dedicated to Timothy Leary. Later, the hard bop revival of the mid 1980s saw the measured intelligence and drive of Wilen's early achievements back in fashion. However, in retrospect the larger part of Wilen's creative legacy in France is to be found in the openness of attitude which he displayed in the 1960s.

It is this openness of attitude which characterises representative albums of the 1970s and 1980s by François Jeanneau and Michel Portal (both b. 1935), two of the leading French saxophonists of Wilen's generation. Recorded in 1977 by the Coltrane-influenced Jeanneau, *Ephemere* is an atmospheric album of diverse originals, including creative use of electronics, while *Turbulence* (1987) is a typically wide-ranging affair from the genre-crossing Portal. A further point to make about the creative legacy of Wilen is that the extensive research trip which he made in Africa at the end of the 1960s could be seen to presage much of what was later to be experienced there by one of France's most exploratory contemporary players, Louis Sclavis (b. 1953).

In the mid-to-late 1990s Sclavis recorded a brace of melodically and rhythmically arresting albums for Label Bleu – *Carnet De Routes* (1995) and *Suite Africaine* (1999) – which documented the African tours he had undertaken with bassist Henri Texier, drummer Aldo Romano and photographer Guy Le Querrec. Like Jeanneau and Portal, Sclavis is a multi-instrumentalist, with a distinctive voice on soprano and bass clarinet, often expressed in ostinato figures. The more abstracted European aspects of his approach are documented on such ECM albums as *Rouge* (1991) and *Les Violences De Rameau* (1995-96).

Embracing distinctive aspects of local atmosphere and culture, the work of Jeanneau, Portal and Sclavis offers a stimulating variety of perspectives on the question of how a European saxophonist might develop a voice redolent of something more than familiarity with the American tradition. Sclavis has spoken, for example, of wanting to create an imaginary folklore, integrating the sophistication of contemporary jazz and archaic Mediterranean melodies, the moods of music hall and concert stage. In Portal, the melodies of European folk music can merge with the ultra-disciplined dynamics of contemporary classical composition, within rhythms and textures which at times conjure images of North Africa.

Equally representative here are the Italian multi-instrumentalist Gianluigi Trovesi, Frenchman André Jaume and the Spanish tenorist and sopranist Pedro Iturralde. Trovesi (b. 1944) brings the folk melodies of his country into creative relation with the sort of jazz that can take its emotional temper from both early Ornette Coleman and late Coltrane, as well as the sort of pensive mood one might associate with singer Paolo Conte or film director Federico Fellini. The poetry of his clarinet playing, especially, is evident in his wide-ranging duos with accordionist Gianni Coscia on the ECM recording *In Cerca Di Cibo* (1999). Like Trovesi, the Marseilles-born multi-instrumentalist André Jaume (b. 1940) has worked in many contexts. His medium-weight tenor fluency is well captured on the aptly named 'Mediterranean Blues', from *Iliade* (1996), where his measured obbligatos serve some impassioned, at times Arab-inflected vocal invocations to the spirit of "la grande bleue".

Louis Sclavis, one of the most important bass-clarinet innovators since Eric Dolphy, is also a gifted saxophonist.

Born in the northern Spanish town of Falcas, Pedro Iturralde (b. 1929) is in part a harmonically sophisticated hard bopper. He once held his own with such a master of this genre as pianist Hampton Hawes, as documented by *Pedro Iturralde Quartet Featuring Hampton Hawes* (1968, Spanish Blue Note). However, Iturralde's lasting claim to fame lies in his response to the seminal inspiration of Miles Davis's and Gil Evans's *Sketches Of Spain* and Coltrane's *Olé* albums. The modally-oriented, jazz-meets-flamenco albums which he made with guitarist Paco de Lucia in 1966-67 are striking examples of Iturralde's dramatic mixing of the spirit of jazz and blues with the Andalusian flavour of what Federico Garcia Lorca called cante jondo (deep song) and the duende.

Peter Brötzmann (b. 1941), from Germany, was an early member of pianist Alex von Schlippenbach's Globe Unity Orchestra; his contributions to

Pedro Iturralde made a fruitful connection between modal jazz and Spanish flamenco. The Ganelin Trio began as a barely-tolerated underground band in Soviet Russia, while the Swede Mats Gustafsson developed solo free improvisation.

his own *Machine Gun* (1968) and trumpeter Manfred Schoof's *European Echoes* (1969) gave rampaging notice of the huge saxophone sound and relentless, blatting "power play" that would mark much of his subsequent work. The 1971 live album *The Message* revealed the more variegated inclinations of Dutchman Willem Breuker (b. 1944). A more than capable saxophonist and multi-instrumentalist, Breuker's free-jazz energy is often leavened by a knowing admixture of diverse European popular melody and theatrically realised structure, the whole rinsed in the sort of humour that can recall the irony of Kurt Weill – to whom the Dada-esque Breuker is often compared.

Undoubtedly, free jazz of the 1960s and beyond did much to stimulate European saxophonists to discover and develop a voice of their own. Connoisseurs of freely improvised music in its most radical or extreme forms have no difficulty in distinguishing the layered lucidity of the tenor and soprano multiphonics of Britain's pioneering Evan Parker (b. 1944) from the Slavic keening of Russia's Vladimir Rezitsky (b. 1944) and Vladimir Chekasin (b. 1947) or the fragmented, volatile yet poetic eruptions of Swedish multi-instrumentalist Mats Gustafsson (b. 1964). Gustafsson's *Impropositions* (1996), released as a beautifully designed and illustrated 80-page CD/book, exemplifies the solo ambitions and achievements of a form of music-making which has also engendered much organically conceived collectivism – as on the legendary *Karyobin* recording of 1968 by the Spontaneous Music Ensemble of Kenny Wheeler, Evan Parker, Derek Bailey, Dave Holland and John Stevens.

Whatever the nature of free jazz, the question of its origin and impact is a complex matter. For example, did free jazz begin with Ornette Coleman, or the West Indian, British-domiciled Joe Harriott (1928-73)? Harriott was an urgent, spiky yet lyrical altoist whose *Free Form* (1960) and *Abstract* (1962) reveal an almost painterly treatment of free-flowing dynamics, tonalities and tempi. Or should the origins of free jazz be traced further back, past Cecil Taylor, Steve Lacy and Paul Bley to the more even-tempered music (in several senses of the term) which pianist Lennie Tristano improvised with saxophonists Warne Marsh and Lee Konitz at the end of the 1940s?

For German trombonist Albert Mangelsdorff, writing in 1963 in the album sleevenote of the appropriately titled *Tension*, freedom in jazz meant the possibility of going forward while reserving the right to reference all periods of the music. The contributions which his post-bop compatriots Günter Kronberg (alto), Heinz Sauer and Gerd Dudek (tenor) made to Mangelsdorff's wide-

ranging music on albums like *Tension* and *Birds of Underground* (1972) reveal a congruent sensitivity to the many expressive possibilities available both on and around the Coltrane/Coleman/ Dolphy axis of jazz saxophone.

Much the same point applies to the Polish altoist and multi-instrumentalist Zbigniew Namyslowski (b. 1939). Namyslowski first came to international attention through *Lola* (1964) and *Astigmatic* (1965), key records of Polish modern jazz. The latter was made with two other outstanding Polish musicians: pianist and composer – and leader – Krzysztof Komeda (1931-69) and trumpeter Tomasz Stanko (b. 1942). Aware of the jazz potential within the folk melodies of his native land, Namyslowski has always maintained that jazz must nevertheless retain a strong core of American rhythm, and spent some time in the US in the late 1970s. In his finely crafted and characterful music a poetic feeling for the lilting melodies and staggered rhythms of the Polish folk tradition can sit happily next to a (respectfully) humorous reading of a piece of Americana like 'Ol' Man River', as heard on *Lola*, or an up-tempo jazz-rock workout.

Other European saxophonists who have distinguished themselves in jazz-rock include the German Klaus Doldinger (b. 1936) whose group Passport made one of the best albums in that genre of the 1970s, *Cross Collateral* (1974), and the British multi-instrumentalist Barbara Thompson (b. 1944). Thompson's work with her jazz-rock group Paraphernalia has reached a wide audience, although not as wide as her writing and playing for the 1990s British TV drama series *A Touch Of Frost*. Less well known, unfortunately, are such rolling, relaxed pieces of hers as 'Blues For Adolphe Sax' (1978) which

Barbara Thompson and Don Rendell (far left), top British saxophonists of different generations. Veteran Austrian saxophonist Hans Koller (sleeves, centre and right) survived the Nazi period and emerged as a post-war leader. Hungarian guitarist Attila Zoller and Algerian-born pianist Martial Solal (above) are two further important figures in European jazz.

she recorded as a single for a small label with the much-respected British tenorist and multi-instrumentalist Don Rendell (b. 1926).

The sort of consciously conceived diversity that one finds in Namyslowski is also to be heard in the work of such accomplished Central European saxophonists as Wolfgang Puschnig, Florian Bramböck, Andy Sherrer and Harry Sockal – plus a healthy dose of high-energy, free-jazz anarchy and humour. Over the past two decades these players – "with Dolphy and Ellington marching alongside" – have contributed much to the eclectic, genre-spanning music of Mathias Rüegg's Vienna Art Orchestra. Such material that distinguishes the VAO's three-volume *20th Anniversary 1977-1997* (1997) is rich testimony to the maturity of contemporary European jazz.

If the music of Rüegg's mainly Austrian orchestra might be seen as "post-

Altoist Mike Osborne (above) and baritone saxophonist John Surman (right) made up two-thirds of the innovative electro-acoustic trio SOS.

modern" in its often quicksilver eclecticism, the work of Austrian multi-instrumentalist Hans Koller (b. 1921) exemplifies the structured, tradition-conscious yet innovative freedom of expression which European saxophonists have been able to achieve within the gradual and diverse evolution of post-bop modernism. Koller was one of the leaders of post-war jazz in Austria and Germany, and his early, Tristano-school tenor work could evince a beautifully weighted sense of tone, time and line, as on the title track of *Some Winds* (1955). A decade later Koller made *Zo-Ko-So* with Hungarian guitarist Attila Zoller and French-Algerian pianist Martial Solal. The album is one of the classic recordings of modern chamber jazz, and its many qualities led producer Joachim Ernst Berendt to speak in his sleevenote of the courage these musicians had to be in jazz what they were born to be in life: Europeans.

Recorded in 1962, *Multiple Koller* is another classic, this time a tenor and piano quartet, with Koller's tenor sound much fuller than in the 1950s. The music features a range of both poised reflections and swinging, blues-charged Koller compositions, reflecting his interests in painting and poetry as well as an appreciation of such modern jazz masters as Charles Mingus and Eric Dolphy, Oscar Pettiford (an old playing partner) and Zoot Sims. With some overdubbing of Koller's tenor, parts of the record presage the rhythm-section-less approach of *Out On The Rim* (1991), a representative example of Koller's more abstract latter-day work, often on soprano. The record closes with the bonus of a lengthy live tenor duet with Warne Marsh from 1984.

Few if any saxophonists have made more creative use of multitracking than the English multi-instrumentalist John Surman (b. 1944), in both recording and live situations, and including extensive use of loops. Surman first came to international attention with the Mike Westbrook Concert Band with which he won the Best Soloist award at the 1968 Montreux Jazz festival. Americans as diverse as Charlie Parker and Eric Dolphy, John Coltrane and Harry Carney have meant much to him. However, as shown on his own *How Many Clouds Can You See?* and British guitarist John McLaughlin's *Extrapolation* (both 1969), Surman's playing was distinguished early on by the

sort of combination of (structured) free-jazz energy and limpid lyricism which speaks in large part of a European sensibility.

One of Surman's many achievements, from the late 1960s onwards, has been his expansion of the baritone's expressive register. The variety of tone colour, dynamics and rhythmic interplay in the rhythm-section-less 'Bouquet Garni' (from *Jazz in Britain 1968-1969*) documents the fine understanding Surman shared at this time with two other distinctive British saxophonists, altoist Mike Osborne (b. 1941) and tenorist Alan Skidmore (b. 1942). Their understanding would soon be developed in the all-saxophone SOS trio where Surman's interest in church chorales and organ fugues is at times clear.

The richness of saxophone talent which emerged in Britain at this time included multi-instrumentalists Stan Sulzmann (b. 1948), whose mature, fully-rounded qualities as both saxophonist and flautist are to the fore on British pianist Dave Saul's *Reverence* (1999), and Trevor Watts (b. 1939). Watts moved from an early and intense involvement with free jazz to make eventual hypnotic use of extended riffs in the richly textured and strongly rhythmic work of his Moiré Music ensemble, as on *A Wider Embrace* (1993) on ECM.

Established by Manfred Eicher in 1969, the Munich-based ECM label has done a considerable amount both to document and to help develop European sensibilities in jazz. *On Reflection* (1979) was John Surman's first – and all-solo – recording for the label. Since then he has appeared on several diverse quartet albums with, among others, Czech bassist Miroslav Vitous and Norwegian vocalist Karin Krog, led the fine quartet of his own – with pianist John Taylor, bassist Chris Laurence and drummer John Marshall – which can

Three items from British saxophonist John Surman's early career: with Mike Westbrook's Concert Band; as leader of a group largely composed of Westbrook players; and in a collaboration with composer-arranger John Warren.

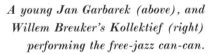

A young Jan Garbarek (above), and
Willem Breuker's Kollektief (right)
performing the free-jazz can-can.

be heard on *Stranger Than Fiction* (1993), and recorded the songs of John Dowland with English early-music vocalist John Potter.

Surman's mastery of baritone and soprano saxophone, bass clarinet, recorder and looped synthesised patterns has distinguished a variety of albums, such as the solo *Withholding Pattern* (1985). So has the tonally rooted, sometimes Vaughan Williams/Frank Bridge-like aura of his compositions, as on *Proverbs And Songs* (1998), featuring organ and choir, and *Coruscating* (1999), which premiered Surman's writing for string quintet.

At the same time, he has continued to participate in projects of a more spontaneously improvised nature: a 1991 session with pianist Paul Bley, bassist Gary Peacock, and drummer Tony Oxley yielded two albums, *Adventure Playground* and *In The Evenings Out There*. Here can be discerned distant echoes of the free-flowing world of The Trio, the explosive group which Surman co-led two decades earlier with Barre Phillips (bass) and Stu Martin (drums).

Surman's role in the development and establishment of a fully European jazz aesthetic on the saxophone has been matched by only one other musician of his generation: his fellow ECM recording artist, the Norwegian Jan Garbarek (b. 1947). Together with such partners as guitarist Terje Rypdal, pianist Bobo Stenson, electric bassist Eberhard Weber and drummer Jon Christensen, Garbarek has created an increasingly broad-based yet intensely poetic music. Aspects of his work, such as the liquid soprano treatment of an old Norwegian folk song on *Folk Songs* (1979) with American bassist Charlie Haden and Brazilian guitarist Egberto Gismonti, can recall the folk-tinged aura of much of the cool-school work of Swedish altoist Arne Domnérus (b. 1924) and his compatriot, the great baritonist Lars Gullin (1928-76).

However, other aspects of Garbarek's work, as on the ground-breaking *Afric Pepperbird* (1970) or *Witchi Tai To* (1973), feature the hotter, high-energy voice which he developed early on from the stimulus he had received as a teenager from John Coltrane and Albert Ayler, Pharoah Sanders and Archie Shepp – as well as from the excellent Swedish multi-instrumentalist, Bernt Rosengren. Rosengren (b. 1937) played high-quality Swedish hard bop

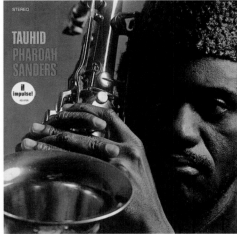

CHAPTER TWENTY-TWO

Pharoah Sanders, a strong US influence on the European free-jazz scene.

in the latter half of the 1950s, and was a member of the 1958 Newport International Youth Orchestra. He went on to contribute atmospheric tenor to Krzysztof Komeda's 1962 soundtrack for Roman Polanski's film *Knife In The Water* (reissued in 1996 as part of Komeda's *Crazy Girl*). In the 1970s Rosengren recorded exploratory albums with Lars Gullin, Don Cherry and Maffy Falay's Turkish-Swedish band Sevda: *Notes From Underground* (1973) is a fine example of his post-Coltrane, folk-tinged Nordic jazz.

Recently, Rosengren has won the attention of a new jazz audience through his contributions to Tomasz Stanko's *Litania* (1997), a sextet reworking of the music of Komeda. Also deserving mention here is the Swede Börje Fredriksson (1937-68). His album *Progressive Movements* (1962-65), with its blend of Coltrane-like authority and folk elements, intimates much of what Garbarek would later bring to more refined (and much less directly swinging) synthesis.

Keith Jarrett has said that he has never heard a better saxophonist than Garbarek. The multi-instrumentalist contributed to such memorable Jarrett albums as *Belonging* and *Luminessence*, both in 1974, with the latter setting Garbarek's tenor and soprano against a string orchestra. Certainly, few players have evolved a more personal voice, whether on tenor or soprano. Only the alto work of the Danish-Congolese John Tchicai (b. 1936) comes close to Garbarek's plangent power. Tchicai played a significant role in the New York Contemporary Five and New York Art Quartet of the early-to-mid 1960s, but

Bobby Wellins (above) has one of the most beautiful and distinctive tenor sounds in jazz. Socttish saxophonist and composer Tommy Smith (right) is pictured at the Cheltenham jazz festival in 1999.

his sculpted intensity is best captured on albums such as *Real Tchicai* (1977).

Allied to Garbarek's scrupulous approach to factors of (highly vocalised) tone and (reflective) time, space is a key element in the Norwegian's mature aesthetic. Some may prefer more notes than those to be heard in the slowly-unfolding, questing melodies of the wind harp-assisted *Dis* (1976), the solo *All Those Born With Wings* (1986) or *Officium* (1993), a million-selling collaboration with The Hilliard Ensemble, Britain's early music vocal specialists. They could turn to *Electronic Sonata For Souls Loved By Nature* (1969) or *Triptykon* (1972). The former is a vibrant document of Garbarek's apprentice years with George Russell, the latter a lyrical example of the fluid free jazz which Garbarek created in the early 1970s with fellow Norwegian Arild Andersen on bass and the Finnish Edward Vesala on drums, and with Norwegian poet Jan Erik Vold sometimes guesting in concerts.

Something of the spirit of Garbarek's border-crossing work, such as that heard on *Song For Everyone* (1984) with Indian violinist Shankar or *Madar* (1992) with Tunisian 'ud virtuoso Anouar Brahem, can be discerned today in Scandinavian saxophonists as diverse as Norway's Tore Brunborg, Bendik Hofseth and Karl Seglem, Finland's Juhani Aaltonen and Eero Koivistoinen and Sweden's Jonas Knutsson and Joakim Milder – the last-named featuring on Tomasz Stanko's *Litania* (1997).

Garbarek's example has been of particular importance for England's Andy Sheppard (b. 1957), as is apparent on *Inclassificable* (1994) and *Learning To Wave* (1998), and Scotland's Tommy Smith (b. 1967). Smith's recent output ranges from the Ellington-Strayhorn tribute *The Sound Of Love* (1997) and

Blue Smith (1999), which includes some driving contributions from guitarist John Scofield, to the more European-sounding *Azure* (1995), an album dedicated to the painter Joan Miró, and *Gymnopédie* (1997). This last features saxophone and piano readings of a variety of pieces in the modern classical vein, including work by Satie and Bartók, and two of Smith's own concertos for saxophone and piano.

While *Gymnopédie* may bring to mind the classically trained English saxophonist John Harle (b. 1956) and such various excursions into jazz of his as the Ellington tribute *The Shadow Of The Duke* (1992), the overall blend of poetry and power in Smith's work serves to recall the achievements of Smith's compatriot, Bobby Wellins. Today, British jazz saxophone has many things to commend it: the spacious lyricism of ex-Loose Tubes member Ian Ballamy, as

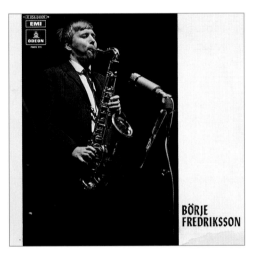
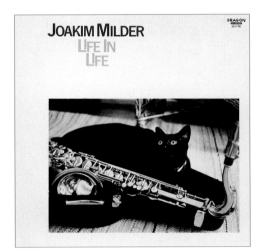

heard on *Food* (1998); the mature mix of material, including the poetry of Langston Hughes and the energy of a streetwise DJ, which can be enjoyed on *Modern Day Jazz Stories* (1996) by the Coltrane-fired Courtney Pine (b. 1964); or the passionate, jazz-meets-Africa quest of Alan Skidmore's *The Call* (1999), for example. However, it is possible to argue that the main event in recent British saxophone history has been the recording renaissance of Wellins.

Bobby Wellins (b. 1936) has never doubled up his instruments, remaining firmly committed to the tenor. Over the years he has cultivated an enigmatic, compressed yet open sound. Combined with his song-like phrasing, this can produce music as distinctive in emotional register as that of Surman or Garbarek. Wellins's work first revealed a simultaneously European and American-inflected synthesis of rhythmic mastery, harmonic sophistication and lyrical introspection in the Stan Tracey Quartet – around the time of Courtney Pine's birth. His latter-day mastery is evident on albums like *Birds Of Brazil* (1989), *Nomad* (1992), *Don't Worry 'Bout Me: Live At The Vortex* (1996) and *The Satin Album* (1996), a wonderfully weighted quartet reading of Billie Holiday's 1958 valedictory "with strings" recording.

Wellins has never ceased to explore the manifold potential of the saxophone, as evident on such rare and, unfortunately, deleted albums as *Jublilation!* (1978) and *Dreams Are Free* (1979), or the 1997 first-time issue of 1983's *Making Light Work*. Without recourse to the window-dressing of some of today's so-called world music, the art of Bobby Wellins reminds us that, whether it be European or American in flavour, the sound of the saxophone can speak to (and of) the deepest currents of our common humanity.

Zbigniew Namyslowski's quartet was the first Polish jazz group to tour western Europe. Swedish tenor saxophonists Börje Fredriksson and Joakim Milder developed a distinctive European style, initially from the approach of John Coltrane.

THE NEW SWING

THE VIGOROUS AND EXPRESSIVE SAXOPHONE STYLES OF THE SWING ERA AND BEFORE DID NOT DIE WITH THEIR CREATORS, THANKS TO A NEW GENERATION OF TALENTED PLAYERS. NOT ONLY DID THEY ADOPT THE IDIOM, THEY REVITALISED IT WITH THEIR OWN DISTINCTIVE IDEAS.

If there was ever such a thing as the golden age of jazz, it was the 1950s, the last decade in which virtually all the great figures of the music were still playing. The oldest had barely reached the age of 70 by the close of that decade, and most were in the prime of life. This meant that every style of jazz – from New Orleans street music to the new-born avant-garde – was alive and kicking at the same time. It was quite possible, as late as 1963, for a saxophone fancier to spend a few evenings club-hopping in New York and take in performances by, say, Bud Freeman, Coleman Hawkins, Zoot Sims, Hank Mobley and Eric Dolphy. The average jazz listener at the time would

Scott Hamilton, born 1954, has released a steady stream of albums and CDs since his early 20s. His following is particularly strong in Europe.

feel quite comfortable with the assortment of styles and enjoy each on its own terms. For some reason it was assumed that this happy state of affairs could go on indefinitely. New musicians would regularly turn up, introducing new ideas, while the established players would continue to mellow and ripen. Jazz would luxuriate forever in its rich and fluid diversity. But human mortality made this impossible. By the end of the century all the above were long dead, together with the early masters, the great swing players and most of the bebop generation. If every newcomer had been intent on being innovative and up-to-date, that would have been the end of swing and so on as living musical styles. Fortunately, this was not the case.

The story of tenor saxophonist Scott Hamilton (b. 1954) can serve as an introduction to the subject of what, for want of a better term, we can call neo-classical jazz.

Hamilton announced his arrival on the jazz scene at the age of 23 with his first album, *Scott Hamilton Is A Good Wind Who Is Blowing Us No Ill*, in 1977,

CHAPTER TWENTY-THREE

The ever-dapper Scott Hamilton in concert.

and caused an instant sensation. It was unusual then for young people of that age to be playing jazz of any kind, but this was almost beyond belief. Hamilton was playing pure swing tenor, and doing so with poise, assurance and understanding far beyond his years. There were times, at this early stage, when he could almost have been taken for a reincarnation of Ben Webster. Webster himself had died in 1973, Don Byas in '72, Paul Gonsalves in '74. One by one, the great figures were leaving the stage, and here was this neat, quiet, slightly dandyish young white man from Providence, Rhode Island, stepping into the breach. Middle-aged jazz fans everywhere fell upon him with cries of delight and hugged him almost to death.

The big question was, how had this phenomenon come about? The answer, in Hamilton's case and a number of similar ones that followed, features that stock character, the jazz-loving parent. Scott Hamilton's teenage years were the years of Beatlemania and the high tide of pop and rock, during which teenagers were subjected to unprecedented media and peer pressure to conform to a pop-fan stereotype. Yet Hamilton seems hardly to have noticed. His father, a painter, continually played jazz records of the classic era as he worked and the child absorbed the cadences of the music in the same way that he learned to speak. It became his natural idiom. After a brief period spent blowing a harmonica with a local blues band, he acquired a tenor saxophone at 16 and played his first gig on it a month later. He remains entirely self-taught.

In his career so far, Hamilton has recorded something in the region of 60 albums, either as leader or featured soloist. They document his progress from juvenile phenomenon to mature artist, and demonstrate that it is perfectly possible to grow artistically while working in an established idiom. The Scott Hamilton of today is instantly recognisable as himself, not just an amalgam of

Harry Allen's playing has matured impressively in recent years. Shown here are two particularly fine recorded examples. Alan Barnes leads an occasional quintet with trumpeter Bruce Adams.

influences. His solos are fluent, direct, adventurous and immensely varied in mood. He is probably the finest exponent alive of the slow-to-medium-tempo ballad, as he amply demonstrates on *Scott Hamilton Plays Ballads* (1989).

As with all music, Scott Hamilton's playing sounds best when experienced in person. He is also a phenomenally consistent player who rarely if ever seems to have an off night. He keeps his recorded output fresh by choosing different contexts in which to work. *Radio City* (1990) finds him in company with veteran pianist Gerry Wiggins; for *East Of The Sun* (1993), recorded in London, he has the rhythm section which regularly accompanies him when he visits Britain; a duet album with guitarist Bucky Pizzarelli, *The Red Door* (1998), is dedicated to the memory of Zoot Sims. There is even a Christmas album, *Christmas Love Song* (1997), with full string orchestra.

Hamilton, by virtue of his timely arrival and high profile, staked out the ground for what is now a sizeable tract of contemporary jazz performance, often referred to by the somewhat slippery term "mainstream". This is more a state of mind than a definable style. Mainstream jazz adheres to the repertoire of classic American song, composed mainly between World War I and the end of the 1950s, together with the blues and an occasional original piece composed on the old swing-riff pattern. It is neither antiquarian nor experimental, but in other respects it is inclusive, touching on the fringes of Dixieland in one direction and bebop in the other. Although it is vastly popular around the world, mainstream jazz tends to be un-newsworthy. It has no connection with fashion and therefore receives little publicity. One of its most articulate spokesmen and most eloquent practitioners is tenor saxophonist Harry Allen (b. 1966). Like Hamilton, he grew up in a house full of swing. His father had been a professional drummer and swing records provided the regular background to daily life. "When I was a little boy, my father would play jazz records for me each morning before I went to kindergarten," says Allen. "We'd listen to Benny Goodman, Louis Armstrong, Bunny Berigan, Ella Fitzgerald – 'Elafitz Gerald', as I thought then – and Duke Ellington." Although he was born the year before The Beatles released *Sergeant Pepper*, swing, he says, "sounded like more fun" than the music his contemporaries enjoyed.

His own playing reveals traces of the players he has listened to and admired since childhood, notably Stan Getz, Ben Webster, Flip Phillips and his father's boyhood friend, Paul Gonsalves. At the same time, and this

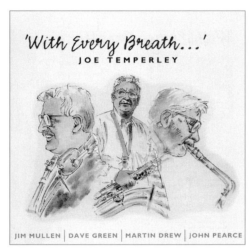

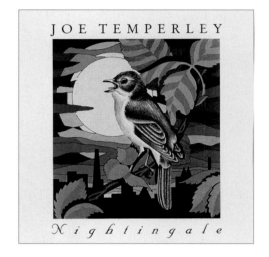

applies equally to Hamilton and many others, there are elements in his playing that would not have been there 50 years ago – little turns of phrase, hints of bebop harmony, touches of bossa nova, and so on. Swing, in his hands, remains a dynamic, growing idiom. Particularly impressive are two albums with the John Pizzarelli Trio, *Harry Allen Meets The John Pizzarelli Trio* and *Tenors Anyone* (both 1996). Pizzarelli's mellow guitar acts as the perfect foil for Allen's tenor and the light texture of the drum-less trio emphasises the fibrous warmth of his tone.

"There's always something fresh to do," Allen insists. "People ask, 'Why do you play in an older style?' But what's new and what's old? Most times what they call 'new' is just another version of John Coltrane, and he died the year after I was born. So if 30-plus years is 'new', how old is 'old'? Fifty years? Eighty years?" It is largely a question of delivery, he believes. A rugged, abrasive approach is perceived by some as somehow modern and "challenging" (a term of high approval among jazz publicists, although virtually devoid of meaning), while softness, warmth and a smooth surface are condemned as safe "easy listening".

In contrast to Hamilton, Allen received a formal musical education, specialising in jazz at Rutgers University. His predilection for swing was a source of puzzlement to his teachers and pity to his fellow students. They were convinced that, despite his obvious talent, he was bound for a life of unemployment, because nobody wanted to hear that old stuff. As it turned out, that old stuff was precisely what people did want to hear and, by his mid 20s, Allen was touring the world as a featured soloist. Many of his

Best known for his alto saxophone and clarinet playing, Alan Barnes has a special fondness for the baritone. Joe Temperley's tough-tender baritone is unfailingly moving.

Bob Wilber (above) pioneered the scrupulous revival of earlier jazz styles. Joe Temperley (right) is a founder-member of the Lincoln Center Jazz Orchestra, led by Wynton Marsalis.

contemporaries, he recalls in carefully neutral tones, seemed to be occupied mainly in playing for wedding parties in hotel ballrooms.

Scott Hamilton's generation was not the first to produce jazz musicians with a neo-classical bent. Bob Wilber (b. 1928) is of the generation which grew up with bebop, yet his career has been almost exclusively involved with styles of jazz which the bebop revolution seemed intent on sweeping away. A pupil of Sidney Bechet while still a teenager, Wilber plays mainly soprano saxophone, along with clarinet and occasionally alto. Few jazz musicians have moved with such intelligence and authority through the panorama of jazz history, creating music which is at the same time both contemporary and traditional. Among his many projects was Soprano Summit (1973-75), featuring himself and Kenny Davern on sopranos and clarinets. This band performed with such zest and high good humour that it regularly stole the show at festivals and concerts. The first task of music, as Wilber has often remarked, is to make people enjoy it. A later band, Bechet Legacy (1981-86), brought off the same trick.

Wilber has been pursuing his particular path for a long time, in the course of which he has developed a viewpoint which directly challenges what the American writer Gary Giddins calls "the tyranny of the new" in jazz.

"There's all this music called 'jazz' that was made since the beginning of the 20th century," says Wilber. "Luckily for us, somebody invented the phonograph at about the same time. So we have the music documented on records in the same way that classical music is documented in scores. This music is just as valid today as Mozart is, so why not play it, celebrate it?

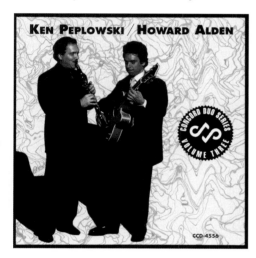

Ken Peplowski (two record jackets, left) combines sparkling clarinet playing with warm and breathy tenor saxophone.

Why just have it on old records?" Re-creation, says Wilber, can be a creative act in itself. He himself has a great gift for recreating the sounds and ambience of early jazz through transcription and through expert direction. His re-creation of Duke Ellington's first band for the film *The Cotton Club* (1984) was simply uncanny.

Playing baritone saxophone in that re-creation, taking the role of Harry Carney, was Joe Temperley (b. 1929), a musician whose rich tone and poetic turn of phrase have intensified with the passing years. Scottish-born, Temperley worked for a long time in the London profession, spending seven years (1958-65) with Humphrey Lyttelton's band before emigrating to the US. Subsequently he played in the bands of Woody Herman, Buddy Rich, Mercer Ellington and many others. He is a founder-member of Wynton Marsalis's Lincoln Center Jazz Orchestra, dedicated to performing jazz of all styles and eras. Temperley is a magnificent soloist – grave, sonorous and moving – and his playing has the timeless, universal quality that distinguishes jazz musicians who have passed beyond the narrow categories of style and period.

It is still comparatively rare to find players who can move easily from one jazz style to another, but their numbers are increasing. Among saxophonists, a notable example is Ken Peplowski (b. 1959). Although he is best known as a clarinet virtuoso, Peplowski also plays tenor saxophone, and occasionally alto. In appreciating the work of such a wide-ranging player, it is impossible to separate the roles of the instruments in any meaningful way.

Peplowski began playing the clarinet with polka bands in his native Cleveland at the age of nine (for money!). At 19 he was leading the saxophone section of the posthumous Tommy Dorsey orchestra, then under the direction of trombonist Buddy Morrow. During his travels with this band he met and became a pupil of Sonny Stitt. Settling in New York in 1981, he worked in Dixieland bands and in Peggy Lee's accompanying group, played with Bob Wilber and cornettist Ruby Braff, and spent two years with that remarkable singer, humorist and musical archaeologist Leon Redbone. It may have been a haphazard process, but it is difficult to imagine a more comprehensive and practical education in the jazz tradition, from ragtime to bebop – albeit in reverse order.

Peplowski's versatility is not achieved by adopting the mannerisms of various different styles. It is more a question of having a personal style so broad and comprehensive that it can embrace the most diverse material. A mere glance through the contents list of a typical Peplowski CD can be a bracing experience. Ancient ballads by Irving Berlin, Dixieland favourites, Ellington tunes, jazz themes by John Coltrane, and even Ornette Coleman – all emerge sounding as though they had been custom-made for the Peplowski treatment. This eclecticism has been a particular feature of his long and fruitful partnership with guitarist Howard Alden. Their two duet albums, *Ken Peplowski / Howard Alden* (1993) and *Encore!* (1995), recorded live at concerts, are both wonders of virtuosity and musical intelligence.

The teenaged Michael Hashim (b. 1956) was learning the alto saxophone at school in Geneva, in upstate New York, when he heard Johnny Hodges for the first time and was instantly smitten. He was lucky in his place of birth because, for reasons that no one can satisfactorily explain, New England has turned out to be the undisputed centre of latter-day swing. Hashim teamed up with bassist Phil Flanagan and guitarist Chris Flory in nearby Rhode Island and quickly developed his own distinctive and ebullient style. In 1977 he joined The Widespread Depression Orchestra, a nine-piece band dedicated to presenting swing music in an entertaining format. The band proved highly successful, scoring particularly well on European tours, and Hashim eventually took over the leadership. He later found that the outfit's jokey name was causing confusion among more literal-minded members of the public, and so dropped "Depression" from the title.

On leaving the orchestra Hashim became a freelance, gaining as much experience as possible by working with surviving members of the swing generation, such as drummers Jo Jones and Sonny Greer and trumpeter Roy Eldridge. By the beginning of the 1990s he had, like Hamilton and Allen, embraced the life of the travelling soloist. His engaging personality and good-humoured style of presentation have proved valuable assets in this career. He has made a number of superb recordings, in particular *Lotus Blossom* (1990), devoted to the compositions of Billy Strayhorn, *Transatlantic Airs* (1995), recorded in Britain with vocalist Tina May, and *Keep A Song In Your Soul* (1996), also featuring pianist Richard Wyands.

Plenty of young jazz players today begin by learning an instrument, play in student bands of various kinds, and gradually take to jazz in the process. Their jazz listening experience is often surprisingly patchy and sometimes almost non-existent. By contrast, all the artists mentioned here became musicians because they loved jazz. They were discerning listeners, sometimes at a bizarrely young age, before they seriously took up playing, and many of them continue to listen avidly to jazz of all periods. Thus, valuable contact is maintained and the music of the past continues to resonate in the music of the

Alan Barnes (left) duets with Charles
McPherson at London's 100 Club, 1989.

present. Among saxophonists, no clearer example could be found than
Britain's Alan Barnes (b. 1959), who firmly declares: "If I had not been a jazz
fan in the first place I would have had no interest at all in becoming a
musician." His stylistic range is quite phenomenal, from Dixieland to post-
bop, and must be attributed in some measure to an insatiable and lifelong
appetite for listening to jazz records. "It's a question of language, really," he
says. "Bebop is a language; you can't play a Charlie Parker tune and follow it
up with a swing-style solo, because it wouldn't work – like starting a sentence
in one language and finishing in another. Once you understand that, you can
play in any style you like and still be yourself."

Barnes plays all the saxophones, plus clarinet and bass clarinet, although
most of his work is on alto, baritone and clarinet, and he has won numerous
awards for these three. He has a wonderful capacity for suggesting a given
style without actually imitating anyone. Johnny Hodges, for instance, is a
great favourite with Barnes, and he could, presumably, produce a near-perfect
facsimile if asked. But what he actually does is to drop in a series of feathery,
soft-tongued notes in the Hodges manner as a discreet reference and leave it
at that. The rest of the solo will be pure Alan Barnes. The ability to inhabit a
style in this way, to include it as an active ingredient in one's own playing, is
a rare, valuable and largely unrecognised gift.

Jazz journalists and publicists (the terms are often interchangeable) have
made a fetish of innovation. This is quite understandable, given the constant
need to find something new to write about, but it gives rise to a curious
system of values in which novelty is confused with originality. Since the
number of original geniuses, in jazz or anywhere else, is strictly limited, it
follows that most of the revolutionary, mould-breaking, convention-defying
innovations with which we are regularly presented are more or less a waste of
everyone's time.

Most artists, even hugely talented ones, work best inside established forms.
Scott Hamilton, Harry Allen and the others mentioned in this chapter have
grown and matured while working in the idiom of latter-day swing. For them
it not a restriction but a liberation.

CONTEMPORARY TRADITIONALISTS

A JAZZ REVIVAL IN THE EARLY EIGHTIES WAS LED BY THE CLEAN-LIVING WYNTON AND BRANFORD MARSALIS. AS RECORD COMPANIES PROMOTED THE "YOUNG LIONS", MANY NEW PLAYERS ENJOYED OPPORTUNITIES UNAVAILABLE TO THEIR PREDECESSORS ONLY A FEW YEARS EARLIER.

Branford Marsalis (opposite, and above) has a remarkable all-round talent, as a jazz, classical and pop saxophonist, as a composer, as a musical director and as a record producer.

Many groundbreaking saxophonists of the last 20 years of the century emerged from the jazz "revival" of the early 1980s. Those highlighted here uphold stylistic, tonal and repertory traditions of the instrument and the jazz legacy, at the same time borrowing from contemporary musical trends. Most use largely acoustic ensembles, with the odd exception of an electric keyboard for effect and a variety of guitars. It is not unusual for them to record songs from the recent popular music repertoire.

One attribute evident in many contemporary players is their ability to extend beyond the normal highest note of the instrument, the standard high F. During the 1950s and 1960s, high-note specialists such as Sam Donahue and Eddie Harris rose above the crowd, often playing a full octave beyond the normal range. Although they were respected by their fellow musicians, this proclivity was often dismissed as a freakish stunt.

However, when the saxophone was assimilated into rock, funk and jazz-fusion during the late 1960s and 1970s, use of the high altissimo register grew steadily. The volume and intensity of electric instruments obliged saxophonists to play in a high, screaming register in order to cut above the backing and emerge as the soloist. Stylists such as David Sanborn, Michael Brecker and Grover Washington Jr were blazing new pathways in the development of altissimo artistry. This way of playing gradually became conventional for many of the newer players. While it grew out of rock- and R&B-influenced music, many contemporary jazz saxophonists have effectively assimilated high-note playing into more mainstream and modern jazz settings, even in the absence of electric instruments.

Joe Lovano (b. 1952) comes from a musical family, and was encouraged by his father Tony "Big T" Lovano, also a tenor saxophonist. Joe's warm, dark but fiery sound reflects the influence of Coleman Hawkins and Joe Henderson, along with a virtuosic command of the altissimo register and a fleet technique to match. His ballad playing reveals a reflective side, demonstrated on his unaccompanied treatment of 'Prelude To A Kiss' on *Rush Hour* (1995).

Lovano's special quality comes from his versatility both as an instrumentalist and as a purveyor of diverse musical styles and settings. The tenor is his main horn, but the alto and soprano, together with flute and alto clarinet, also figure in his work. Like several other saxophonists – Michael Brecker, Steve Grossman, David Liebman – he is also a talented drummer, and has often recorded on drums.

Lovano's eight recordings so far on Blue Note are set in a variety of musical contexts, with each CD taking a dynamic stylistic turn compared to the previous one. His 1991 debut *Landmarks* was recorded at the seasoned age

of 39, in contrast to the plethora of still-teething "young lions" debuting in their early 20s. It featured pianist Kenny Werner and guitarist John Abercrombie. Following quickly after that came *From The Soul* (1992) with the late New Orleans drummer Ed Blackwell. *The Wind Ensemble* (1993) was introduced on Universal Language and featured other 1960s stalwarts such as Charlie Haden, Steve Swallow and Jack DeJohnette. Soprano singer Judi Silvano and the angularly melodic trumpeter Tim Hagans also make important contributions to this group which continued to tour through the turn of the century.

Larger ensemble settings figure importantly in Lovano's output, which is not surprising considering his lengthy stints in the jazz orchestras of Woody Herman and Mel Lewis. *Rush Hour*, his album arranged and conducted by Gunther Schuller, includes strings and woodwinds in colourful, innovative settings for a variety of old ballads and new original compositions, while *Celebrating Sinatra* (1997) shows off his robust tenor largely supported by veteran orchestrator Manny Albam's charts. While this may have begun as a producer's idea for combining Lovano's Italian heritage with Sinatriana, the resulting music amounts to a high-quality tribute to the 20th century's most influential crooner.

Lovano also figures in jazz education, being a regular performer-clinician at schools and universities around the world. His ability to interpret and relate what he does to students is one that not all musicians share. He tells developing players of all ages to build technique directly from the music. Lovano also stresses that the melodies, rhythms and harmonies of specific pieces should help shape technical mastery, and urges musicians to question the practising of patterns for its own sake. All this is evident in his own playing: Lovano has an original melodic and rhythmic vocabulary which appears to have developed organically.

Another important saxophonist to emerge in the 1990s was Joshua Redman, a Harvard-educated son of "Texas Tenor" Dewey Redman. Joshua (b. 1969) toured briefly with his father in 1990-91 before winning in 1991 the prestigious Thelonious Monk Competition for young musicians, which helped jump-start his career as a leader.

Principally a tenorist, Redman also plays alto and soprano. He possesses a phenomenal technique, although his regular forays into the altissimo register are sometimes overdone, at the expense of the deeper, broader sound he achieves in the normal range. Like his father, Redman produces a full, bright sound reminiscent of Coleman Hawkins or Dexter Gordon. As an extremely emotive player he often plays extended versions of pieces, bringing out the dramatic side of the music and providing excitement for audiences.

Redman's recorded output features a wide variety of material and musical companions. *Wish* (1993) has him with Pat Metheny, Charlie Haden and Billy Higgins (not the first Redman to record with these two) and features music by Metheny, Stevie Wonder and Eric Clapton. A tour featuring that group followed the album's release. *Timeless Tales For Changing Times* (1998) is probably his most remarkable release to date. It's a collection of popular tunes, old and new, joined by connecting interludes. The supporting cast consists of Brad Meldau (piano), Larry Grenadier (bass) and Jorge Rossy (drums). Distinctive treatments of classics such as 'Summertime', 'Yesterdays' and 'How Deep Is The Ocean' are integrated with more recent songs like Bob Dylan's 'The Times They Are A-Changin' and Stevie Wonder's 'Visions' in a

seamless production. Redman has played duets with other tenor saxophonists, but without the traditional view of such meetings as battles or contests (as were the Kansas City "cutting sessions" of the 1930s). 'Leap Of Faith' from *Beyond* (1999) is a Redman composition that also features tenor saxophonist Mark Turner. Redman said, "We transcend the classic tenor-battle mode when we play together. It's not about competition. It's about communication. Everything on this track happened organically. We had no preconceived ideas and this was a first take." Redman guested on Joe Lovano's *Tenor Legacy* (1994) with similarly cordial results.

Mark Turner (b. 1965) is a contemporary of Redman's but a distinctively different player – although he does have an equally blinding control of the high register. Raised in California, Turner studied at the Berklee School Of Music in Boston, Massachusetts, in the late 1980s, befriending Redman at that time. Redman recalled, "We came up playing together. Over the years I've probably learned more from him than from any of my other peers."

Turner is one of the few – perhaps the only – modern saxophonist today to incorporate the linear fluidity of the great Warne Marsh with the more robust sounds of Joe Henderson and Joe Lovano. Marsh is an overlooked tenor

Joshua Redman, whose sudden and devastating appearance on the jazz scene caused a sensation, is pictured (above) performing in London during 2000 with bassist Reuben Rogers.

saxophonist whose best-known work was with Lennie Tristano and Lee Konitz; he was an innovative stylist in his own right.

Marsh's ease in seamlessly negotiating a four-octave range while emphasising the smooth trajectory of the melodic line has clearly left a lasting mark on Turner, whose blending of Marsh's relentless linearity and the slightly harder, robust tone with a distinctively more modern edge has brought together old and new in a highly individual way. A good example of this is Turner's rendering of Victor Feldman's ballad 'Falling In Love' on Tana Reid's *Looking Forward* (1994). While his tone maintains an open, airy intensity, his nimble-fingered negotiation of the harmony sets up a tension in this reflective piece that results in an eloquent interpretation.

Turner's three CDs for Warner Brothers – *Mark Turner* (1997), *In This World* (1998) and *Ballad Session* (1999) – are the best examples of his recorded work. *In This World* is particularly interesting for its inclusion of 'Lennie Groove', a melodically linear Turner composition that pays tribute to both Tristano and Marsh. His treatment of Henry Mancini's 'The Days Of Wine And Roses' is compelling in its unusually spirited tempo and the key-change in the second half of the tune. The album also features creative Fender-Rhodes piano playing by Brad Meldau, leaning on that instrument's introduction to jazz in the early 1970s.

Turner's voice is still developing in some ways, but he provides an important benchmark for the role of the saxophone in jazz. His clear acknowledgement of the contributions of past innovators is combined with a special ability to fuse that with today's music, giving renewed hope for the future of the art.

The talented and much celebrated saxophonist Branford Marsalis (b. 1960) has like Mark Turner blended together old and new influences both in his style and in his general approach. Marsalis's tributes to the 1950s sounds of Sonny Rollins and Charles Mingus, coupled with his work with Sting as well as other contemporary artists, show once again how versatile the saxophone can be in capable hands.

The oldest of the four musical progeny of renowned pianist and teacher Ellis Marsalis, Branford was born in Beaux Bridge, Louisiana, and as a

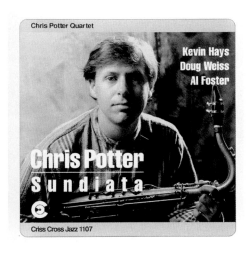

Two fresh and original saxophonists breaking through in the new century: Mark Turner and Chris Potter.

teenager was active in sports and many different forms of music. His main horns are soprano and tenor, although like many saxophonists he owns and plays them all. Sporting a big, full tone, he counts among his influences Sonny Rollins, John Coltrane and King Curtis. His own groups have borrowed stylistically from many idioms, but with the exception of Buckshot LaFonque – a funky ensemble he formed in the 1990s – he has mostly been featured in acoustic trios and quartets.

Marsalis's work as a sideman has been extremely varied. He started off with short stints in the big-bands of Art Blakey (on baritone saxophone) and Clark Terry (on alto) in 1980-81. He first came to prominence playing with his brother Wynton's quintet for three years from 1982. During this time he also played with Miles Davis, and then in 1985 joined the new band of English singer-songwriter Sting, which included keyboardist Kenny Kirkland, a long-standing colleague until his untimely death in 1998. Marsalis's association with Sting lasted on and off until 1988, around which time he appeared on the soundtracks of two Spike Lee films, *School Daze* (1988, which included a credible acting role) and *Mo' Better Blues* (1990), the latter scored by trumpeter Terence Blanchard.

In addition to his work in films, Marsalis hosted a jazz programme for National Public Radio during the late 1980s, and in 2000 presented a series *Jazz Legends* for BBC radio. His national celebrity was heightened when he joined *The Tonight Show* featuring Jay Leno on NBC TV in 1992 as musical director. After two years as a sidekick to the juvenile antics of the show's host, Marsalis felt it was time to move on. He formed his Buckshot LaFonque jazz group, incorporating the influences of 1960s R&B artists James Brown and Aretha Franklin, and Cannonball Adderley (who originally invented the name Buckshot Le Fonque as a recording pseudonym).

Some of Branford Marsalis's key recordings as a sideman are *Wynton Marsalis* (1981), Miles Davis's *Decoy* (1984) and Sting's *Bring On The Night* (1986). His own groups feature in a variety of recordings, starting with *Scenes From The City* (1983), his re-creation of a suite composed and recorded by Charles Mingus many years earlier. *Romances For Saxophone* (1986) has him exclusively on soprano performing a variety of late 19th century and early 20th century French classical pieces, effectively arranged by Michel Colombier for chamber orchestra.

A completely different side of Marsalis is exemplified on *Trio Jeepy* (1988), a blistering trio of tenor, bass and drums that takes up where the Sonny Rollins trio recordings at the Village Vanguard in 1957 left off. *Requiem* (1999) is a particularly moving tribute to the late Kenny Kirkland, the pianist who contributed so much to Marsalis's own recorded work.

Another remarkable technician, altissimo virtuoso and creative musician is multi-saxophonist Chris Potter (b. 1971). Born in Chicago, he was raised in South Carolina where as a precocious 15-year-old he was "discovered" by trumpeter Red Rodney. He worked with the Red Rodney Quintet, starting in 1989 and lasting until the leader's death in 1996, and at the same time earned a degree from the Manhattan School Of Music.

Equally at home on tenor, alto and soprano sax, Potter occasionally adds bass clarinet. While many players have mastered more than one horn, he clearly "owns" each instrument so completely that it is difficult to describe him as a tenor player or as an alto player. For instance, most tenorists give themselves away when playing alto. They tend to lose the "centre" and pitching of the sound in the top five notes of the normal register of the horn. These notes are unique to the alto, and often suffer in the hands of someone who is used to moving the air for a bigger, lower-pitch instrument. Not so with Potter. His talent and abilities enable him to adapt to each horn's idiosyncrasies. Very few if any saxophonists today are able to move between the three horns with such ease.

As well as his work with Rodney, Potter has long-term associations with the Mingus Big Band, on alto saxophone and largely playing in a section, with the occasional solo feature. With few big-bands around to provide a training ground for developing players, this association is no doubt an important one for Potter. The discipline of blending and interacting with other saxophonists in a section is rewarding in ways similar to that of playing with a rhythm section. The pursuit of a common musical goal in close proximity to one's fellow musicians is evident in both cases, and many of Potter's compositions and recordings exemplify this ensemble-oriented focus and sensibility.

Potter has also toured and recorded with Steely Dan, taking the mantle from key saxophone soloists Tom Scott, Michael Brecker and Pete Christlieb, all of whom have recorded in the past with this innovative band. On Steely Dan's most recent studio album, *Two Against Nature* (2000), Potter's improvised tenor solos add a distinctive new-jazz flavour to the group's recorded output, and are much more extended as well as being looser in scope than his predecessor's efforts.

Other notable recorded work by Potter includes Red Rodney's *Then And Now* (1992) which features his impressive rendering of Ralph Burns's 'Early

Discovered as a teenage prodigy, Chris Potter has equal virtuosity on all the saxophones and clarinets.

Autumn' among the largely bebop-themed recording. His own *Pure* (1992) provides an excellent cross-section of the saxophonist's talents. For example, there are blistering tenor versions – with bass and drums – of Mingus's 'Boogie Stop Shuffle' and Cole Porter's 'Easy To Love', but these are offset by his tranquil, reflective bass clarinet on Lennon & McCartney's 'The Fool On The Hill'. The recording has many sides and shapes, and features Larry Goldings moving between the Hammond organ and piano effectively to complement Potter's solo voice.

These five contemporary jazz saxophonists – Lovano, Redman, Turner, Marsalis and Potter – have borrowed from and upheld many aspects of the tradition. Their compositions also form an important part of their identity, creating a link with the great players who influenced and inspired them. Their mastery of the altissimo range and their overall technical skill have set new standards for future generations, and while technique in itself is not everything, these players clearly have it balanced within their own original forms of expression.

They have a wealth of experience as sidemen, but their contributions as leaders are distinctive and fresh. Their ability to honour and celebrate the traditional strongholds of the music, while redefining it with their own contemporary treatments and interpretations, point to a bright future.

MARK GILBERT **THE FUTURE OF JAZZ SAXOPHONE**

INTO A NEW CENTURY, AND DEBATE RAGES ON THE STATE OF JAZZ: IS IT DEAD, OR JUST SIMPLY MOTIONLESS? MEANWHILE, PLAYERS – WITH SOME TALENTED, INDIVIDUAL SAXOPHONISTS AMONG THEM – GET ON WITH MAKING THE MUSIC.

The outstandingly gifted David Murray (opposite) covers a vast range of jazz genres, from big-band to free. In 1991 he was awarded the prestigious Danish Jazzpar Prize. Albums pictured here are the Big Band live (1984) and Shakill's Warrior (1991).

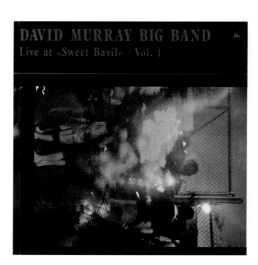

Saxophonist David Liebman is a veteran of the New York loft scene of the 1960s, of Miles Davis's 1970s fusion band, and of the jazz classroom. In a blindfold test organised for *Jazz Review* magazine in the summer of 2000 he was in a suitably millennial, end-of-an-epoch mood. In Liebman's well-travelled opinion, the work of jazz is largely done. "The history of jazz is over," he said during the test. "We had our 60 to 80 years of wonderful innovations, at an incredible rate, from Armstrong to fusion. This is a time of collection and gathering and of absorption, and also of spreading out to the world. Jazz may be the main influence on a new music, but jazz as we know it, that's over with."

The end of an age is invariably followed by a period of reflection, and if Liebman is right, then jazz has been in just such a phase these past few years. One only has to look to the wide array of jazz styles that now seem to co-exist in relative peacefulness.

The jazz scene has traditionally been split by any number of factions at any given time. But today, with no revolution or new thing in sight – and thus no threat to the established conventions – there's a sense of business-like tolerance rather than factional, missionary zeal. It's as if jazz has become a big, friendly festival programme offering something for everyone. A survey of the scene since the last major jazz development, the jazz fusion of the 1970s and 1980s, certainly suggests that the engine of forward motion in jazz has stalled or, at the very least, faltered.

With maturity comes self-awareness, and over the last 20 years jazz, along with other popular idioms, has reached a point where it has become acutely

conscious of its past, and in a way that was unthinkable in the progressive 1970s. In the early 1980s, as on a repentant, chastened morning after a bibulous adolescent party, jazz seemed to be taking a look back on its excesses – both of freedom and of flirtations with rock'n'roll juvenilia – and to be pulling in its stylistic horns.

In the United States this new awareness of the past was chiefly focused on the trumpeter Wynton Marsalis, and in Britain on the saxophonist Courtney Pine. In order to identify itself as a strong reaction against rock'n'roll in all its diverse forms, the so-called jazz revival of the 1980s consisted therefore in a substantial return to an earlier era – along with the dress and to a smaller extent the culture and manner.

It was at first chiefly a return to the music and suits of the hard bop

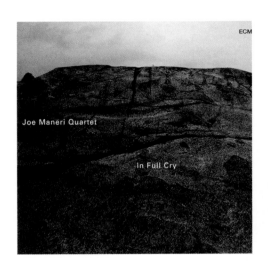

Joe Maneri (right) and his 1997 album (above) In Full Cry.

period of the late 1950s and the early 1960s. Happily, sartorial taste has moved along since then, but the musical effect of that outlook has turned out to be been wide-ranging as well as long-lived. Although the initially fanatical revivalism has subsided, it has left a distinct mark on the attitudes of many players in and around the jazz scene. As older styles came to be re-absorbed and given new validity by the Marsalis crowd, so that philosophy was in turn absorbed by those musicians who otherwise would have had a progressive, non-traditional approach.

The result was a curious series of "returns" of all kinds in the ensuing years. Fusion players, for example, began to pay tribute to the blues and funk of Eddie Harris and Maceo Parker. Greg Osby, one of the chief architects of the funky, urban, electrified sound of M-BASE in the late 1980s, signed up with Blue Note in the mid 1990s and began to make acoustic jazz records, including old standards such as 'Tenderly' in his repertoire. Wynton Marsalis dipped even further back into the repertory of jazz, until he arrived at Louis Armstrong, and began to present jazz like a classical concert form. And revivalism threatened to catch its own tail when such a recent grouping as The Brecker Brothers – only disbanded in 1982 – reconvened in 1991.

But fusion specialists like saxophonist Bill Evans and guitarist Scott Henderson continued almost regardless of the revivalism around them, pursuing the funky, megawatt muse set free by Joe Zawinul and Miles Davis during the 1970s. Compared with earlier decades, when with small exceptions jazz seemed to be in a perpetual state of forward motion with only very infrequent glances back over its shoulder, the late 1980s and the 1990s presented a fragmented landscape. This was not only the case in jazz, but also in popular culture generally.

This state of peaceful co-existence between genres old and new is frequently given a positive spin by calling it pluralism, yet one might just as

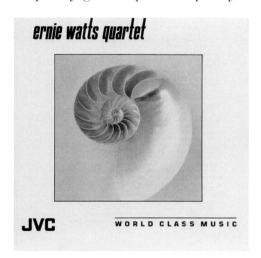 

Ernie Watts's 1988 album World Class Music, plus Roots And Fruits (1996) by Austrian saxophonist Wolfgang Puschnig.

easily refer to it as fragmentation or, more simply, a lack of direction. At the time of writing, in the absence of a unifying figure or movement, it seems that every kind of jazz is given what amounts to equal weight, resulting in a certain bland aesthetic correctness.

When art forms reach self-awareness, a kind of codification or inventory-taking of the constituent elements is likely to take place. Just such a process has happened apace in jazz over the last two decades. Nobody knows whether jazz retrospection or jazz education came first, but the two are linked and mutually perpetuating. Although Berklee college in Boston has been teaching jazz since at least the late 1950s, in the last 15 years there has been an explosion around the world of college courses and materials which will teach the receptive student to play in virtually any jazz style – as long as it's already been played.

There are two clear dangers here for creativity among musicians. The first is that teaching music will at some level involve the suggestion that there is a right way and a wrong way to play. The second danger is that in setting up a course to teach an idiom called "jazz", teachers must inevitably focus on the jazz that has happened.

David Liebman the pedagogue has some salutary thoughts about this. He points out that there is no case for ignorance, and that academia will never stifle the creative individual. Although he remains sceptical about the likelihood of a new and far-reaching revolution in jazz, Liebman does not rule out the advent of new stylists within the familiar idioms of the music. "There's always room for someone to have an individual voice," he says, "as there is always room for all the human beings on this planet to have different fingerprints. If there is a spark, it will be found. You cannot stamp out individuality; it will not be subsumed by an academic procedure."

Clearly, as the rest of this book has shown, the present period of reflection doesn't signify the end of the road for the reed in jazz. On the contrary, and as noted in the fusion chapter, the real saxophone is being played more now than the synthesised version, and probably more in general by jazz-inclined instrumentalists than in the 1970s, when the guitar and keyboard were in the ascendancy. One of the most highly touted newcomers is the young American James Carter. Like many avant-garde players before him, Carter is happy to be seen in the company of any of the 14 originally-patented members of the

`Bennie Wallace has a unique style, containing elements from several jazz eras. His albums shown here are Twilight Time, from 1985, and The Art Of The Saxophone, released in 1987.

saxophone family. On his *Chasin' The Gypsy* album (2000), alongside the commonplace bass, tenor and soprano instruments, Carter also makes use of the rare f-mezzo saxophone.

But while the instrument is evidently not going out of fashion, does the saxophone have any more to add to the language of jazz? Or is the future for jazz saxophone a long period of recycled and recombined swing, bop and free-jazz clichés? Where, if anywhere, are the new pioneers? There are plenty of record companies purporting to present ground-breaking players, but how well do these musicians measure up?

The gauging of novelty is a subjective matter. Perceptions of surprise are filtered through the ear of the beholder and governed by cultural context. Followers of Scott Hamilton will, for example, tell you that the saxophonist isn't just a Ben Webster clone. Like his younger colleague Harry Allen, Hamilton incorporates modern spices (though perhaps no more modern than Stan Getz) which give his supporters a frisson of excitement at just the level that their tastes will tolerate. However, those attuned to more challenging sounds may hear no such nuance of modernism in the music, and instead find Hamilton and Allen to be corny and conservative.

Many of the flavours of contemporary and recent saxophone playing have been comprehensively detailed in preceding chapters: the free playing of Evan Parker and Anthony Braxton; the funk and fusion of Eddie Harris, Michael Brecker and David Sanborn; the smooth jazz of Eric Marienthal and Art Porter; the young fogeyism of Scott Hamilton and Harry Allen; the particularly European interest in pastoral lyricism found at various points in Jan Garbarek, John Surman, Andy Sheppard and Tommy Smith; and the modern traditionalism of Chris Potter and Mark Turner. But a few more names have been floating around in recent times with tags such as "new" or "pioneering" attached, together with some others who, while unattended by claims of pioneering quality, do at the very least help to fill out a more complete picture of the contemporary jazz saxophone scene.

Within the fully avant-garde spectrum, Tim Berne, John Zorn and Joe Maneri received a good deal of attention in the 1990s. Free improvisation is associated indelibly with the cultural and political upheavals of the 1960s and 1970s. Its philosophy of the emancipation of harmony, pitch and instrumental roles stands like a musical analogue to the real business of politics. However, it has flourished anew in recent years, manifested in particular by the

Tim Berne, an uncompromising member of the avant-garde.

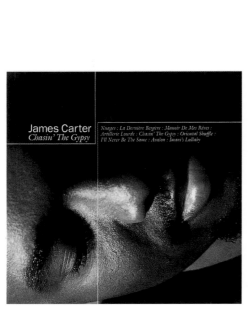

Greg Osby (right) in concert, 1996, and the remarkable, young, multi-talented James Carter (above).

activities of The Knitting Factory, a venue on New York's Lower East Side which also spawned a prolific record label.

Altoist Tim Berne (b. 1954) is one of the newer breed of avant-garde players who temper their free explorations with elements of composition – albeit highly angular ones. Berne is also keen to retain in his music the sense if not the substance of the raw, bluesy quality he enjoyed when listening to Stax and Volt recordings as a child. The saxophonist discovered the same mixture of earthy blues and free improvisation in his chief inspiration, Julius Hemphill, and in 1993 recorded *Diminutive Mysteries*, an album that largely consisted of Hemphill compositions – and also featured a bluesy if unlikely guest in David Sanborn.

Berne was himself a guest on John Zorn's *Spy Vs Spy* (1989), a tribute to the music of Ornette Coleman. Its atmosphere was typical of the exhilarating, punky, high-energy quality that Zorn (b. 1954) brings to avant-garde and free improvised material. The same approach acquired a special focus in Zorn's extraordinary work in the group Naked City in the early 1990s, when on albums such as *Grand Guignol* (1992) he produced thoroughly nasty, spiky little packets of compressed rage. Here were gruesome 20- or 30-second collisions of ranting alto saxophone, crashing speed-metal guitar, smooth lounge jazz, and caterwauling, blood-curdling vocals. Tying in with David Liebman's notion that jazz is finished, these musical glimpses were often described as post-modernist, mainly because they seemed to state that the only avenue left once all had been played was to produce burlesques of what had gone before. Liberal genre-crossing and a milder form of satire is also heard in some of the playing and writing of the Austrian saxophonist Wolfgang Puschnig, both in the Vienna Art Orchestra and in his set as leader, *Roots And Fruits* (1996).

Joe Maneri (b. 1927) is hardly a young radical, but he has belatedly been hailed for discovering a new angle on avant-garde saxophone playing. In contrast to Zorn and Berne he has a relatively reserved approach, the sort that usually attracts the description "chamber jazz". On the face of it, his

The adventurous and hugely influential Courtney Pine, who inspired a whole new generation of young jazz musicians.

nervy, burbling saxophone playing on albums such as *In Full Cry* (1997) and *Tales Of Rohnlief* (1999) appears little different from the pointillistic sounds produced by many free improvisers.

However, one of the causes of the celebration of Maneri is his claim to be playing microtonally – that is, playing notes in between the usual 12 semitones of the octave. Of course, a theory such as this might well earn immediate credibility in the jazz world, where the bent, in-between notes of the blues are considered a cornerstone of the music. In fact, Maneri's austere, icy sound couldn't be further from the intrinsic warmth of the blues, but it has the stark if one-dimensional beauty that can be found in the work of many similarly-styled players.

A notch inward from such uncompromising avant-gardists as Zorn, Berne and Maneri lies a school of players who soften the hard edges of the avant-garde by combining it with the mainstream. The style is typified by David Murray, Bennie Wallace and James Carter. These three saxophonists are essentially traditionalists in that they largely bypass fusion, undermining the certainties of swing and bebop with such avant-garde effects as squeals, screams, tonguing and random intervallic leaps.

David Murray (b. 1955) began as a disciple of Albert Ayler and his idiosyncratic freedoms. But by the 1990s, signed to the DIW label, Murray's early waywardness had abated to the extent that he was applying his unpredictable approach to standards, and even to the occasional electric funk setting. With the World Saxophone Quartet he also pioneered the concept of the modern unaccompanied saxophone group.

Bennie Wallace (b. 1946) emerged as a leader in the late 1970s on the Enja label with his album *The Fourteen Bar Blues* (1978) and later received considerable exposure through the Blue Note and Denon labels before subsiding into film work on the West Coast of the United States. His approach suggests again the influence of Ayler and also of Eric Dolphy, his basic blues licks rubbing shoulders with curious and unexpected explosions of apparently unrelated theatricality.

A very recent addition to the roster of traditionalists with a taste for avant-garde decoration is James Carter (b. 1969) who has shown an awareness of the continuing currency of post-modernism. On the three albums that he

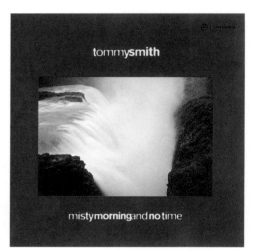

Tribute to Ornette Coleman by John Zorn and Tim Berne; David Liebman's collaboration with guitarist Pat Metheny; and some atmospheric Celtic jazz by Scotland's Tommy Smith.

recorded between 1998 and 2000, Carter moved apparently effortlessly from Dixieland, swing and free-jazz orthodoxies through a Django Reinhardt tribute to a set of funk grooves. His command of particular instrumental techniques is secure, and he has made a show of reorganising existing dialects and applying a strong sense of theatre.

Beyond the theatrical, and related to such contemporary traditionalists as Chris Potter and Mark Turner, is the large school of saxophonists which continues to work in the long shadow of John Coltrane and associated players such as Sonny Rollins, Joe Henderson and Wayne Shorter. Michael Brecker is prominent in this group, but others include Bob Berg (b. 1951), Jerry Bergonzi (b. 1950), George Garzone (b. 1950), Bob Mintzer (b. 1953), Bob Malach (b. 1954) and Bob Sheppard (b. 1957). All these players have done and continue to do sterling work in advancing the language mapped out by Coltrane. Prime examples include Jerry Bergonzi's *Lost In The Shuffle* (1998), George Garzone's *Fours And Twos* (1996), Bob Mintzer's *One Music* (1991) and Bob Berg's *Another Standard* (1996).

There are other, younger players who also show the enduring influence of Coltrane. On *Melaza* (2000), David Sanchez (b. 1969) works hard to find a novel intersection between Coltrane-type tenor saxophone and Latin rhythm. Courtney Pine (b. 1964) on *Back In The Day* (2000) lays soprano and tenor lines derived from Coltrane over retro funk beats, from Lee Morgan's 'The Sidewinder' onward. And Coltrane's own son, Ravi Coltrane (b. 1965), demonstrates a cooler, more oblique version of his father's style on *From The Round Box* (2000). Ernie Watts is another player whose yearning if sometimes

Britain's Andy Sheppard (left) covers everything from straightahead jazz to reggae in a highly personal style. Puerto Rican-born David Sanchez (below) combines high-energy bop with Latin rhythms.

overwrought tone has recalled Coltrane on several albums, including *The Ernie Watts Quartet* on JVC in 1988. For David Liebman, Coltrane was the last jazz musician to transform the music at every level, not just as a saxophone stylist but as a composer and conceptualist, and the existence of players such as these – a mere handful of the total number still under Coltrane's spell – offers sound confirmation of his diagnosis.

All the players discussed in this chapter have their dedicated audiences. But many who have been touted at various points as Important New Players could be seen more straightforwardly as musicians who recombine old material in relatively novel contexts – James Carter's avant-garde licks over funk basslines, for example – rather than saxophonists who are breaking new ground for their horn.

The saxophone's defining role in jazz is as a solo voice. In that sense, it is players such as Chris Potter and Mark Turner who are closest to developing a new voice for the saxophone, by demonstrably expanding the vocabulary of the instrument and widening its technical resources. Liebman may be right about the end of jazz as we know it. But Potter, Turner and the like have introduced a striking new dimension to playing over chord changes – a business that might have been considered as "over with" many years ago.

RECOMMENDED LISTENING

INDEX

ACKNOWLEDGEMENTS

"Master your horn, that's all you've got to do. And it's hard to do, you better believe that" COLEMAN HAWKINS *1967*

RECOMMENDED LISTENING

This is a list of recommended records, compiled by the contributors to this book. It is certainly not a complete discography; rather, it is designed to help your quest for new listening pleasures and to supplement the information to be found in the body of *Masters Of Jazz Saxophone*.

The saxophonists are arranged in alphabetical order. Shown first under each artist are any recommended recordings by them as leader, followed by any relevant work with other artists and leaders (noted as "with…"). Everything is arranged alphabetically.

Each record listing shows album title (*in italics*) or piece title ('In Single Quotes'). In brackets are given a date or dates, where available and/or relevant, and the record label. The date given is generally the date of the recording and/or original release. Occasionally (and, we hope, obviously) the date is a reissue date. The label given is usually for the most recent release, where available. Many records have been released on a number of different labels over the years, so be on the lookout for the same artist or for specific records on labels other than those noted. Now, open your ears.

George Adams
with Don Pullen:
Live At The Village Vanguard (1983 Soul Note)
with Gil Evans:
Little Wing (1978 DIW)

Pepper Adams
with Thad Jones:
Mean What You Say (1966 Original Jazz Classics)

Julian "Cannonball" Adderley
Live! (1965 Capitol)

Gerald Albright
Givin' Myself To You (1995 Atlantic)
Just Between Us (1987 Atlantic)
Live At Birdland West (1991 Atlantic)
Smooth (1994 Atlantic)

Harry Allen
A Little Touch Of Harry (1997 Mastermix)
Day Dream (1998 RCA)
Tenors Anyone (1996)
with John Pizzarelli Trio:
Harry Allen Meets The John Pizzarelli Trio (1996)

Gene Ammons
Boss Tenor (1960 Prestige)
In Chicago (1961 Prestige)
with Sonny Stitt:
Boss Tenors (1961 Verve)

Georgie Auld
with Charlie Christian:
The Genius Of The Electric Guitar (1939-41 Columbia)

Albert Ayler
Live In Greenwich Village (1966-67 Impulse)
Spiritual Unity (1964 ESP)

Alan Barnes
A Dotty Blues (1997 Zephyr)
with David Newton:
Summertime (2000 Concord)

Sidney Bechet
'Dans les Rues d'Antibes' (1952 Vogue) on *Salle Pleyel 31 January 52* CD (Vogue).
with Mezzrow-Bechet Quintet:
'Out Of The Gallion' (1945 King Jazz) on *King Jazz Volume 1* CD (King Jazz).
with New Orleans Feetwarmers 'Maple Leaf Rag' (1932 Victor) on *Complete Sidney Bechet Volumes 1 & 2 1932-41* CD (RCA).
with Red Onion Jazz Babies: 'Cake Walking Babies' (1924 Gennett) on *Clarence Williams 1924-36* CD (Classics),
with Spanier-Bechet Big Four: 'China Boy' (1940 HRS) on *Sidney Bechet 1940* CD (Classics).

Bob Berg
Another Standard (1996 Stretch)
Short Stories (1987 Denon)

Jerry Bergonzi
Lost In The Shuffle (1998 Double-Time)

Tim Berne
Diminutive Mysteries (1993 JMT)

Chu Berry
Chu Berry 1937-41 (Classics)
Giants of The Tenor Sax (Commodore)
with Spike Hughes, Fletcher Henderson, Cab Calloway:
Blowing Up A Breeze (1933-41 Topaz)
with Lionel Hampton:
Hot Mallets/The Jumpin' Jive (1937-39 Bluebird)

Arthur Blythe
In Concert (1977 India Navigation)
with Chico Freeman:
Luminous (1989 Jazz House)
The Unspoken Word (1993 Jazz House)

Florian Bramböck
with Vienna Art Orchestra:
20th Anniversary 1977-1997 (Amadeo/Verve)

Anthony Braxton
with Derek Bailey:
First Duo Concert (1974 Emanem)

Michael Brecker
Don't Try This At Home (1988 MCA/Impulse)
Michael Brecker (1987 MCA/Impulse)
Now You See It... (Now You Don't) (1990 GRP)
Tales From The Hudson (1996 Impulse)
Two Blocks From The Edge (1998 Impulse)
with Chet Baker:
You Can't Go Home Again (1977 A&M/Horizon)
with The Brecker Brothers:

The Brecker Brothers (1975 Arista)
Heavy Metal Bebop (1978 Arista)
Out Of The Loop (1994 GRP)
Return Of The Brecker Brothers (1992 GRP)
with Billy Cobham:
A Funky Thide Of Sings (1975 Atlantic)
with Chick Corea:
Three Quartets (1981 Warner Bros)
with Dreams:
Dreams (1968 Columbia)
with Hal Galper:
Speak With A Single Voice (1978 Enja)
with Hugh Marsh:
The Bear Walks (1986 veraBra)
with Pat Metheny:
80/81 (1980 ECM)
with Claus Ogerman:
Cityscape (1981 Warner Bros)
with Horace Silver:
Pursuit Of The 27th Man (1972 Blue Note)
with Steps Ahead:
Steps Ahead (1983 Elektra Musician)

Tina Brooks
True Blue (1960 Blue Note)

Peter Brötzman
Machine Gun (1968 FMP)

Marion Brown
Vista (1974 Impulse)

Don Byas
Walkin' (1963 Black Lion)
Jazz At The Philharmonic In Europe Vol 1 (1960 Verve)
with Budd Powell:
Tribute to Cannonball (1961 Columbia)

Harry Carney
with Duke Ellington:
Duke Ellington 1928 (Classics)

Benny Carter
All Of Me (1940-41 Bluebird)
Cosmopolite (1952-54 Verve)
Further Definitions (1961-66 Impulse)

James Carter
Chasin' The Gypsy (2000 Atlantic)
In Carterian Fashion (1998 Atalantic)
Layin' In The Cut (2000 Atlantic)

Arnett Cobb
Arnett Blows For 1300 (1947 Delmark)
Blow, Arnett, Blow! (1959 Prestige)

Ornette Coleman
Beauty Is A Rare Thing (1959-61 Rhino)
The Best Of The Blue Note Years (1965-68 Blue Note)
Body Meta (1975 Verve/Harmolodic)
Free Jazz (1960 Atlantic)
Friends & Neighbors (1970 BMG/RCA)
In All Languages (1987 Verve/Harmolodic)
Something Else! (1958 Original Jazz Classics)
Sound Museum: Hidden Man (1996 Verve/Harmolodic)
Tone Dialing (1995 Verve/Harmolodic)
with Joachim Kuhn:
Colors (1996 Verve/Harmolodic)
with Pat Metheny:
Song X (1985 Geffen)

John Coltrane
Ascension (1965 Impulse)
Ballads (1962 Impulse)
Blue Train (1957 Blue Note)
Giant Steps (1959 Atlantic)
A Love Supreme (1964 Impulse)
My Favorite Things (1960 Atlantic)
with Duke Ellington:
Duke Ellington And John Coltrane (1962 Impulse)
with Miles Davis:
Round About Midnight (1955-56 Columbia)
Milestones (1958 Columbia)
Kind Of Blue (1959 Columbia)
with Thelonious Monk:
With John Coltrane (1957 Original Jazz Classics)

Ravi Coltrane
From The Round Box (2000 BMG)

Alix Combelle
with Django Reinhardt:
Swing de Paris (1995 Charly)

Junior Cook
with Horace Silver:
Finger Poppin' (1959 Blue Note)

Bob Cooper
with Stan Kenton:
The Innovations Orchestra (1950-51 Capitol)
Retrospective (1943-68 Capitol)

Lol Coxhill
with Steve Lacy, Evan Parker:
Three Blokes (1992 FMP)

Sonny Criss
I'll Catch The Sun (1969 Prestige)
Portrait (1967 Prestige)

Ronnie Cuber
Love For Sale (1998 Koch)
with Three Baritone Saxophone Band
Plays Mulligan (1998 Dreyfus)

Eddie "Lockjaw" Davis
The Cookbook Vol 1 (1958 Prestige)
with Count Basie:
The Complete Atomic (1957 Roulette)
Standing Ovation (1969 Sequel)
with Oscar Peterson:
At Montreux 1977 (Original Jazz Classics)

Elton Dean
Newsense (1997 Slam)
with Soft Machine:
Third (1970 Columbia)

Paul Desmond
Easy Living (1964 Bluebird)
Like Someone In Love (1975 Telarc)
Paul Desmond And The Modern Jazz Quartet (1971 Columbia)
with Dave Brubeck:
Jazz At Oberlin (1953 Original Jazz Classics)
Jazz At The College Of The Pacific (1953 Original Jazz Classics)
Time Out (1959 Columbia)
with Gerry Mulligan:
Gerry Mulligan-Paul Desmond Quartet (1957 Verve)

Eric Dixon
with Count Basie:
L'il' Ol' Groovemaker (1963 Verve)

Eric Dolphy
Far Cry (1960 Original Jazz Classics)
Live At The Five Spot (1961 Original Jazz Classics)
Out To Lunch (1964 Blue Note)

Jimmy Dorsey
'Dorsey Dervish' (1936) on ASV
Pennies From Heaven CD.

Tommy Douglas
with Julia Lee:
Kansas City Star (1923-57 Bear Family)

Gerd Dudek
with Albert Mangelsdorff:
Birds of Underground (1973 MPS)

Paul Dunmall
Desire & Liberation (1996 Slam)

Teddy Edwards
with Milt Jackson:
At The Kosei Nenkin (1976 Pablo)

André Ekyan
with Django Reinhardt:
Swing de Paris (1995 Charly)

Booker Ervin
The Freedom Book (1963 Prestige)

Bill Evans
Push (1993 Lipstick)

Herschel Evans
with Count Basie:
The Original American Decca Recordings (1937-39 MCA GRP)
Basie Rhythm (1936-39 Hep)

Stump Evans
with Jelly Roll Morton's Red Hot Peppers:
'Wild Man Blues' (1927 Victor) on *Jelly Roll Morton 1924-26* CD (Classics).

Wilton Felder
with The Crusaders:
Those Southern Knights (1976 MCA)
with The Jazz Crusaders:
Freedom Sound (1961 Pacific Jazz)

Jimmy Forrest
Night Train (1951-53 Delmark)

Frank Foster
with Count Basie:
Easin' It (1960 Roulette)

Chico Freeman
Destiny's Dance (1981 Original Jazz Classics)
Luminous (1989 Jazz House)
The Unspoken Word (1993 Jazz House)

Kenny G
Duotones (1986 Arista)
Breathless (1994 Arista)
G-Force (1993 Arista)

Jan Garbarek
I Took Up The Runes (1990 ECM)
with Keith Jarrett:
Luminessence (1975 ECM)

George Garzone
Fours And Twos (1996 NYC)

Herb Geller
Herb Geller Quartet (1993 VSOP)
Plays The Al Cohn Song Book (1996 Hep)
That Geller Feller (1957 Fresh Sound)
You're Looking At Me (1997 Fresh Sound)

Stan Getz
Another World (1977 Columbia)
The Brothers (1949 Prestige)
The Complete Roost Recordings (1950-54 Roost)
Focus (1961) Verve
Getz/Gilberto (1963 Verve)
Pure Getz (1982 Concorde)
Sererity (1987 Emarcy)
Stan Getz With The Oscar Peterson Trio (1958 Verve)
The Steamer (1956 Verve)

Benny Golson
Tenor Legacy (1996 Arkadia)

Dexter Gordon
Go! (1962 Blue Note)
The Homecoming (1976 Columbia)

Wardell Gray
Memorial Volume 1/Volume 2 (1949-53 Original Jazz Classics)

Johnny Griffin
Way Out! (1958 Original Jazz Classics)

Lars Gullin
The EMI Years 1964-1976 (EMI)
Lars Gullin Vol. 2 (1953 Dragon)
Portrait Of My Pals (1964 Swedish EMI)

Mats Gustafsson
Impropositions (1997 Phono Suecia)

Scott Hamilton
After Hours (1997 Concord)
At The Brecon Jazz Festival (1995 Concord)
Christmas Love Song (1997 Concord)
East Of The Sun (1993 Concord)
Gene Harris/Scott Hamilton Quintet At Last (1990 Concord)
Plays Ballads (1989 Concord)
Radio City (1990 Concord)
Scott Hamilton Is A Good Wind Who Is Blowing Us No Ill (1977 Concord)
with Bucky Pizzarelli:
The Red Door (1998 Concord)

John Handy
At Monterey Jazz Festival (1965 Koch)

Joe Harriott
Abstract (1961-62 Redial)
Free Form (1960 Redial)

Eddie Harris
The Electrifying Eddie Harris (1967-68 Atlantic)

Michael Hashim
Guys & Dolls (1992 Stash)
Keep A Song In Your Soul (1996 Hep)
Lotus Blossom (1990 Stash)
Transatlantic Airs (199533 Records)

Coleman Hawkins
Bean & The Boys (Fantasy/Prestige)
Coleman Hawkins 1943-44 (Jazz Chronological Classics)
Coleman Hawkins Retrospective 1929-63 (BMG/RCA)
Coleman Hawkins, Verve Jazz Masters 1944-62 (Verve)
Hawk In Europe 1934-37 (ASV Living Era)
Today & Now (1962 Impulse)
Ultimate Coleman Hawkins (Verve)

Tubby Hayes
Down In The Village (1962 Redial)

Jimmy Heath
Really Big! (1960 Original Jazz Classics)

Joe Henderson
Inner Urge (1964 Blue Note)
Lush Life (1991 Verve)

Ernie Henry
with Thelonicus Monk:
Brilliant Corners (1956 Original Jazz Classics)

Johnny Hodges
with Duke Ellington:
Duke Ellington 1928-29 (Classics)
Duke Ellington 1940-41 (Classics)
Duke Ellington 1941 (Classics)
Duke Ellington 1946 (Classics)
New Orleans Suite (1970 Atlantic)

George Howard
Do I Ever Cross Your Mind? (1994 GRP)
A Nice Place To Be (1986 MCA)
Steppin' Out (1983 TBA)

Pedro Iturralde
with various:
Jazz Meets Europe (1968 MPS)

Willis Jackson
Bar Wars (1977 Muse)

Illinois Jacquet
The Complete Illinois Jacquet 1945-50 (Mosaic)
Flying Home: The Best of the Verve Years (1951-58 Verve)
Jacquet's Got It (1987 Atlantic)
with Lionel Hampton:
Lionel Hampton 1929-1940 (Jazz Classics)

Joseph Jarman
Equal Interest (1999 OmniTone)

with Art Ensemble Of Chicago:
Art Ensemble 1967-68 (Nessa)

Bobby Jaspar
At Ronnie Scott's – 1962 (Mole Jazz)

François Jeanneau
Ephemere (1977/93 Owl)

Jerry Jerome
Something Old, Something New (1939-96 Arbors)

Budd Johnson
Let's Swing (1960 Original Jazz Classics)

Louis Jordan
Best Of (1942-45 MCA)

Peter King
Brother Bernard (1988-92 Miles Music)

Roland Kirk
The Inflated Tear (1967 Atlantic)
We Free Kings (1961 Emarcy)

Hans Koller
Multiple Koller (1980 L+R)

Lee Konitz
Live At The Half Note (1959 Verve)
Motion (1961 Verve)
Sound Of Surprise (1999 BMG)
Subconscious-Lee (1949-50 Original Jazz Classics)
with Miles Davis:
Birth Of The Cool (1949-50 Capitol)
with Stan Kenton:
Retrospective (1943-68 Capitol)

Steve Lacy
Scratching The Seventies/Dreams (1969-77 Saravah)
with Lol Coxhill, Evan Parker
Three Blokes (1992 FMP)

Harold Land
The Fox (1959 Original Jazz Classics)

Don Lanphere
Stop (1983-86 Hep)

Ronnie Laws
Pressure Sensitive (1975 Blue Note)

David Liebman
Miles Away (1994 Owl)

Charles Lloyd
Forest Flower (1966 Atlantic)

Joe Lovano
Celebrating Sinatra (1997 Blue Note)
From The Soul (1992 Blue Note)
Landmarks (1991 Blue Note)
Rush Hour (1995 Blue Note)
Universal Language (1993 Blue Note)

Bob Malach
Mood Swing (1990 Go Jazz)

Joe Maneri
In Full Cry (1997 ECM)
Tales Of Rohnlief (1999 ECM)

Charlie Mariano
Alto Sax For Young Moderns (1955 Bethlehem)
Mariano (1987 Intuition)

Eric Marienthal
Crossroads (1990 GRP)
Oasis (1991 GRP)
Walk Tall (1998 ie Music)

Branford Marsalis
Music From Mo Better Blues (1990 Sony)
Requiem (1999 Sony)
Romances For Saxophone (1986 Columbia)
Scenes In The City (1983 Columbia)
Trio Jeepy (1988 Columbia)

Warne Marsh
The Complete Atlantic Recordings Of Lennie Tristano, Lee Konitz & Warne Marsh (1954-58 Mosaic)
Live At The Montmartre Club Vol 2 (1975 Storyville)
Tenor Gladness (1976 Disco-Mate)

Jackie McLean
Bluesnik (1961 Blue Note)
One step Beyond (1963 Blue Note)
Right Now! (1965 Blue Note)

Big Jay McNeely
Road House Boogie (1949-52 Saxophonograph)

Charles McPherson
First Flight Out (1994 Arabesque)

Joakim Milder
with Tomasz Stanko:
Litania (1997 ECM)

Eddie Miller
with Bob Crosby:
Bob Crosby 1937 To 1938 (Jazz Classics)
Bob Crosby's Bob Cats Vol 2 (1939 Swaggie)

Bob Mintzer
Latin From Manhattan (2000 DMP)
One Music (1991 DMP)
Quality Time (1998 TWT)

Billy Mitchell
with Count Basie:
Chairman Of The Board (1959 Roulette)

Roscoe Mitchell
Sound Songs (1994 Delmark)
with Art Ensemble Of Chicago:
Art Ensemble 1967-68 (Nessa)

Hank Mobley
Soul Station (1960 Blue Note)
with Art Blakey's Jazz Messengers:
At The Café Bohemia (1955 Blue Note)

James Moody
Something Special (1986 Novus)
with Dizzy Gillespie:
Something Old, Something New (1964 Verve)

Gerry Mulligan
The Complete Pacific Jazz Recordings Of The Gerry Mulligan Quartet With Chet Baker (1952-57 Pacific Jazz)
Lonesome Boulevard (1989 A&M)
What Is There To Say? (1958-59 Columbia)
with Miles Davis:
Birth Of The Cool (1949-50 Capitol)

David Murray
Fast Life (1991 DIW)
The Hill (1986 Black Saint)

Vido Musso
with Benny Goodman:
Benny Goodman 1936 Vol 2 (Classics)
with Stan Kenton:
Stan Kenton 1945 (Classics)

Zbigniew Namyslowski
Kujaviak Goes Funky (1976 Power Bros)

Oliver Nelson
The Blues And The Abstract Truth (1961 Impulse)

Lennie Niehaus
The Octet No. 2, Volume 3 (1954 Original Jazz Classics)
Patterns (1989 Fresh Sound)

Greg Osby
Art Forum (1996 Blue Note)
The Invisible Hand (2000 Blue Note)
Man-Talk For Moderns, Volume X (1991 Blue Note)

Charlie Parker
The Charlie Parker Story (1945 Savoy)
Diz 'n' Bird At Carnegie Hall (1947 Blue Note)
Jazz At The Philharmonic 1946 (Verve)
On Dial: The Complete Sessions (1945-47 Spotlite)
The Quintet / Jazz At Massey Hall (1953 Original Jazz Classics)
South Of The Border (1948-52 Verve)
With Strings (1947-52 Verve)
with Dizzy Gillespie:
Groovin' High (1945-46 Savoy)
The Complete RCA Victor Recordings (1937-49 Bluebird)
with Jay McShann:
Blues From Kansas City (1941-43 MCA)

Evan Parker
Saxophone Solos (1975 Chrononoscope)
with Barry Guy, Paul Lytton:
Imaginary Values – Nine Improvisations (1993 Maya)
with Lol Coxhill, Steve Lacy
Three Blokes (1992 FMP)
with Spontaneous Music Ensemble:
Karyobin (1968 Chronoscope)

Leo Parker
Let Me Tell You 'Bout It (1961 Blue Note)

Cecil Payne
with Woody Herman:
Concerto For Herd (1967 Verve)

Dave Pell
with Joe Williams:
Prez & Joe (1979 GNP)

Ken Peplowski
It's A Lonesome Old Town (1995 Concord)
The Natural Touch (1992 Concord)
with Howard Alden
Ken Peplowski / Howard Alden (1993 Concord)
Encore! (1995 Concord)

Art Pepper
Art Pepper Meets The Rhythm Section (1957 Original Jazz Classics)
Art Pepper Plus Eleven (1959 Original Jazz Classics)
The Artistry Of Pepper (1956-57 Pacific Jazz)
Winter Moon (1980 Original Jazz Classics)
with Stan Kenton:
The Innovations Orchestra (1950-51 Capitol)
Retrospective (1943-68 Capitol)

Bill Perkins
Just Friends (1956 Pacific Jazz)
Perk Plays Prez (1995 Fresh Sound)

Houston Person
Basics (1987 Muse)

Flip Phillips
Flip Wails (1947-57 Verve)

Courtney Pine
Back In The Day (2000 Blue Thumb)

Michel Portal
Turbulence (1987 Harmonia Mundi)

Art Porter
Pocket City (1992 Verve)
For Art's Sake (1998 Verve)

Joe Poston
with Jimmie Noone's Apex Club Orchestra:
'*I Know That You Know*' (1928 Vocalion)
'*Monday Date*' (1928 Vocalion) both on *Apex Blues 1928-30* CD (Decca).

Chris Potter
Moving In (1995 Concord)
Pure (1992 Concord)
Vertigo (1998 Concord)

Red Prysock
with Tiny Bradshaw:
Walk That Mess!: The Best of the King Years (c1950-54 Westside)

Wolfgang Puschnig
with Vienna Art Orchestra:
20th Anniversary 1977-1997 (1997 Amadeo/Verve)

Ike Quebec
Heavy Soul (1961 Blue Note)

Gene Quill
with Phil Woods:
Phil & Quill (1957 Original Jazz Classics)

Paul Quinichette
The Kid From Denver (1956-59 Biograph)
with John Coltrane:
Cattin' With Coltrane & Quinichette (1952-57 DCC)

Nelson Rangell
Playing For Keeps (1989 GRP)
Truest Heart (1993 GRP)

Dewey Redman
with Ed Blackwell:
Red & Black In Willisau (1980 Black Saint)

Joshua Redman
Beyond (1999 Warner Bros)
Timeless Tales (For Changing Times) (1998 Warner Bros)
Wish (1993 Warner Bros)

Sam Rivers
Fuschia Swing Song (1964 Blue Note)
Trio Live (1973 Impulse)
Waves (1978 Tomato)

Prince Robinson
with McKinney's Cotton Pickers:
'*Four Or Five Times*' (1928 Victor)

Adrian Rollini
with Bix Beiderbecke & His Gang:
'*At The Jazz Band Ball*' (1927 Okeh)
'*Jazz Me Blues*' (1927 Okeh)

Sonny Rollins
The Complete Sonny Rollins On RCA (1962-64 RCA)
The Cutting Edge (1974 Milestone)
The Freelance Years: The Complete Riverside & Contemporary Recordings (1956-58 Riverside)
Newk's Time (1957 Blue Note)
On Impulse! (1965 Impulse)
Saxophone Colossus (1956 Prestige)
Sonny Rollins Plus Four (1956 Prestige)
Trio/Brass (1958 Verve)
with Bud Powell:
The Amazing Bud Powell Volume 1 (1949-51 Blue Note)
with Dizzy Gillespie:
Sonny Side Up (1957 Verve)
with Miles Davis:
Bags' Groove (1954 Prestige)
with Miles Davis and others:
Collector's Item (1953 Esquire)
with Thelonious Monk:
Work (1954 Prestige)

Bernt Rosengren
with Tomasz Stanko:
Litania (1997 ECM)

Charlie Rouse
with Art Blakey:
Introducing Joe Gordon (1954 Verve)

with Benny Carter:
Further Definitions (1962 Impulse)

David Sanborn
As We Speak (1982 Warner Bros)
Close-Up (1988 Reprise)

David Sanchez
Melaza (2000 Columbia)

Pharoah Sanders
Black Unity (1971 Impulse)
Crescent With Love (1992 Evidence)

Heinz Sauer
with Albert Mangelsdorff:
Birds of Underground (1973 MPS)

Louis Sclavis
Carnet de Routes (1995 Label Bleu)

Ronnie Scott
All Stars At Montreux (1977 Pablo)
The Night Is Scott (1966 Redial)
with Clarke-Boland Big Band:
Sax No End/All Blues (1967 MPS)

Tom Scott
with The LA Express:
Tom Cat (1974 Epic)

Gene Sedric
with Fats Waller:
The Joint Is Jumpin' (1934-42 Bluebird)

Bud Shank
After You, Jeru (1998 Fresh Sounds)
The Pacific Jazz Bud Shank Studio Sessions (1956-61 Mosaic)

Archie Shepp
Fire Music (1965 Impulse)

Andy Sheppard
Learning To Wave (1998 Provocateur)

Andy Sherrer
with Vienna Art Orchestra:
20th Anniversary 1977-1997 (1997 Amadeo/Verve)

Sahib Shihab
with Clarke-Boland Big Band:
Sax No End/All Blues (1967 MPS)

Wayne Shorter
Atlantis (1985 Columbia)
JuJu (1964 Blue Note)
with Art Blakey:
Buhaina's Delight (1961 Blue Note)
with Weather Report:
I Sing The Body Electric (1972 Columbia)
Heavy Weather (1976 Columbia)

Zoot Sims
And The Gershwin Brothers (1975 Original Jazz Classics)

Buster Smith
with Hot Lips Page:

Hot Lips Page 1938-40 (Classics)

Tommy Smith
Azure (1997 Linn)

Willie Smith
The Complete Jazz At The Philharmonic On Verve 1944-1949 (Verve)

Gary Smulyan
Saxophone Mosaic (1994 Criss Cross)
With Strings (1997 Criss Cross)

Harry Sockal
with Vienna Art Orchestra:
20th Anniversary 1977-1997 (1997 Amadeo/Verve)

James Spaulding
Brilliant Corners (1988 Muse)
with Sun Ra:
Jazz In Silhouette (1958 Evidence)

Sonny Stitt
Only The Blues (1957 Verve)
with Gene Ammons:
Boss Tenors (1961 Verve)
with Oscar Peterson:
Sits In With the Oscar Peterson Trio (1959 Verve)

John Surman
Coruscating (2000 ECM)
Withholding Pattern (1985 ECM)

Buddy Tate
The Ballad Artistry Of Buddy Tate (1981 Sackville)
Count Basie 1939 (Classics)
Jumpin' On The West Coast (1947-49 Black Lion)
with Milt Buckner:
When I'm Blue (1967 Black & Blue)

Steve Tavaglione
with MVP:
Centrifugal Funk (1991 Heading West)

John Tchicai
Real Tchicai (1977 Steeplechase)

Joe Temperley
Nightingale (1992 Hep)
With Every Breath I Take (1998 Hep)

Gary Thomas
By Any Means Necessary (1989 JMT)

Lucky Thompson
Tricotism (1956 Impulse)
with Art Blakey:
Soul Finger (1965 Limelight)

Gianluigi Trovesi
Les Boîtes à Musique (1988 Splasch)

Frankie Trumbauer
with Bix Beiderbecke:
'Singing The Blues' (1927 Okeh)
'Trumbology' (1927 Okeh) both on *Bix Beiderbecke Vol 1 Singin' The Blues* CD (Columbia).

Mark Turner
Ballad Session (1999 Warner Bros)
In This World (1998 Warner Bros)
Mark Turner (1997 Warner Bros)

Stanley Turrentine
La Place (1989 Blue Note)
That's Where It's At (1962 Blue Note)
Up At Minton's (1961 Blue Note)

Various artists (free)
Document: The 80s; New Music In Russia (1989 Leo)
For Example: Workshop Freie Musik (1978 FMP)

Various artists (R&B)
Groove Station: King-Federal-DeLuxe Saxblasters Vol 1 (1999 Westside)
Honkers & Bar Walkers Vols 1 & 2 (1992 Delmark)
1942-45 The R&B Hits (Indigo)
1946 The R&B Hits (Indigo)
1947 The R&B Hits (Indigo)
1948 The R&B Hits (Indigo)
1949 The R&B Hits (Indigo)

Charlie Ventura
In Concert (1949 MCA)

Bennie Wallace
The Fourteen Bar Blues (1978 Enja)

David S Ware
Surrended (2000 Columbia)

Grover Washington Jr.
Inner City Blues (1972 Kudu)
Mister Magic (1975 Kudu)
Strawberry Moon (1987 Columbia)
Winelight (1980 Elektra)

Ernie Watts
The Ernie Watts Quartet (1988 JVC)

Trevor Watts
with Derek Bailey, John Stevens:
Dynamics Of The Impromptu (1974/99 Entropy)
with Spontaneous Music Ensemble:
Karyobin (1968 Chronoscope)

Ben Webster
Music for Loving (1954-55 Verve)
The Soul Of (1957-58 Verve)
with Duke Ellington:
Duke Ellington 1940 (Classics)
The Blanton-Webster Band (1940-42 Bluebird)
with Oscar Peterson:
Meets Oscar Peterson (1959 Verve)
with Art Tatum:
Group Masterpieces Volume 8 (1956 Pablo)

Bobby Wellins
Don't Worry 'Bout Me: Live At The Vortex (1997 Cadillac)

Frank Wess
with Count Basie:
Chairman Of The Board (1959 Roulette)

Kirk Whalum
The Promise (1988 Columbia)

Bob Wilber
with Soprano Summit
Soprano Summit (1976-77 Chiaroscuro)
Live At Concord '77 (1977 Concord)
with Dick Hyman:
A Perfect Match (1997 Arbors)

Barney Wilen
Jazz Sur Seine (1958 Philips)

Dick Wilson
with Andy Kirk:
Andy Kirk 1936-1940 (Classics)
with Mary Lou Williams:
Mary Lou Williams 1927-1940 (Classics)

Phil Woods
Real Life (1990 Chesky)
with Gene Quill:
Phil & Quill (1957 Original Jazz Classics)

Lester Young
Lester Young's recorded output has been issued and reissued innumerable times, in various formats, and this will continue to be the case. Our selection is from three compilations.
From *The Lester Young Story* (1936-49 Proper):
with Jones-Smith Inc:
'Shoe Shine Boy'/'Lady Be Good' (1936)
with Count Basie:
'Taxi War Dance' (1939)
'Clap Hands, Here Comes Charlie' (1939)
'Tickle Toe' (1939)
'You Can Depend On Me' (1939)
with Billie Holiday:
'Me, Myself & I' (1937)
'A Sailboat In The Moonlight' (1937)
'When You're Smiling' (1938)
with Nat Cole:
'Tea For Two' (1942)
Lester Young Quartet:
'Just You, Just Me' (1943)
'Sometimes I'm Happy' (1943)
'Ghost Of A Chance' (1944)
Lester Young & his Band:
'These Foolish Things' (1945)
'DB Blues' (1945)
with Jazz At The Philharmonic:
'Lester Leaps In' (1949)
From *The Complete Lester Young Studio Sessions* (1944-55 Verve):
Lester Young Quartet:
'Polka Dots & Moonbeams' (1949)
'Undercover Girl Blues' (1951)
From *Lester Young In Washington DC, Vol 3* (1956 Original Jazz Classics):
Lester Young Quartet:
'Gs, If You Please' (1955)

John Zorn
The Big Gundown (1984-85 Elektra Nonesuch)
Filmworks 1986-1990 (Elektra Nonesuch)
Spy Vs Spy (1989 Elektra Musician)
with Naked City:
Grand Guignol (1992 Avant)

ACKNOWLEDGEMENTS

Thanks to the following for the loan of CD inserts and record sleeves for illustration in this book: Kevin Alexander; Balafon Image Bank; Stan Britt; Steve Day; Dave Gelly; Mark Gilbert; Ray's Jazz Shop; Peter Symes; Mike Tucker; David Wood.

PHOTOGRAPHS were supplied by the following (number indicates page):
Sonny Rollins (**front jacket**) Peter Symes; *opening shot* (**2**) Val Wilmer; *Freeman* (**4**) Charles Peterson; *Dorsey* (**7**) Charles Peterson; *Robinson* (**8**) Charles Peterson; *Trumbauer* (**9**) Charles Peterson: *Bechet* (**10**) Charles Peterson; *Carter/Procope* (**11**) Charles Peterson; *Hawkins* (**13**) Charles Peterson; *Hawkins* (**14**) Ray Avery; *Hawkins* (**15**) Charles Peterson; *Hawkins/Carter/Sims* (**17**) Mike Doyle/Symil Library; *Hawkins* (**18**) Val Wilmer; *Carney* (**21**) Val Wilmer; *Hodges* (**22**) Val Wilmer; *Webster* (**24**) Randi Hultin; *Webster* (**25**) Charles Peterson: *Phillips* (**27**) Charles Peterson; *Smith* (**28**) Charles Peterson; *Carter* (**29**) Charles Peterson; *Brown* (**31**) Charles Peterson; *Edwards* (**32**) Peter Symes; *Freeman/Hodges/Berry* (**33**) Charles Peterson; *Tate/Shavers/Coleman* (**34**) Mike Doyle/Symil Library; *Tate* (**34**) Val Wilmer; *Auld* (**36**) Charles Peterson; *Procope* (**37**) Charles Peterson; *Young* (**39**) Charles Peterson; *Young* (**40**) Charles Peterson; *Young* (**42**) Institute of Jazz Studies; *Young* (**45**) Ray Avery; *Parker* (**47**) E Levinsohn/Val Wilmer; *Parker* (**48**) Steve Race/Val Wilmer; *Gillespie* (**49**) Peter Symes; *Parker* (**50**) Ray Avery; *Roach* (**50**) Peter Symes; *Parker/Baker* (**53**) Ray Avery; *Byas* (**55**) Val Wilmer; *Stitt* (**56**) Val Wilmer; *Gordon* (**57**) Randi Hultin; *Gray* (**59**) Ray Avery; *Moody* (**60**) Peter Symes; *Criss* (**61**) Val Wilmer; *Scott* (**63**) Val Wilmer; *Konitz* (**65**) Val Wilmer; *Marsh* (**66**) Mike Doyle/Symil Library; *Mulligan* (**67**) Val Wilmer; *Pepper* (**69**) Dennis Austin; *Desmond* (**71**) Val Wilmer; *Getz* (**72**) Randi Hultin; *Sims* (**74**) Mike Doyle/Symil Library; *Sims/Cohn/Giuffre* (**75**) Val Wilmer; *Cohn* (**76**) Peter Symes; *Gordon/Getz* (**78**) Randi Hultin; *Cobb* (**80**) Mike Doyle/Symil Library; *Forrest* (**81**) Val Wilmer; *McNeely* (**84**) Ray Avery; *Jordan* (**87**) Val Wilmer; *Rollins* (**89**) Val Wilmer; *Rollins* (**91**) Val Wilmer; *Rollins* (**92**) Randi Hultin; *Rollins* (**93**) Peter Symes; *Rollins* (**95**) Peter Symes: *Mobley* (**97**) Institute of Jazz Studies; *McLean* (**98**) Val Wilmer; *Griffin* (**100**) Randi Hultin; *Golson* (**101**) Peter Symes; *Gilmore/Allen/Thompson* (**102**) Val Wilmer; *Cook* (**103**) Peter Symes; *Hayes* (**104**) Val Wilmer; *Woods* (**105**) Howard Denner; *Eddie 'Lock Jaw' Davis* (**107**) Dennis Austin; *Smith* (**109**) Peter Symes; *Harris* (**110**) Ray Avery; *Felder* (**112**) Ray Avery; *Miles Davis* (**114**) Mike Doyle/Symil Library; *Coltrane* (**116**) Val Wilmer; *Jones* (**119**) Mike Doyle/Symil Library; *Alice Coltrane* (**120**) Peter Symes; *John Coltrane* (**120**) Randi Hultin; *Adderleys* (**123**) Val Wilmer; *Lloyd* (**125**) Val Wilmer; *Shorter* (**126**) Peter Symes; *Henderson* (**128**) Peter Symes; *Blythe* (**131**) Val Wilmer; *Freeman* (**132**) Peter Symes; *Dolphy* (**133**) Val Wilmer; *Rivers* (**135**) Peter Symes: *Kirk* (**136**) Val Wilmer; *Kirk* (**137**) Brian O'Connor: *Redman/Coleman* (**138**) Val Wilmer; *Cherry* (**141**) Peter Symes; *Schuller* (**142**) Peter Symes; *Coleman* (**145**) Peter Symes; *Ayler* (**147**) Val Wilmer; *Lowe* (**148**) Val Wilmer; *Shepp* (**150**) Dennis Austin; *Harriott* (**151**) Val Wilmer; *Brötzmann* (**152**) Dennis Austin; *Lacy* (**153**) Val Wilmer; *Zorn* (**153**) Peter Symes; *Breckers* (**155**) Peter Symes; *Brecker* (**156**) Peter Symes; *Brecker* (**161**) Howard Denner; *Sanborn* (**162**) Peter Symes; *Turrentine* (**164**) Ray Avery; *Scott* (**166**) Ray Avery; *Bartz* (**168**) Ray Avery; *Watts* (**169**) Ray Avery; *Washington* (**171**) Ray Avery; *Marienthal* (**173**) David Sinclair; *Rangell* (**174**) David Sinclair; *Porter* (**177**) David Sinclair; *Sclavis* (**179**) Peter Symes; *Osborne* (**182**) Peter Symes; *Surman* (**182**) Peter Symes; *Garbarek* (**184**) Peter Symes; *Breuker/Kollektief* (**184**) Peter Symes; *Sanders* (**185**) Peter Symes: *Wellins* (**186**) Peter Symes; *Smith* (**186**) Howard Denner; *Hamilton* (**189**) Peter Symes; *Wilber* (**192**) Mike Doyle/Symil Library; *Temperley* (**192**) Dennis Austin; *Barnes/McPherson* (**195**) Peter Symes; *Marsalis* (**197**) Peter Symes; *Lovano* (**199**) Peter Symes; *Redman* (**200**) Peter Symes; *Potter* (**203**) Peter Symes; *Murray* (**205**) Dennis Austin; *Maneri* (**206**) New Note; *Berne* (**209**) Peter Symes; *Osby* (**210**) David Sinclair; *Pine* (**211**) Peter Symes; *Sheppard* (**213**) Peter Symes; *Sanchez* (**213**) Sony Music; *closing shot* (**215**) Val Wilmer; **rear jacket:** *Ben Webster*, Randi Hultin; *Tony Coe*, Peter Symes; *Peter King*, Peter Symes; *Gilmore/Allen/Thompson in Sun Ra Arkestra*, Val Wilmer; *Tommy Smith*, Howard Denner

BIBLOIOGRAPHY

Ian Carr et al Jazz, The Rough Guide (1995 Rough Guides)
John Chilton The Song Of The Hawk (1990 Quartet)
Richard Cook & Brian Morton The Penguin Guide To Jazz On CD (1998 Penguin)
Stanley Dance The World Of Swing (1974 Da Capo)
George Duvivier Bassically Speaking (1993 Scarecrow Press)
Michael Erlewine et al All Music Guide To Jazz (1998 Miller Freeman)
Leonard Feather Inside Bebop (1949 Robbins)
Gil Goldstein Jazz Composer's Companion (1993 Advance)
Barry Kernfield (ed) The New Grove Dictionary Of Jazz (1994 Macmillan)
Donald Maggin Stan Getz: A Life In Jazz (1997 Morrow)
Lewis Porter John Coltrane, His Life And Music (1998 University of Michigan Press)
George Russell The Lydian Chromatic Concept Of Tonal Organization In Improvisation (1959)
Arnold Shaw Honkers And Shouters – The Golden Years of Rhythm & Blues (1978 Collier)

"The best part of playing jazz is letting the music really take over. And then it's beyond me: I'm just standing up there holding an instrument and putting air into it." **Sonny Rollins, 1996**